Building Vocabulary for College

Instructor's Annotated Edition

Instructor's Annotated Edition

Building Vocabulary
for College

Seventh Edition

R. Kent Smith

Houghton Mifflin Harcourt Publishing Company   Boston • New York

Executive Publisher: Patricia Coryell
Senior Sponsoring Editor: Joann Kozyrev
Senior Marketing Manager: Tom Ziolkowski
Discipline Product Manager: Giuseppina Daniel
Development Editor: Amy Gibbons
Associate Project Editor: Carrie Parker
Art and Design Manager: Jill Haber
Cover Design Director: Tony Saizon
Senior Photo Editor: Jennifer Meyer Dare
Senior Composition Buyer: Chuck Dutton
New Title Project Manager: James Lonergan
Editorial Associate: Daisuke Yasutake
Marketing Assistant: Bettina Chiu
Editorial Assistant: Jill Clark

Cover image: © Travis Foster Illustration

Printed in the U.S.A.

Library of Congress Control Number: 2008926619

Instructor's Annotated Edition
   ISBN-10: 0-618-97959-X
   ISBN-13: 978-0-618-97959-2
For orders, use student text ISBNs
   ISBN-10: 0-618-97905-0
   ISBN-13: 978-0-618-97905-9

123456789- CRW -12 11 10 09 08

Contents

College English instructors, like English instructors at all levels, are keenly aware of the strong correlation between the breadth of students' vocabulary and their academic performance. However, given the reality that students often take college reading, writing, and study skills courses for only one or two semesters, it can be challenging for instructors to find adequate time for vocabulary concerns. *Building Vocabulary for College* was conceived and developed as a practical, rewarding, and efficient means for helping students gain the general and specialized vocabulary that they need to flourish academically, both in English and in other courses.

The word parts, challenging words, and academic terms featured in *Building Vocabulary for College* were selected based on a thorough consultation of numerous textbooks, standardized tests, dictionaries and other reference books, journals and periodicals, and college instructors and students. Through the years, they have enabled thousands of high-school, college-preparatory, community-college, and four-year college students to dramatically improve their vocabularies.

NEW TO THE SEVENTH EDITION

The following new features have made *Building Vocabulary for College* even more student- and instructor-friendly.

- **A streamlined organization** (twenty-nine chapters total) now covers *Word Parts* and related *Challenging Words* (Part One) in the same chapter to emphasize the connection between them and combines all *Academic Terms* (Part Two) from a single discipline into one chapter.

- **An updated design** with color accents, descriptive exercise headings, and photos and other visuals illustrating selected terms enhances the text's visual appeal and pedagogical utility.

- **A new mathematics chapter** (Chapter 25), added in response to instructor requests, familiarizes students with the terms and symbols used in introductory mathematics courses.

- **New, varied, and engaging cloze passages** in every chapter allow students to assess their comprehension and progress while practicing using new vocabulary in an interesting context.

- **New *Featured Word* boxes** in every chapter present the origin and connotation of a word from the chapter, family words (such as "caprice" and "capriciously" for "capricious"), and an associated image to serve as a memory aid.

- **New *Mastering Confusing Words* boxes** in every chapter help students master the distinctions between frequently-confused pairs of words such as *accept/except* and *affect/effect* with the aid of sample sentences and practice exercises.

- **New cumulative reviews** featuring crossword puzzles and a variety of other exercise types, including analogies, are included after Chapters 5, 10, 17, 23, and 29.
- **Numerous revisions to sentences and exercises** throughout the text enhance students' learning and retention of individual word parts, challenging words, and academic terms.

ORGANIZATION AND CONTENT

Each of the seventeen chapters in **Part One** features ten common word parts (prefixes, suffixes, and roots) and ten college-level challenging words containing these word parts. Each word part and challenging word is introduced in two sentences that offer context clues as to its meaning. Visual aids accompanying selected words provide additional clues. A multiple-choice question after each pair of sentences gives students an immediate opportunity to use the context clues to determine the meaning of the word part or challenging word. Consistently structured exercises—including matching, fill-in, and multiple-choice exercises as well as cloze passages and prompts for writing original definitions—provide abundant opportunities for students to enhance and evaluate their understanding. Cumulative review tests cover Chapters 1–5, 6–10, and 11–17.

The twelve chapters in **Part Two** introduce the basic vocabulary terms from a wide range of humanities, science, and social-science disciplines, including literature, U.S. history and political science, psychology, and biology, as well as from more specialized fields such as law, computer science, and medicine, that students are likely to encounter in introductory courses in these areas. As with the vocabulary in Part One, each term in Part Two is introduced in two sentences that provide students with additional opportunities to practice using context clues, and selected terms are accompanied by visuals. An engaging blend of exercises structured similarly to those in Part One reinforces the definitions. There are cumulative reviews for Chapters 18–23 and 24–29.

Indexes for the word parts, challenging words, and academic terms, as well as appendices covering parts of speech and tips for using the dictionary, are included at the end of the text.

ANCILLARIES

Building Vocabulary for College Annotated Instructor's Edition
The *Building Vocabulary for College* Annotated Instructor's Edition contains on-page answers for all of the chapter exercises in the text.

Building Vocabulary for College Instructor Website (college.hmco.com/pic/smithBVC7e)
The *Building Vocabulary for College* instructor website features suggestions for effectively teaching from this text and a *Test Bank* of additional tests.

***Building Vocabulary for College* Student Website
(college.hmco.com/pic/smithBVC7e)**

The *Building Vocabulary for College* student website provides interactive flashcards for vocabulary terms from the text, additional crossword puzzles, and access to the exercises and resources of *Total Practice Zone.*

ACKNOWLEDGMENTS

The Houghton Mifflin editorial staff, as always, provided me with expert guidance and steadfast support, and I am most appreciative of both. In particular, the skills, dedication, and graciousness of Amy Gibbons, Development Editor, made the work on this new edition a delightful as well as a rewarding experience; her insightful suggestions are incorporated throughout.

My gratitude continues to extend to the reviewers, colleagues, students, and editors whose assistance made possible the previous editions. For this edition, I am especially indebted to the following people for their conscientious feedback and helpful suggestions:

Bonnie Bailey, Arapahoe Community College
Sylvia Boyd, Phillips Community College of the University of
    Arkansas—Stuttgart
Kathleen A. Carlson, Brevard Community College
Dorothy D. Chase, Community College of Southern Nevada
Marie G. Eckstrom, Rio Hondo College
Margaret W. Fox, Oregon State University
Laura McCracken, North Seattle Community College
Phyllis Prawl, Laramie County Community College
Betty Raper, Pulaski Technical College
Jeffery L. Siddall, College of DuPage
Marguerite Stark, Monterey Peninsula College
Steve Stewart, West Central Technical College
David A. Strong, Jr., Dyersburg State Community College

Finally, the abiding support and interest I have received from colleagues, students, friends, and family is noted and deeply appreciated.

—R. Kent Smith
vocabteach@gmail.com

College success requires you to attend class regularly, follow good study habits, set and achieve short- and long-term goals, complete your assignments on time, maintain contact with your instructors and advisors, and most of all, take responsibility for your own success. It also requires that you develop literacy and thinking skills. But few things are likely to help you as much as you progress through your education as a good vocabulary. (For proof, look no further than the studies that have shown that an extensive vocabulary is associated with outstanding grades.)

The good news is that no one is born with more word knowledge than anyone else—which means that if you are willing to work at it, the benefits of a broad vocabulary can be yours. As an adult, you do have to make a deliberate effort to increase your vocabulary if it is to grow significantly. One way you can achieve this is to read a lot and look up any words you come across that you do not know. Another is to study vocabulary with the aid of a book, preferably one that provides many opportunities for you to actually practice using the words (like this one).

This book is designed to help you increase your vocabulary in a systematic, practical, and interesting way. You are probably already familiar with some of the vocabulary words and terms it contains, but most of them will be new to you. In any event, your vocabulary will only continue to grow as you work through the chapter exercises and review tests. **Part One** will deepen your understanding of common prefixes, suffixes, and roots (also known as *word parts*), which will make it easier for you to decipher the challenging words that are also featured in this part of the book. **Part Two** is devoted to helping you master the academic terms associated with many of the college subjects that you will be required (or will elect) to take.

The more words you learn, the easier it will be to unlock the meaning of other unfamiliar words that you encounter in the future. And with your newly enhanced vocabulary will come greater academic achievements. I wish you much success in that endeavor.

—R. Kent Smith
vocabteach@gmail.com

Part **ONE** Word Parts and Challenging Words

WORD PARTS: INTRODUCTION

Our vocabularies have two intertwining branches: *recognition* and *expression*. The *recognition* branch includes those words we may not personally use but we know what they mean when we hear them spoken or encounter them in our reading ("frenzy" may be an example); our *expression* branch includes those words we personally use when we speak or write ("dilapidated" may be an example).

Knowledge of word parts can play a vital role in increasing the size of both branches of our vocabularies, and prefixes, suffixes, and roots are the major elements of words. These word parts are defined in this way:

A **prefix** is a word part added at the beginning of a word, and it can dramatically alter a word's meaning, such as changing a word to its opposite meaning: correct—*in*correct; regard—*dis*regard.

A **suffix** is a word part added at the end of a word. A suffix can change a word's part of speech: jump (verb)—jump*er* (noun); poison (noun)—poison*ous* (adjective), and knowing a word's part of speech can contribute to your understanding of its definition:

An *ohmmeter* is needed to reassure electric resistance. (The suffix *-er* indicates *ohmmeter* is a noun, and this knowledge, coupled with the sentence's context, makes clear that *ohmmeter* is an instrument to measure electric resistance.)

A **root** is the base part of a word that conveys the bulk of the word's meaning. A prefix and a suffix can be attached to a root to form variants of the root: *in-* (a prefix meaning "not") + *cred* (a root meaning "believe") + *-ible* (a suffix meaning "capable of") = *incredible* (not capable of being believed).

Although word parts are usually consistent in their meaning, this isn't always the case. For example, *pre* means "before" in *pre*view and *pre*caution, but not in *pre*cise or *pre*cious; nevertheless, prefixes, suffixes, and roots are sufficiently consistent in their meanings to make it definitely worthwhile to learn their usual meanings. This knowledge will enable you to unlock unfamiliar words that you encounter in a reading assignment, such as "monolithic." When you know the prefix *mono-* means "one" and the root *lith* means "block of stone," and the suffix *-ic* means "having the characteristic of," you will understand that "monolithic" refers to an object made from a single block of stone, or, if used in a general sense, to something that is massive, rigid, and uniform throughout.

Obviously, the ability to analyze unfamiliar words in the preceding way, referred to as **word analysis,** depends on a comprehensive understanding of prefixes, suffixes, and roots, an understanding you will have an opportunity to acquire in **Part One.**

- Carefully read the two sentences illustrating the meaning of each word part; in some instances, more than one word part is underlined because it is one you have studied in a previous chapter.
- Then select what you believe is the correct meaning for the word part by writing either **a** or **b** in the space provided.

DOING THE EXERCISES

- After you have studied the word parts in the preceding manner, follow the directions for completing the chapter's four sets of exercises for the word parts.

CHALLENGING WORDS: INTRODUCTION

Mastering the definitions of the challenging words in each chapter will contribute to your ability to comprehend college-level material because these words frequently appear in textbooks, newspapers, periodicals, and standardized tests. You will have an opportunity to learn these words by applying your knowledge of the word parts previously studied and by using context clues, that is, by studying the relationship between a challenging word and the words surrounding it. Becoming familiar with these types of context clues will prove particularly helpful to you now and in the future.

- **Direct Definition**

  It's rare these days to see anyone wear a *monocle,* an eyeglass for just one eye.
  Intrinsic motivation is a desire for action coming from within an individual.
  (Both sentences provide straightforward definitions of the italicized words.)

- **Indirect Definition**

  Although the pain is not intense, it is *chronic,* having bothered me <u>for the past two months</u>.

  Her desire for financial security, she realized, was <u>not a sufficient</u> *rationale* for accepting his marriage proposal.

  (In the first sentence, "for the past two months" indicates that *chronic* describes a condition lasting a long time; in the second sentence, "not a sufficient *rationale*" suggests that *rationale* is a reason or a motive.)

- **Examples**

  Arthropods, <u>such as crabs and lobsters</u>, live in water.

  Unrestricted television viewing can have *deleterious* effects on children, including <u>sluggishness and insensitivity</u>.

  (In the first sentence, the examples of "crabs and lobsters" indicate that *arthropods* are animals with a hard outer covering and jointed legs. In the second sentence, "sluggishness and insensitivity" suggest that *deleterious* describes something undesirable or even harmful.)

- **Synonyms**

  The *arbitrator*, <u>or</u> judge, ruled in favor of the club owners.

  As a result, the players were *irate*; <u>in other words</u>, they were furious.

  (In the first sentence, "or" makes it clear that *arbitrator* and *judge* are synonyms, that is, words with similar meanings. In the second sentence, "in other words" makes it obvious that *irate* and *furious* are also synonyms.)

- **Antonyms**

  Early in her career, she was <u>careless</u> in her public remarks, <u>but</u> today she is much more *discreet.*

  <u>Although</u> the mayor was *churlish* yesterday, he was <u>pleasant and agreeable</u> at today's news conference.

  (In the first sentence, "but" indicates *careless* and *discreet* are antonyms, that is, words with opposite meanings. In the second sentence, "Although" signifies *churlish* has an opposite meaning to those of *pleasant* and *agreeable.*)

- **Key Phrases Plus Knowledge of Word Parts**

  The military leaders who seized control of the government <u>intended to rule with absolute authority</u>, but their attempt to *subjugate* the country eventually led to their overthrow.

  (The phrase "intended to rule with absolute authority" and knowing that *sub-* means "under" provide clues for understanding *subjugate,* which means "to put under authority.")

  Infidelity is the <u>only grounds for divorce</u> in that country.

  (The phrase "only grounds for divorce" and knowing *in-* means "not" and *fid* means "faith" provide the clues for understanding *infidelity,* or "unfaithfulness.")

Specific context clues like the ones in the preceding examples are not always present to help unlock the meaning of an unfamiliar word. When that is the case, a reasonable inference about the unknown word can often be made <u>by concentrating on what is being said about the subject of the sentence</u> and by <u>identifying the word's part of speech</u>. Here is an example of this technique:

Bereft of money, friends, and jobs, numerous <u>immigrants struggled to survive</u> in the New World.

(The subject of the sentence is *immigrants* who "struggled to survive," probably because they were "*bereft* of money, friends, and jobs." *Bereft* is an adjective, so concentrating on what is being said about the subject, *immigrants,* we can infer *bereft* means "lacking"; and the sentence does make sense if you use *lacking* instead of *bereft:* "*Lacking* money, friends, and jobs, numerous immigrants struggled to survive in the New World.")

LIMITATIONS OF CONTEXT CLUES

Although using context clues is generally reliable and is the most practical way of unlocking the meanings of unfamiliar words, this approach has limitations. Specifically, context clues

- often reveal vague rather than precise meanings;
- usually reveal a single meaning, whereas many words have several meanings;
- are sometimes absent or too obscure to be helpful;
- seldom provide certainty of definition.

It should be clear, then, that there are times when you should consult a dictionary (see **Appendix B,** pages 396–397), particularly when you need complete and precise meanings of words or when context clues are lacking or insufficient in a sentence.

STUDYING THE CHALLENGING WORDS

- Take advantage of pictures and other visual aids that may be available to acquaint you with some of the challenging words.
- Familiarize yourself with each word's pronunciation, part of speech, and definition, noting that (1) a word part you have studied is underlined; (2) the word is presented phonetically in parentheses with a space separating each syllable; (3) the accented syllable is printed in capital letters; (4) vowels with long sounds have a line over them; (5) the schwa sound—*uh*—in unaccented syllables is represented by ə, which resembles an upside-down e; and (6) the word's part of speech is presented (see **Appendix B,** beginning on page 396, if you need to review parts of speech).
- Carefully read the two sentences illustrating the appropriate use of each word; be alert to the types of context clues that have been discussed in addition to applying your knowledge of the underlined word part or parts.
- Select your definition for each challenging word by writing either **a** or **b** in the space provided.

DOING THE EXERCISES

- Follow the directions for completing the chapter's four sets of exercises for the challenging words, including those for Featured Word and Mastering Confusing Words.
- Note that the third set of exercises always ends with three analogy questions. **Analogies are pairs of words with a similar relationship,** so the analogy questions require you to study a pair of words to discover the relationship between them. Then, choosing from several options, you are to select the pair having the same relationship in the first pair of words. Consider this example:

  failure : ridicule :: success : praise

Analogies are read and understood in this manner: **failure** *is to* **ridicule** as **success** *is to* **praise.** Now think about the <u>relationship</u> between the first pair of words; that is, if you fail, people may ridicule you. Notice that the same type of <u>relationship</u> exists between success and praise; that is, if you succeed, people may praise you.

Keep in mind, then, that the relationship of the second pair of words must *always* be the *same* as it is in the first pair, as in these examples (: represents *is to* and :: represents *as*):

Similar meanings	café: restaurant :: clothes : garments
Opposite meanings	cloudy: clear :: straight : crooked
Part to whole	toe: foot :: finger : hand
Place and activity	mall : shopping :: highway : driving
General to specific	car : Ford :: sport : basketball
Noun and its association	clown : silly :: winter : cold
Adjective and its association	generous : good :: tricky : unfair

As the preceding examples demonstrate, the key to doing well on the analogy questions is to discover the relationship between the two words given, then to select the pair of words having a similar relationship.

FEATURED WORD

This brief component of each chapter presents interesting information about one of the more intriguing words you have just studied. Specifically, you will learn of the featured word's history, words in its family, and words and images associated with it. You will then be given another opportunity to demonstrate your mastery of this word by writing an original sentence featuring it.

MASTERING CONFUSING WORDS

This component is another bonus of each chapter. It focuses on words often confused with one another—*affect/effect, council/counsel, desert/dessert,* and many others. However, the brief but practical information and exercises presented in this concluding section of each chapter will enable you to quickly and easily learn the distinctions between such frequently misused words.

REVIEW TESTS

Review tests are included in Part One. In addition to the type of exercises featured in the chapters, the review tests also include word-completion passages and crossword puzzles. If you periodically review the chapters you have completed, you should do well on the review tests.

Chapter 1

Learning Word Parts from Context Clues

1. sta

- My aunt's *station* in life seems to be taking care of her elderly parents.
- The *statue* in the park is in honor of all military veterans from this community.

sta is closest in meaning to (a) position (b) fame _____ *a* _____ .

2. co, col, com, con, cor

- In an impressive display of civic pride, the downtown merchants *cooperated* when they remodeled their storefronts in the same style.
- This summer, three of my friends and I have decided to *collaborate* in painting houses.
- Luis Rodriguez, my *companion* in college, is now a dentist in Minnesota.
- George Washington and Benjamin Franklin were *contemporaries*.
- Coughing is positively *correlated* to smoking.

co, col, com, con, and **cor** mean to (a) separate (b) combine _____ *b* _____ .

3. il, im, in, ir

- Did you know it's *illegal* for businesses to open on Sundays in my community?
- The day after playing softball for the first time this spring, I was practically *immobile* from soreness.
- The celebrity was *inconspicuous* at the football game because she was wearing sunglasses and a heavy long coat as well as a hat.
- The judge dismissed the evidence as *irrelevant*.

il, im, in, and **ir** change a word to its (a) original (b) opposite meaning _____ *b* _____ .

4. de

- How much does a new car *depreciate* in value the first year?
- The trees that had been toppled by storms through the years were in various stages of *decomposition*.

de means move (a) toward (b) away from _____ *b* _____ .

5. er, or, ist

- My cousin is a *rancher* in Montana.
- Adele would like to become a high school *counselor*.
- Vic is fun to be around because he's such a *humorist*.

er, or, and **ist** refer to a person who (a) does (b) doesn't do what the base word indicates _____*a*_____ .

6. pre

- After the *previews* were shown, the feature movie began.
- The staff had *prearranged* the room for the banquet, so the guests were able to be seated immediately.

pre means (a) before (b) after _____*a*_____ .

7. re

- Mr. Lucas had to *revarnish* the table after it was stained by candle drippings.
- The Rapozas had such a good vacation in British Columbia that they are planning to *revisit* this Canadian province next year.

re means to (a) avoid (b) repeat _____*b*_____ .

8. ex

- The dentist reluctantly decided he would have to *extract* the patient's tooth.
- Oranges, which are shipped in abundance from Florida and California, are a major *export* of the United States.

ex means (a) in (b) out _____*b*_____ .

9. mono

- The term *monogamy* means having only one wife or husband.
- Working on the assembly line was *monotonous* work because I did the same thing hour after hour.

mono refers to (a) one (b) many _____*a*_____ .

10. un

- The defense lawyer contended the accident was caused by the waiter, so he feels it would be *unjust* to make his client pay damages.
- The cows wandered out of the pasture when the gate was left *unlatched*.

un means (a) with (b) not _____*b*_____ .

Matching Word Parts and Definitions

Match each definition with the word part it defines; some definitions are used more than once.

_f_	**1.** sta	**a.** one
_h_	**2.** co, col, com, con, cor	**b.** person who does something
_c or d_	**3.** il, im, in, ir	**c.** not; opposite
_c or d_	**4.** de	**d.** do the opposite of; away from
_b_	**5.** er, or, ist	**e.** before
_e_	**6.** prc	**f.** stand; position
_i_	**7.** re	**g.** out
_g_	**8.** ex	**h.** with; together
_a_	**9.** mono	**i.** again
_c or d_	**10.** un	

Fill-Ins with Word Parts

Select the appropriate word part so the proper word is formed in each sentence.

sta	in	ist	re	mono
con	de	pre	ex	un

1. The belief in only one God is known as _____ *mono* _____ theism.

2. The doctor _____ *con* _____ curred with his colleague's diagnosis.

3. I hope Frank and Teresa will _____ *re* _____ tell their hilarious story about their first camping experience.

4. A(n) _____ *in* _____ competent mechanic attempted to fix my car, much to my regret.

5. Did the optometr _____ *ist* _____ say you needed glasses?

6. The judge ordered the government official to _____ *de* _____ classify the document labeled "Top Secret."

7. People are guilty of _____ *pre* _____ judice when they make judgments before they know all of the facts.

8. Vickie rides a(n) _____ *sta* _____ tionary bike for exercise.

9. Fortunately, the window was _____ *un* _____ broken after it suddenly slammed shut.

10. After the baseball struck Jake in the chest, breathing was painful for him when he _____ *ex* _____ haled.

Matching Words and Definitions

Use your knowledge of the underlined word parts to match the definitions and words.

__h__	**1.** <u>re</u>juvenate	**a.** to free from blame
__d__	**2.** <u>un</u>chaste	**b.** person's standing or condition
__f__	**3.** <u>de</u>fection	**c.** not able to read or write
__j__	**4.** suffra<u>gist</u>	**d.** not pure; corrupted
__a__	**5.** <u>ex</u>onerate	**e.** railway system using a single rail
__g__	**6.** <u>commun</u>icable	**f.** abandonment of one's duty or loyalty
__b__	**7.** <u>stat</u>us	**g.** capable of being transmitted, such as
__e__	**8.** <u>mono</u>rail	a disease, when people come together
__c__	**9.** <u>il</u>literate	**h.** make fresh again; breathe new life into
__i__	**10.** <u>pre</u>amble	**i.** an introduction appearing before the main
		message
		j. person concerned with voting rights

Writing Your Own Definitions

Write the definitions of the words after noting the underlined word parts and studying the context of the sentences; if you are still uncertain, feel free to consult a dictionary.
Typical responses:

1. A <u>*stabilizer*</u> was installed to prevent the machine from rolling about.

   stabilizer _____ device that keeps something from moving _____

2. A number of supervisors were asked to accept <u>*demotions*</u> as a cost-saving step.

   demotions _____ lower positions with less pay _____

3. Our long-awaited trip had an <u>*inauspicious*</u> start because it started to sleet just as we drove out of our driveway.

   inauspicious _____ not favorable; not promising _____

4. According to the game warden, trout, bass, and perch can <u>*cohabit*</u> in the same body of water.

   cohabit _____ live together _____

5. Most drive-in movies became <u>*defunct*</u> in the 1970s.

   defunct _____ no longer in business or in existence _____

6. *Narcissists* never miss an opportunity to gaze fondly at themselves when they come across a mirror or a reflecting store window.

narcissists _____ people who are in love with themselves _____

7. My *predecessor* won three league championships in five years, so I knew I would be under a lot of pressure when I accepted this coaching position.

predecessor _____ person coming before _____

8. Some homeowners were so upset that they threatened legal action if their homes were not *reappraised*.

reappraised _____ reevaluated _____

9. The construction crew will *excavate* the property to put in a new drainage system.

excavate _____ to dig or scoop out _____

10. The game was canceled because the rain had been *unremitting*.

unremitting _____ continuous; unending _____

Learning Challenging Words from Context Clues

1. **stature** (STACH ər)—noun
   - My brother's *stature* as an outstanding athlete accounts for much of his popularity in our small community.
   - Her *stature* in the community rose even higher when she was appointed principal of the new high school.

   stature has to do with (a) regard (b) health _____ a _____ .

2. **compliance** (kəm PLĪ əns)—noun
   - Because the restaurant was not in *compliance* with the state's fire code, it was closed while the necessary changes were made.
   - The judge's decision was that the defendant was in *compliance* with the terms of the contract.

   compliance has to do with (a) praise (b) obedience _____ b _____ .

3. **incongruous** (in KONG GROO əs)—adjective

- Juan's friends think it's *incongruous* that he can't stand the sight of blood even though he's planning to become a doctor.
- It's *incongruous* to me that Lucia, who never goes out of her way to make friends, is often the person others turn to for advice.

incongruous is related to (a) inconsistency (b) intelligence _____ *a* _____ .

4. **debilitate** (də BIL ə tāt)—verb

- Fad diets not only don't work, but they may also *debilitate* one's health.
- Glenn's hard life as a cross-country trucker began to *debilitate* his health when he was in his early forties.

debilitate means (a) weakening (b) strengthening _____ *a* _____ .

5. **hedonist** (HĒ don ist)—noun

- When John first went to college, he became such a *hedonist* he almost flunked out after his first semester as his endless partying gave him little time for studying.
- The movie star has the reputation of being a *hedonist* because she is often pictured in newspapers and magazines in nightclubs and gambling casinos with other celebrities.

A **hedonist** is best known for seeking (a) support (b) fun _____ *b* _____ .

6. **precocious** (prə KŌshəs)—adjective

- Mozart was a *precocious* child as he was giving piano concerts and composing classical music before he was ten years old.
- My grandfather thinks his three-year-old granddaughter is *precocious* because she can count to twenty, but I don't think such ability is unusual for a child her age.

precocious has to do with demonstrating ability at an (a) early stage of life (b) unusual place _____ *a* _____ .

7. **replicate** (REP lə kāt)—verb

- The researchers *replicated* the experiment many times before they were sure the same results would occur.
- Is it legal to *replicate* a couple of my favorite CDs so I can give copies to my friends?

replicate is associated with (a) starting (b) copying _____ *b* _____ .

8. extricate (EK strə kāt)—verb

- Pete says the only way he can *extricate* his car from the ditch is by calling a tow truck.
- Justin *extricated* himself from the embarrassing situation by pretending he had to make a telephone call.

extricate is associated with (a) separating (b) repairing _____ *a* _____ .

9. monomania (MON ə MĀ nē ə)—noun

- My cousin is suffering from *monomania* as he spends all of his time trying to avoid germs.
- I decided to limit myself to no more than one hour per day on my computer as I was starting to have a *monomania* about playing computer games.

monomania is similar to an (a) obsession (b) obligation _____ *a* _____ .

10. unseemly (un SĒM lē)—adjective

- Didn't you think it was *unseemly* of her to ask why he and his wife were divorcing?
- Using vulgar language is particularly *unseemly* when children are present.

unseemly means being (a) bold (b) discourteous _____ *b* _____ .

Matching Challenging Words and Definitions

Write each word before its definition.

stature	incongruous	hedonist	replicate	monomania
compliance	debilitate	precocious	extricate	unseemly

precocious	**1.** advanced in mind or skills at an early age
monomania	**2.** an intense preoccupation with one subject
extricate	**3.** free from a difficult situation
debilitate	**4.** to make weak or feeble
unseemly	**5.** unbecoming, impolite, inappropriate
hedonist	**6.** one who seeks pleasure above all else
replicate	**7.** copy, duplicate
incongruous	**8.** out of step with one another, not in agreement
compliance	**9.** act of cooperating or obeying
stature	**10.** rank, standing, position

Fill-Ins with Challenging Words

In each space, write the appropriate word from those listed below.

stature	incongruous	hedonist	replicate	monomania
compliance	debilitate	precocious	extricate	unseemly

1. At the age of seven, Anders displayed _____*precocious*_____ ability to handle many of the chores associated with operating his grandfather's farm.

2. Ancient Romans seldom bathed because they believed frequent baths would _____*debilitate*_____ their strength.

3. I hope I'm not being _____*unseemly*_____ by asking, but how much do you pay per month for renting this dump?

4. Gretchen is constantly checking to see whether she left her stove on; she's showing all the signs of _____*monomania*_____ when it comes to this concern.

5. Austin, Texas, enjoys the _____*stature*_____ of being a wonderful city in which to live.

6. The golfer had difficulty trying to _____*extricate*_____ his ball from the sand trap.

7. After extensive renovations, the majestic old inn was finally in _____*compliance*_____ with the state's new safety code.

8. Ron was quite a(n) _____*hedonist*_____ in his younger days, but he's given up his wild ways since he got married.

9. Ashley finds it _____*incongruous*_____ that her roommate complains all the time about her boyfriend, yet she continues to go out with him.

10. The investigators were attempting to _____*replicate*_____ the conditions existing before the accident to see if they could discover the cause of the tragedy.

Checking Your Word Power

After selecting your response, put the letter in the space provided.

____*b*____ 1. The *opposite* of **compliance** is
   a. obedience
   b. defiance
   c. acceptance
   d. submission

____*a*____ 2. The *opposite* of **debilitate** is
   a. improve
   b. ruin
   c. inspect
   d. deceive

_____c_____ **3.** The *opposite* of **extricate** is
  a. trust
  b. explain
  c. hold
  d. free

_____d_____ **4. Incongruous** suggests
  a. smoothness
  b. stubbornness
  c. dishonesty
  d. disharmony

_____b_____ **5. Replicate** suggests
  a. exhaustion
  b. duplication
  c. destruction
  d. exception

_____a_____ **6.** At what age is someone most likely to be **precocious?**
  a. eight
  b. eighteen
  c. forty-eight
  d. seventy-eight

_____a_____ **7.** If people behave in an **unseemly** manner, they act
  a. inappropriately
  b. humorously
  c. intelligently
  d. politely

_____d_____ **8. hedonist : pleasure ::** **a.** teacher : school
                b. athlete : joy
                c. comedian : crying
                d. judge : seriousness

_____b_____ **9. stature : prominence ::** **a.** fame : wealth
                b. reputation : importance
                c. size : height
                d. desire : acquire

_____b_____ **10. monomania : sensible ::** **a.** fad : popularity
                b. foolishness : reasonable
                c. disturbance : unpleasantness
                d. nonsense : ridiculous

Completing a Passage

After reading the selection, fill in each space with one of the words listed below.

compliance	replicate	extricate	debilitate	unseemly
stature	monomania	precocious	incongruous	hedonist

JEFF

With his ability to read and to play the guitar when he was only three years old, Jeff was a(n) ___precocious___ youngster, but, unfortunately, also a headstrong one. In fact, by the time he reached his mid-twenties, Jeff had become a confirmed ___hedonist___ as his only apparent goal in life was that of self-gratification, regardless of whether this goal led him to commit illegal or immoral acts. As a result, Jeff's ___monomania___ for "pleasure only" eventually landed him in prison. When he was released on parole after two years, Jeff was soon discovered not to be in ___compliance___ with the conditions of his release, so he was sent back to prison to serve his full sentence. Not surprisingly, his once respectable ___stature___ in the small community where he lived was left in tatters.

Some of us who were high-school classmates of Jeff suspected his disgraceful, ___unseemly___ life may have been due to his failure to ___replicate___ the impressive successes of his older brother. But whatever the cause of his shameful conduct, Jeff's behavior seemed simply ___incongruous___ to his heartbroken parents, whose other children were highly respected and successful.

His family, relatives, and friends still cling to the hope that Jeff will someday ___extricate___ himself from the destructive hole he now finds himself in and that he will not continue to ___debilitate___ his health and future by making "personal pleasure regardless of cost" his sole aim in life.

Hedonist—one who believes that pleasure or happiness is the highest good; one who devotes his or her life to pleasure above all else:

- Some historians believe the decline of the Roman Empire began with Nero, who was thought to be mentally unbalanced and more interested in being a <u>hedonist</u> than a wise ruler.

Origin: 1855–1860 <Greek—*hedone*—pleasure

Family words: hedonism (n), hedonistic (adj), hedonistically (adv)

Connotation: *negative*—suggests an *excessive* devotion to pleasure

Image to remember: a playboy

Write an original sentence using *hedonism*:

_____

_____

_____

MASTERING CONFUSING WORDS | advice / advise

advice   a noun meaning a suggestion or an opinion:

Ming's <u>advice</u> is never buy a car with more than 30,000 miles on it.

advise   a verb meaning to provide suggestions:

Did Professor Morrison advise you to switch your major to biology?

Circle the correct answer:

1. Yasmin appears to be in great shape, so I don't know why anyone would <u>advice / (advise)</u> her to lose weight.

2. I took my sister's <u>(advice) / advise</u> and borrowed some money from our parents to pay off my credit card bills.

Write original sentences using these words:

1. **advice:** _____

2. **advise:** _____

Chapter 2

Learning Word Parts from Context Clues

1. sub

- Because the sergeant was *subordinate* in rank to the lieutenant, he obeyed the order.
- You will have to *submerge* the shirt in some water and bleach to remove the stain.

sub means (a) above (b) below _____ *b* _____ .

2. pro

- My folks have always been *pro-music,* so they are delighted I'm taking guitar lessons.
- The Luthers, who often complain about the property taxes they have to pay, surprised me when they became leading *proponents* for a new community swimming pool.

pro means (a) for (b) against _____ *a* _____ .

3. uni

- Everyone said in *unison,* "Let's go!"
- This clock is *unique* because it is the only one ever made of bamboo.

uni means (a) one (b) many _____ *a* _____ .

4. inter

- Our team plays a number of *intercollegiate* basketball games with California teams.
- A network of *interstate* highways links all sections of our country.

inter means (a) huge (b) between _____ *b* _____ .

5. mis

- A run was scored when the shortstop *misplayed* the ball.
- The cylinders in my car are *misfiring*.

mis is closest in meaning to (a) action (b) inefficiency _____ *b* _____ .

6. dis

- Logan has been working long hours, but that is no excuse for him to be *discourteous* to customers.
- The Mustangs will be at a *disadvantage* in the game because two of their best players are injured.

dis means (a) reverses (b) emphasizes a word's meaning _____a_____ .

7. ob, op

- The lawyer's *objection* to the police officer's testimony was overruled by the judge.
- The Hawkeyes should be a tough *opponent* for the Buckeyes.

ob and **op** mean (a) support (b) against _____b_____ .

8. ten

- The owners of an auto parts store are the *tenants* of the new building on the corner of Oak and Main Streets.
- Students held in *detention* at the high school I attended had to sit quietly for an hour and do homework.

ten relates to (a) keeping (b) rejecting _____a_____ .

9. tion

- Anya is embarrassed about the ticket she received for a speeding *violation*.
- Jackson can't play golf or tennis until the *inflammation* in his right elbow clears up.

tion relates to the (a) condition of (b) improvement of _____a_____ .

10. logy

- *Sociology* is concerned with the systematic study of society.
- *Zoology* is the branch of biology concerned with the animal kingdom.

logy relates to (a) people (b) study _____b_____ .

Matching Word Parts and Definitions

Match each definition with the word part it defines.

___h___	**1.** sub	**a.** one
___d___	**2.** pro	**b.** not; opposite of
___a___	**3.** uni	**c.** to hold
___f___	**4.** inter	**d.** for; in favor of
___j___	**5.** mis	**e.** study of

_b_	**6.** dis	**f.** between; among
_g_	**7.** ob, op	**g.** against
_c_	**8.** ten	**h.** under
_i_	**9.** tion	**i.** state of; act of; result of
_e_	**10.** logy	**j.** wrong

Fill-Ins with Word Parts

Select the appropriate word part so the proper word is formed in each sentence.

sub	uni	mis	ob	ten	logy
pro	inter	dis	op	tion	

1. Mr. Martin presented a moving recita _____ *tion* _____ of Shakespeare's "Sonnet 29."

2. The scuba divers discovered a(n) _____ *sub* _____ terranean tunnel on the south side of the isolated island.

3. Psycho _____ *logy* _____ is the most interesting subject I've studied so far in college.

4. It was difficult to find Filipe because everyone was wearing _____ *uni* _____ forms.

5. The rain _____ *ob* _____ literated the white lines on the football field.

6. The movie star claims he was _____ *mis* _____ quoted in the newspaper.

7. Mr. Perrochi's _____ *ten* _____ ure as mayor was twelve years, the longest anyone in our community has held that position.

8. The audience was served refreshments during the _____ *inter* _____ lude between the first and second acts.

9. Allen had a(n) _____ *dis* _____ agreement with his parents about his desire to get a job and continue college at night.

10. The candidate's record indicates he's _____ *pro* _____ -labor on most issues, so he should get the support of the industrial states.

Matching Words and Definitions

Use your knowledge of the underlined word parts to match the definitions and words.

_e_	**1.** <u>uni</u>lateral	**a.** wrong name
_f_	**2.** etymo<u>logy</u>	**b.** something taken for granted
_h_	**3.** <u>ob</u>durate	**c.** under the control of another
_b_	**4.** assump<u>tion</u>	**d.** spokesperson in favor of a cause; leading character in a play

_j_	**5.** di<u>sa</u>rray	**e.**	relating to one side; performed by only one side
_c_	**6.** <u>sub</u>servient	**f.**	study of the history of words
_a_	**7.** mis<u>nomer</u>	**g.**	not firm; weak
_i_	**8.** <u>inter</u>val	**h.**	stubborn; unyielding
_d_	**9.** <u>protagon</u>ist	**i.**	period between two events
_g_	**10.** <u>ten</u>uous	**j.**	not in good order; messy

Writing Your Own Definitions

Write the definitions of the words after noting the underlined word parts and studying the context of the sentences; if you are still uncertain, feel free to consult a dictionary. Typical responses:

1. The coroner's clear *articul<u>ation</u>* of the technical terms, as well as her precise explanation of what they meant, helped the jury understand what had happened to the victim.

articul<u>ation</u> _____ pronunciation that is clear and distinct _____

2. The team owners and player representatives finally agreed to have an <u>*inter*</u>*mediary* appointed to settle their dispute.

<u>*inter*</u>*mediary* _____ a go-between person selected to settle differences between those in conflict _____

3. The career counselor said that *audio<u>logy</u>* is a profession worth considering because numerous studies indicate that hearing loss is becoming a problem for many people in our society.

audio<u>logy</u> _____ study of hearing _____

4. The military commander insisted the island was <u>*ten*</u>*able* against any type of attack the enemy might launch.

<u>*ten*</u>*able* _____ capable of being held or defended _____

5. Despite pleas, coaxing, and threats, the <u>*obdurate*</u> youngster refused to open his mouth for the dentist.

<u>*obdurate*</u> _____ stubborn; defiant _____

6. The _miscreant_ was given an additional year in prison for contempt of court.

miscreant _____ criminal; villain; unprincipled person _____

7. Instead of having two legislative branches of government, a few states have a _unicameral_ legislature.

unicameral _____ having one legislative branch _____

8. Our daughter was _submissive_ throughout her elementary school years, but once she was in middle school, she gradually became rebellious.

submissive _____ obedient; agreeable _____

9. The clerk remained _dispassionate_ while the angry customer ranted and raved at him.

dispassionate _____ showing no emotion _____

10. Because he was unable to attend the meeting, Jim officially authorized Miguel to serve as his _proxy_.

proxy _____ substitute; representative _____

Learning Challenging Words from Context Clues

1. subterfuge (SUB tər fūj)—noun

- The athletic director made it clear to the coaches and members of the booster club that no _subterfuge,_ such as money or cars, should be used in the recruitment of athletes.
- Alexandra and her brother used lies and other types of _subterfuge_ to surprise their parents on their twenty-fifth wedding anniversary.

subterfuge has to do with (a) generosity (b) deceit _____ b _____ .

2. proclivity (prō KLIV ə tē)—noun

- A _proclivity_ for desserts of all kinds makes it hard for me to stay on my diet.
- Luke's driving license was suspended because of his _proclivity_ for driving too fast.

proclivity means (a) likeness for (b) suspicion of _____ a _____ .

3. **universally** (ū nə VUR sə lē)—adverb

■ The psychologist said acceptance and love are *universally* longed for by all people everywhere.
■ The assassination of President John F. Kennedy in 1963 was *universally* mourned throughout the world.

universally means (a) widely (b) sadly _____ *a* _____ .

4. **interim** (in tər im)—noun

■ In the *interim* between graduating from high school and serving in the Marines, Javier worked in a plastics factory.
■ Nicole plans to own a restaurant of her own someday, but in the *interim* she will continue working as the chief chef at the Green Lantern Cafe.

interim is associated with (a) consequently (b) meanwhile _____ *b* _____ .

5. **misconstrue** (MIS kən STROO)—verb

■ Please don't *misconstrue* what I'm saying; I would like to help you, but I simply don't have time.
■ Because the elderly clerk was somewhat hard of hearing, he will sometimes *misconstrue* what items customers ask for.

misconstrue indicates a person has (a) gotten the wrong idea (b) been foolish *a* .

6. **dissipate** (DIS ə pāt)—verb

■ Warmer temperatures caused the snow to *dissipate* by the end of the week.
■ The tension that had filled the room began to *dissipate* after the instructor told a few jokes.

dissipate means to gradually (a) increase (b) vanish _____ *b* _____ .

7. **obstreperous** (ob STREP ər əs)—adjective

■ My son had been *obstreperous* all day, so I sent him to bed immediately after supper.
■ This horse should be ridden by only experienced riders because he can be extremely *obstreperous* at times.

obstreperous means (a) disobedient (b) sickly _____ *a* _____ .

8. **tentative** (TENT ə tive)—adjective

■ Rachel wasn't *tentative* when Brent asked her for a date as she immediately said, "Yes!"
■ Mr. Bryson made a *tentative* offer to buy our house; the final decision depends upon whether the bank approves his loan application.

tentative indicates (a) uncertainty (b) confidence _____ *a* _____ .

9. <u>correlation</u> (kor ə LĀ shən)—noun

- A study conducted by a researcher at our college indicates a positive *correlation* between students' grades and their extracurricular activities.
- My math teacher said there is a *correlation* between mathematics skills and computer ability, but this relationship isn't as strong as many people seem to think it is.

correlation is about (a) connections (b) truths _____ *a* _____ .

10. **anthropology** (AN thr ə POL ə jē)—noun

- In my *anthropology* class we are studying the beginnings of civilization in North Africa.
- You will learn about many cultures in *anthropology*.

anthropology involves the study of (a) the solar system (b) human beings __*b*__ .

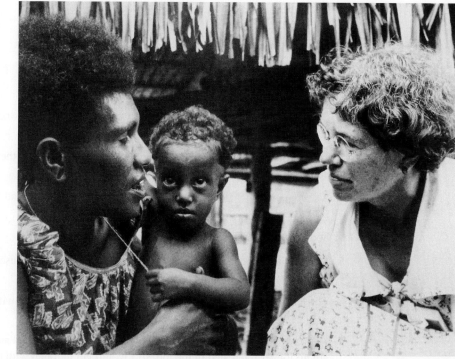

Margaret Mead (1901–1978) was a famous and influential *anthropologist* who studied the people of Samoa and other cultures. *(© Bettmann/ CORBIS)*

Matching Challenging Words and Definitions

Write each word before its definition.

subterfuge	universally	misconstrue	obstreperous	correlation
proclivity	interim	dissipate	tentative	anthropology

___tentative___ **1.** hesitant, uncertain, not final

___interim___ **2.** intermission, temporary period

___dissipate___ **3.** to fade slowly or disappear

___anthropology___ **4.** study of the origin, culture, and development of human beings

___subterfuge___ **5.** deception, secret evasion of the rules

___universally___ **6.** without exception, everywhere, widespread

___correlation___ **7.** a mutual relationship between two or more things, an orderly connection

___proclivity___ **8.** tendency, inclination, fondness for

___obstreperous___ **9.** disorderly, rowdy, unruly

___misconstrue___ **10.** misunderstand, misinterpret, misjudge

Fill-Ins with Challenging Words

In each space, write the appropriate word from those listed below.

subterfuge	universally	misconstrue	obstreperous	correlation
proclivity	interim	dissipate	tentative	anthropology

1. During the _____interim_____ between semesters, Don worked at a small hardware store in his hometown.

2. The accountant's _____subterfuge_____ was discovered by the bank's auditors, and he was eventually convicted of embezzlement.

3. A strong _____correlation_____ exists between mathematical and navigational skills.

4. We thought the fog would eventually _____dissipate_____ during the morning hours, but it didn't, so we decided not to drive into town.

5. Dimitri has decided to major in _____anthropology_____ because of his fascination with early civilizations.

6. The teacher was understandably tense and tired after dealing with a number of _____obstreperous_____ students throughout the day.

7. He may _____misconstrue_____ your failure to return his call as an indication you are no longer interested in the job, so I would get in touch with him right away.

8. Our college is _____universally_____ admired throughout the state for its outstanding music department.

9. Because of Cheung's _____*proclivity*_____ for drawing, his high school counselor suggested he might want to consider majoring in art when he enrolled in college.

10. Leigh is unsure what she's going to do this summer, but she's made _____*tentative*_____ plans to visit some friends in Minnesota if she earns enough money.

Checking Your Word Power

After selecting your response, put the letter in the space provided.

____*d*____ **1.** The *opposite* of **tentative** is
    a. uncertain
    b. hesitant
    c. doubtful
    d. positive

____*a*____ **2.** The *opposite* of **misconstrue** is
    a. understand
    b. disagree
    c. cheat
    d. help

____*c*____ **3.** The *opposite* of **proclivity** is
    a. fondness for
    b. desire for
    c. distaste for
    d. talent for

____*b*____ **4.** The word closest in meaning to **interim** is
    a. maturity
    b. pause
    c. pity
    d. interference

____*b*____ **5.** Which of the following is most closely related to **anthropology?**
    a. astronomy
    b. history
    c. psychology
    d. chemistry

____*a*____ **6.** Which of the following is most likely to be **universally** desired?
    a. acceptance
    b. solitude
    c. simplicity
    d. thriftiness

_____b_____ **7.** The word *not* associated with **dissipate** is
  a. diminish
  b. magnify
  c. evaporate
  d. vanish

_____a_____ **8.** **subterfuge : deception ::** **a.** abbreviation : shortening
  b. reduction : increasing
  c. expectation : surprise
  d. confession : denial

_____d_____ **9.** **obstreperous : behavior ::** **a.** thoughtful : kind
  b. critical : helpful
  c. wealthy : desirable
  d. disobedient : conduct

_____c_____ **10.** **correlation : disharmony ::** **a.** spoil : ruin
  b. shame : disgrace
  c. honesty : dishonesty
  d. agreement : cooperation

Completing a Passage

After reading the selection, fill in each space with one of the words listed below.

anthropology	correlation	dissipate	interim	misconstrue
obstreperous	proclivity	subterfuge	tentative	universally

IDENTITY THEFT

Teenagers, senior citizens, celebrities, school crossing guards, doctors, store clerks, truck drivers, lawyers, college students, and many others from all walks of life have been recent victims of identity theft. This devastating crime is growing not only nationally but also ____universally____ as more and more people throughout the world are experiencing the trauma it inflicts. Because of the treacherous ____subterfuge____ committed by computer hackers and other unprincipled criminals with a(n) ____proclivity____ for thievery, thousands of lives today are in disarray.

Last year's figures relating to identity theft are still incomplete, so only ____tentative____ conclusions can presently be drawn based on them; however, there seems to be no doubt in the minds of law authorities who deal with this crime that it is more common than ever. Though these authorities are confident that foolproof methods to prevent identity theft will someday be developed, it is unlikely that such methods will be available soon, so in the ____interim____, these steps are strongly advised:

- Be extremely protective of your Social Security number. In fact, it's a good idea not to carry your Social Security card in your wallet because if you lose it, it will provide the key information a thief needs to get credit cards, passports, and other important documents in your name.

- Never give out your Social Security number over the phone, even if the caller says you have __misconstrued__ his or her intent or becomes downright __obstreperous__ and threatening.

- If people are waiting to use an ATM after you, be sure to place your hand over your PIN so no one can learn your card number.

- Be especially vigilant when using a computer. Order products online from only well-established businesses with a secure website; otherwise, your credit card number will be in jeopardy.

- Never respond to e-mails requesting your bank account, Social Security number, or insurance card numbers. Identity thieves often pose as bank or government employees, so under no circumstances should you ever reveal such personal information.

- Be wary of downloading any type of "free" software, particularly if you must reveal your e-mail password, as your privacy will likely be compromised if you do.

- Carefully examine your credit card statements. If you spot unauthorized charges, call the credit card issuer immediately.

- Should a monthly credit card statement be late by more than a week, call the credit card issuer to make sure someone hasn't diverted your statements to a different address. You can also opt to receive statements via e-mail instead.

- Always shred, not wad up, all receipts and other papers containing personal information. Identity thieves are always on the lookout for any source, including a trash barrel or a dumpster, that may reveal personal information that they can use to their benefit.

A professor of __anthropology__ made news recently when he asserted that identity theft is no bigger a problem today than it was centuries ago; apparently, the professor is unaware of the clear __correlation__ between the growth of modern technology and the increase in today's identity theft. In any instance, this crime will not soon __dissipate__, so keep in mind the preceding suggestions so that your chances of becoming a victim of identity theft are markedly reduced.

Subterfuge—deception used to avoid a rule, to escape a consequence, to hide something:

- The spy's successful <u>subterfuge</u> enabled him to steal copies of classified government documents for several years before being caught.

Origin: 1565–1575 <Latin—*subterfugium* (an evasion) and *subterfugere* (to evade, escape, flee by stealth) <*subter* (beneath, secretly) and *fugere* (flee; "fugitive" is also derived from *fugere*)

Connotation: *negative*—associated with deception

Image to remember: a spy

Write an original sentence using *subterfuge*:

_____

_____

_____

MASTERING CONFUSING WORDS | **device / devise**

device   a noun that refers to an object:

A stapler can be a handy <u>device</u> to have on your desk.

devise   an action verb meaning to plan, invent, or form in one's mind:

We need to <u>devise</u> a better way of keeping our basketball from rolling down the hill every time we miss a shot.

Circle the correct answer:

1. I'm sure Noreen can device / (devise) an effective method of wrapping that package so nothing will be broken.

2. This is an excellent (device) / devise to use if you have ice on your car's windshield.

Write original sentences using these words:

1. **device:** _____

2. **devise:** _____

Chapter 3

Learning Word Parts from Context Clues

1. able, ible

- My folks believe the most *enjoy<u>able</u>* way of traveling is by train.
- The fiddlehead is an *ed<u>ible</u>,* fernlike plant.

able and **ible** mean (a) capable of (b) incapable of _____ *a* _____ .

2. a, an

- Doug is certainly *<u>a</u>typical* of his brothers; he doesn't enjoy hunting and fishing as they do.
- When the central government was overthrown, no one was able to rule or to enforce the laws, so *<u>an</u>archy* reigned.

a and **an** give words (a) extra (b) opposite meanings _____ *b* _____ .

3. super

- Tyrone is a respected *<u>super</u>visor* at the auto plant.
- The new regulations *<u>super</u>sede* the previous zoning restrictions.

super means (a) over (b) below _____ *a* _____ .

4. trans

- Melanie plans to *<u>trans</u>fer* to a college in Texas.
- Trucks were used to *<u>trans</u>port* the potatoes to market.

trans refers to (a) power (b) change _____ *b* _____ .

5. poly

- Are there any religions that still permit *<u>poly</u>gamy*? I would think one husband or wife would be enough!
- Christie is a *<u>poly</u>glot* because she can speak English, French, Spanish, and Italian.

poly refers to (a) foolishness (b) many _____ *b* _____ .

6. ver

- Can you _verify_ that this wallet is yours?
- Evidence later confirmed that the young children had given _veracious_ testimony at the informal hearing.

ver relates to (a) truth (b) fiction _____ _a_ _____ .

7. log

- Before Mr. Wilkinson showed his slides of China, he gave a _prologue_ explaining why he had traveled to that country.
- The movie has English subtitles for those who can't understand the French _dialogue_.

log is related to (a) words (b) travel _____ _a_ _____ .

8. ism

- Novels featuring _romanticism_ have always been popular.
- The belief that there is no God is called _atheism_.

ism refers to (a) realities (b) beliefs _____ _b_ _____ .

9. chron

- Mike has had a _chronic_ backache since he fell rollerblading two weeks ago.
- Generally, history texts present material in a _chronological_ order.

chron means (a) time (b) changeless _____ _a_ _____ .

10. post

- At the conclusion of the wedding ceremony, Laura played an original _postlude_ on the organ.
- Ahmed added a _postscript_ to his letter because he had forgotten to include the exact time when his plane would be arriving.

post means (a) before (b) after _____ _b_ _____ .

Matching Word Parts and Definitions

Match each definition with the word part it defines.

_g_	**1.** able, ible	**a.**	word; talk
_d_	**2.** a, an	**b.**	many
_c_	**3.** super	**c.**	above; over; beyond
_e_	**4.** trans	**d.**	not; without
_b_	**5.** poly	**e.**	across; change to
_h_	**6.** ver	**f.**	time
_a_	**7.** log	**g.**	capable of; condition of
_i_	**8.** ism	**h.**	true
_f_	**9.** chron	**i.**	belief or doctrine
_j_	**10.** post	**j.**	after

Fill-Ins with Word Parts

Select the appropriate word part so the proper word is formed in each sentence.

able	ism	trans	ver	a	chron
ible	super	poly	log	an	post

1. The belief that things will improve is called optim _____ism_____ , whereas the belief that things will get worse is called pessim _____ism_____ .

2. Have you ever flown at _____super_____ sonic speeds?

3. Autumn is cap _____able_____ of helping you with your problems, so why don't you ask her to?

4. Mr. Wyzinski _____trans_____ planted a maple tree from his backyard to his front yard.

5. The teller said I would have to have two forms of identity _____ver_____ ification before she could cash the check.

6. My uncle's mono _____log_____ ue about his operation went on for almost an hour.

7. A popular singer who had been killed in a car accident was given the prize _____post_____ humously.

8. In geometry class, I learned to construct and measure _____poly_____ gons, which are figures having many angles.

9. A(n) _____an_____ onymous person telephoned my parents to complain about the way I drive my car.

10. My grandparents' old diary provides a(n) _____chron_____ icle of the events leading to their immigration to the United States.

Matching Words and Definitions

Use your knowledge of the underlined word parts to match the definitions and words.

_c_	**1.** habit<u>able</u>	**a.** a chain of many South Pacific islands
_h_	**2.** stoic<u>ism</u>	**b.** not caring about right or wrong
_e_	**3.** <u>super</u>cilious	**c.** can be lived in
_g_	**4.** <u>trans</u>it	**d.** future generations; those coming after
_a_	**5.** <u>Poly</u>nesia	**e.** overly critical; conceited
_i_	**6.** <u>ver</u>itable	**f.** words of praise
_j_	**7.** <u>chrono</u>meter	**g.** passing across or through; a vehicle for transportation
_b_	**8.** <u>a</u>moral	**h.** belief that one should be indifferent to feelings, whether pleasurable or painful
_f_	**9.** eu<u>log</u>y	**i.** true; authentic; genuine
_d_	**10.** <u>post</u>erity	**j.** instrument for measuring time

Writing Your Own Definitions

Write the definitions of the words after noting the underlined word parts and studying the context of the sentences; if you are still uncertain, feel free to consult a dictionary. Typical responses:

1. A colorful picture of the school's mascot was <u>super</u>imposed on the yearbook cover.

   superimposed _____ laid or placed over _____

2. In this computer age, using a typewriter is considered *ana<u>chron</u>istic* by many people.

   anachronistic _____ old-fashioned; out-of-date; not in the right time frame _____

3. The tinted window was still sufficiently *trans<u>luc</u>ent* that I could see figures of people walking by on the sidewalk.

   translucent _____ permitting light to shine through _____

4. After the peace was finally won and the soldiers came home, the *<u>post</u>war* economy boomed.

   postwar _____ after the war _____

5. Snow was such an *<u>a</u>nomaly* in this section of the state that many people had seldom if ever seen it before.

   anomaly _____ abnormality; irregularity _____

6. People with fair skin are especially *susceptible* to sunburn.

susceptible _____ sensitive to; defenseless against _____

7. Though his story was hard to believe, it proved to be <u>veracious</u> in every detail.

<u>veracious</u> _____ truthful _____

8. The board of directors' actions made it clear that male *chauvin<u>ism</u>* would not be tolerated.

chauvin<u>ism</u> _____ partisanship; the feeling that one is superior to others _____

9. Apparently, the *dox<u>ology</u>* that began the service was a familiar one to most of the worshipers, but I had never heard it before.

dox<u>ology</u> _____ an expression of praise to God; a short hymn _____

10. My uncle is a <u>poly</u>math as a result of his unending curiosity, extensive education, wide traveling, and constant reading.

<u>poly</u>math _____ a person of great and varied learning _____

Learning Challenging Words from Context Clues

1. cul<u>pable</u> (KUL pə bəl)—adjective

- Ted actually broke the CD player, but Rosaire felt *culpable* because it was her teasing that had caused the accident.
- Donovan felt *culpable* for his team's bowling loss because if he had made either a strike or a spare, his team would have won.

culpable means (a) interested in (b) responsible for _____ b _____ .

2. <u>apathy</u> (AP ə thē)—noun

- A teacher who delights in what he or she teaches is deeply disappointed when students display *apathy* for the subject.
- I thought Meredith would be eager to talk about her new job, but she showed complete *apathy* when I asked her to tell me about it.

apathy indicates (a) indifference (b) ignorance _____ a _____ .

3. <u>superfluous</u> (soo PUR floo əs)—adjective

- Buying Vanessa a sweater would be *superfluous,* as she must already have at least a dozen.
- Please don't ask him what happened because he goes into such *superfluous* detail.

superfluous means (a) too much (b) too little _____ *a* _____ .

4. <u>transition</u> (tran ZISH ən)—noun

- Going to school for the first time is sometimes a troubling *transition* in a child's life.
- Electricity ushered in a major *transition* in American life.

transition has to do with (a) emotion (b) change _____ *b* _____ .

5. <u>polychromatic</u> (POL ē krō MAT ik)—adjective

- Las Vegas is noted for its flashy, *polychromatic* neon signs advertising its many hotels and gambling casinos.
- The evening sky was *polychromatic,* with brilliant shades of red, orange, pink, blue, and gray covering the horizon.

polychromatic has to do with many (a) noises (b) colors _____ *b* _____ .

6. <u>veracity</u> (və RAS i tē)—noun

- Chad's reputation was such that no one doubted the *veracity* of his story.
- An early biographer of George Washington claimed that Washington once threw a silver dollar across the Potomac River, but most historians question the *veracity* of that story.

veracity means (a) truthfulness (b) anger _____ *a* _____ .

7. <u>epilogue</u> (EP ə log)—noun

- At the end of the book, the author added a short *epilogue* to explain what eventually happened to the young boy featured in the story.
- A speaker gave an *epilogue* after the final act to explain what events had motivated the writing of the play.

epilogue refers to added (a) responsibility (b) information _____ *b* _____ .

8. <u>nepotism</u> (NEP ə tiz əm)—noun

- Many people accused the mayor of *nepotism* after he appointed his brother-in-law chief of the fire department.
- Mr. Healey was obviously guilty of *nepotism* when he appointed his twenty-two-year-old son district manager because there were many other employees who were much better qualified for the position.

nepotism is associated with showing (a) favoritism (b) ignorance _____ *a* _____ .

Peacocks are among the most magnificent *polychromatic* animals. (Stan Osolinski/Getty Images)

9. chronic (KRON ik)—adjective

- Jamie reluctantly gave up basketball because of *chronic* knee problems that had plagued her since her sophomore year.
- The doctor said the *chronic* headache Andrew had suffered from all winter was caused by a sinus infection.

chronic means (a) mysterious (b) long-lasting _____ *b* _____ .

10. posthumously (POS chə məs lē)—adverb

- Shortly after her death, she was *posthumously* honored by the college when the new science building was named after her.
- *Posthumously*, Van Gogh is recognized as one of the world's greatest artists, but this certainly was not the case during his lifetime.

posthumously means (a) while living (b) after death _____ *b* _____ .

Matching Challenging Words and Definitions

Write each word before its definition.

| culpable | superfluous | polychromatic | epilogue | chronic |
| apathy | transition | veracity | nepotism | posthumously |

superfluous **1.** unnecessary, excessive, too much

apathy **2.** lack of interest, absence of emotion

polychromatic **3.** many colored, having a variety of colors

posthumously **4.** after death

nepotism **5.** preference given to relatives

epilogue **6.** concluding information added at the end of a book, poem, play, or other literary work; postscript; supplement

culpable **7.** at fault, deserving blame, responsible for

chronic **8.** continuous, of long duration

veracity **9.** truth; something that is true

transition **10.** movement from one place to another; changeover; passage from one stage to another

Fill-Ins with Challenging Words

In each space, write the appropriate word from those listed below.

| culpable | superfluous | polychromatic | epilogue | chronic |
| apathy | transition | veracity | nepotism | posthumously |

1. Most people don't enjoy being around a(n) _____chronic_____ complainer because hearing constant complaining soon becomes tiresome and depressing.

2. Old photos and letters added _____veracity_____ to his claim that he had once served in the Navy.

3. The judge found the defendants _____culpable_____ for the accident, so they had to pay for all the damages in addition to a large fine.

4. Hannah's _____apathy_____ was obvious during class as she often sighed and yawned during the teacher's lecture, and she wasn't interested in participating in any of the small-group discussions.

5. My mother works at a florist shop, so I guess it would be rather _____superfluous_____ to send her flowers for her birthday, don't you think?

6. Though the actor died shortly after finishing the movie, he was nominated
_____posthumously_____ for an Academy Award.

7. The author of this latest biography about Benjamin Franklin includes an interesting _____epilogue_____ after the last chapter detailing what became of many of Franklin's descendants.

8. The _____transition_____ from an urban to a rural life was a surprisingly easy one for Manuel to make.

9. Some fans believe the coach is guilty of _____nepotism_____ because he recently inserted his daughter into the starting lineup, but I don't agree with them because I think she is clearly one of the better players on the team.

10. When did it become possible to take _____polychromatic_____ snapshots rather than black-and-white ones?

Checking Your Word Power

After selecting your response, put the letter in the space provided.

___c___ **1.** The *opposite* of **epilogue** is
    a. index
    b. chapter
    c. preface
    d. graph

___b___ **2.** The *opposite* of **posthumously** is something done
    a. in anger
    b. while living
    c. before thinking
    d. for revenge

___d___ **3.** The *opposite* of **culpable** is
    a. sober
    b. humorous
    c. guilty
    d. innocent

___a___ **4. Transition** suggests
    a. change
    b. extravagance
    c. indifference
    d. duplication

_____b_____ **5. Superfluous** suggests
  a. power
  b. surplus
  c. dishonesty
  d. weakness

_____d_____ **6. Veracity** suggests
  a. adventure
  b. tenderness
  c. popularity
  d. honesty

_____d_____ **7.** If a person exhibits **apathy,** he or she displays
  a. confidence
  b. fear
  c. joy
  d. unconcern

_____c_____ **8. polychromatic : dull :: a.** flat : dismal
          b. colorful : flashy
          c. colorful : dreary
          d. many : a lot

_____b_____ **9. nepotism : resentment :: a.** optimism : hatred
          b. cooperation : appreciation
          c. bitterness : admiration
          d. abolish : boldness

_____d_____ **10. chronic : persistent :: a.** anger : frequently
          b. happiness : temporary
          c. humor : permanently
          d. ceaseless : continuous

Completing a Passage

After reading the selection, fill in each space with one of the words listed below.

nepotism	culpable	chronic	polychromatic	apathy
veracity	posthumously	epilogue	transition	

TEEN DRIVERS

Possessing the quickest reflexes, keenest eyesight, and most stamina, teenagers could reasonably be expected to be the best drivers on the road, but, in fact, they are ____culpable____ for more serious traffic accidents than drivers in any other age bracket. Specifically, drivers ages sixteen to nineteen are four times more likely than older drivers to have a serious car crash. Tragically, thousands of teenagers die annually in car crashes, accounting for 40 percent of all deaths among this age group. Each spring in high schools across the nation, with graduates resplendent in ___polychromatic___ robes and tasseled mortarboards, diplomas are solemnly awarded ___posthumously___ to seniors who died in car crashes during the school year.

In addition to the many lost lives, a half-million young drivers are seriously injured in car accidents, many of whom will endure permanent disabilities and ____chronic____ pain for the rest of their lives.

Considering their physical advantages, why is it that teenagers have the highest instead of the lowest accident rate? (One thing is certain: it is not due to driving ____apathy____ , as teens consistently rank "driving" at or near the top of their favorite activities.) Studies noted for their ____veracity____ have identified these factors as the major causes of teenage drivers' high accident rate:

- They are more likely than older drivers to speed, run red lights, make illegal turns, and drive after using alcohol or drugs.
- They are the least likely to wear seatbelts.
- Over half of all teenage drivers use cell phones or indulge in other risky behavior (combing their hair, tuning their radios, etc.) while driving.
- They often disregard hazardous driving conditions caused by rain, snow, sleet, fog, traffic congestion, and road repairs.

In an effort to significantly reduce the accident rate of young drivers, a number of states have adopted an approach known as "graduated drivers licensing" (GDL) for applicants under the age of eighteen. While the GDL approach varies from state to state, it generally includes requirements and restrictions like these:

1. An applicant must successfully "graduate" from both the supervised and intermediate states before receiving a full-privileges driver's license. (The ___transition___ period between each stage is commonly three months.)

2. Applicants must sharpen their driving skills for a specific number of hours under the supervision of adult license holders.

3. Night driving is prohibited for the first three months. (Research reveals that 42 percent of teen fatalities occur between 9:00 P.M. and 6:00 A.M.)

4. Chauffeuring other teens is prohibited unless an adult is present. (Over 60 percent of teens killed in crashes are passengers in cars driven by other teens.)

5. There is zero tolerance for drunk driving. (Even if the teen is the son or daughter of politically connected parents, ___nepotism___ has no power to change this policy.)

There is gathering and impressive evidence that the GDL approach is effective; specifically, safety experts in states where GDL has been implemented report drops in teen accidents from 10 percent to slightly over 30 percent.* Because of these encouraging results, it is likely that more and more states will adopt GDL in an attempt to save young drivers from injuries and death.

---

*A(n) ___epilogue___ to one of these reports indicates that a province in Canada experienced a drop of over 60 percent in the accident rate of sixteen-year-olds one year after adopting a graduated licensing law.

FEATURED WORD: nepotism

Nepotism—favoritism shown on the basis of a family relationship:

- The governor was accused of <u>nepotism</u> after he appointed his son-in-law as the new state attorney general.

Origin: 1655–1665 <Italian—*nepotismo* from *nepote* (nephew) <Latin—*nepos*—grandson, nephew (in the Middle Ages, *nepotismo* referred to the privileges granted by a pope to his nephew, who, in some cases, may actually have been his son)

Family words: nepotistic (adj), nepotistical (adj), nepotist (n)

Connotation: *negative*—indicates unfairness

Image to remember: a manager who was appointed to his or her job by a family member who has a high-ranking job in the same company

Write an original sentence using *nepotism*:

_____

_____

MASTERING CONFUSING WORDS | **affect / effect**

affect   a verb meaning "to influence":

Jenna didn't think breaking up with him would <u>affect</u> her so much.
How does working the night shift <u>affect</u> you physically?

effect   a noun meaning "result":

Salary raises had a wonderful <u>effect</u> on the morale of the staff.
Waiting around has a tiring <u>effect</u> on most people.

Circle the correct answer:

1. Eating sensibly and exercising regularly soon had a positive <u>affect /(effect)</u> on his emotional as well as his physical health.

2. Did Connor's angry outburst (affect)/ effect your opinion of him?

Write original sentences using these words:

1. **affect:** _____

2. **effect:** _____

Chapter 4

Learning Word Parts from Context Clues

1. bio

- More _biographies_ have been published about Abraham Lincoln than about any other American.
- Madison is doing extremely well in _biochemistry,_ a course concerned with the chemistry of living matter.

bio means (a) science (b) life _____ _b_ _____ .

2. tele

- Our college needs a more powerful _telescope_ to see the most distant planets in our solar system.
- People are more likely to send an e-mail today to distant friends than a _telegram_ unless the message is particularly urgent.

tele means (a) far away (b) close by _____ _a_ _____ .

3. auto

- In contrast to a carriage pulled by a horse, a car seems to move by its own power; that's why a car is called an _automobile._
- Our furnace will _automatically_ turn on if the temperature in the house falls below sixty-two degrees.

auto means (a) modern (b) self _____ _b_ _____ .

4. eu

- Mr. Sanchez gave a _eulogy_ at the memorial service for his popular neighbor.
- The seniors expressed their _euphoria_ on graduation night by tossing their mortarboards high in the air.

eu means (a) sorrowful (b) praiseworthy _____ _b_ _____ .

5. ante

- Harry Truman's presidency *antedates* John Kennedy's by eight years. Between their terms in office, Dwight Eisenhower was president.
- A pronoun must refer to a previous noun. For example, in the sentence "The package will be expensive to mail because it weighs more than eight pounds," *package* is the *antecedent* of the pronoun *it*.

ante means (a) before (b) after _____ *a* _____ .

6. rect

- A *rectangle* consists of four right angles.
- He has always been a person of high principles and moral *rectitude,* so no one was surprised he entered the ministry.

rect means (a) slanted, intelligent (b) straight, correct _____ *b* _____ .

7. fid

- Chantelle *confided* her secret to Cameron because she knew he wouldn't tell anyone else.
- My sound system has such good *fidelity* you would swear the musicians were in my room.

fid is related to (a) secrets (b) dependability _____ *b* _____ .

8. equ

- Most people *equate* expensive cars with wealth.
- Needless to say, tightrope walkers must have good *equilibrium.*

equ is related to (a) equality (b) equipment _____ *a* _____ .

9. pan

- Athletes from North, Central, and South America participate in the *Pan-American* games.
- Barbara's dream is to have a house on the coast with a *panoramic* view of the ocean.

pan means (a) all, wide (b) few, narrow _____ *a* _____ .

10. sym, syn

- Damian appreciated his friends' expressions of *sympathy* after his grandfather died.
- By *synthesizing* the information and clues revealed by the extensive investigation, the detectives were able to solve the baffling crime.

sym and **syn** mean (a) against (b) with _____ *b* _____ .

Matching Word Parts and Definitions

Match each definition with the word part it defines.

_f_	**1.** bio	**a.**	far; distant
_a_	**2.** tele	**b.**	all
_j_	**3.** auto	**c.**	good; well
_c_	**4.** eu	**d.**	together with
_h_	**5.** ante	**e.**	equal
_i_	**6.** rect	**f.**	life
_g_	**7.** fid	**g.**	faith
_e_	**8.** equ	**h.**	before
_b_	**9.** pan	**i.**	straight, correct
_d_	**10.** sym, syn	**j.**	self

Fill-Ins with Word Parts

Select the appropriate word part so the proper word is formed in each sentence.

bio	auto	ante	fid	pan
tele	eu	rect	equ	syn

1. The earth is divided into two hemispheres at the _____*equ*_____ ator.

2. The police were afraid the large crowd would break into _____*pan*_____ demonium when the concert was canceled.

3. By making it possible to send voices from distant places, the _____*tele*_____ phone revolutionized communications.

4. It's important to have con _____*fid*_____ ence in your doctor.

5. College students have more _____*auto*_____ nomony than high school students, so they must learn to be responsible for themselves.

6. Dr. Morton's _____*ante*_____ room was filled with patients.

7. After our teacher cor _____*rect*_____ ed our essays, we rewrote them one more time.

8. The _____*bio*_____ sphere is the part of the earth's crust, waters, and atmosphere that supports living organisms.

9. *Sanitary engineer* is a(n) _____*eu*_____ phemism for *garbage collector.*

10. Mr. Nickerson formed a(n) _____*syn*_____ dicate with other business people to buy the trucking firm.

Matching Words and Definitions

Use your knowledge of the underlined word parts to match the definitions and words.

_d_	**1.** <u>rect</u>ify	**a.**	time of year when day and night are equal in length
_g_	**2.** <u>synchron</u>ize	**b.**	life of a person written by that person
_j_	**3.** <u>eu</u>thanasia	**c.**	a cure-all; an answer to all problems
_a_	**4.** <u>equi</u>nox	**d.**	to set right; to correct
_h_	**5.** <u>ante</u>diluvian	**e.**	written statement made under oath
_i_	**6.** <u>bio</u>mass	**f.**	communication through distance by thoughts only
_c_	**7.** <u>pan</u>acea	**g.**	make to occur at the same time
_b_	**8.** <u>autobio</u>graphy	**h.**	belonging to the period before the biblical Flood; extremely old
_f_	**9.** <u>tele</u>pathy	**i.**	the total quantity of living matter within a specific area
_e_	**10.** af<u>fid</u>avit	**j.**	the deliberate putting to death painlessly of a person suffering from a fatal disease; mercy killing

Writing Your Own Definitions

Write the definitions of the words after noting the underlined word parts and studying the context of the sentences; if you are still uncertain, feel free to consult a dictionary. Typical responses:

1. Being accountable to no one, the *<u>auto</u>crat* ruled the country with absolute authority.

<u>auto</u>crat _____ dictator; person with complete power _____

2. The weekend *tele<u>thon</u>* raised millions of dollars from people and corporations throughout the country.

tele<u>thon</u> _____ a lengthy television show that raises money for charity _____

3. A small band of rebels attempted to incite an *insur<u>rection</u>* to topple the newly established government.

insur<u>rection</u> _____ rebellion, uprising _____

4. I'm sure many people will *<u>eu</u>logize* Dr. Perez at her retirement party as she's been an excellent teacher for many years.

<u>eu</u>logize _____ to praise highly in speech or writing _____

5. Some religious people in the community considered my grandfather an *infidel* because he never went to church.

infidel _____ non-believer in the dominant religion of the area or culture _____

6. A *synthesis* of durable metals revolutionized the making of golf clubs in the latter part of the 20th century.

synthesis _____ the putting together of separate elements _____

7. Most ancient people practiced *pantheism* rather than *monotheism,* which is the belief in one God.

pantheism _____ belief in many gods _____

8. The federal government and our state government are *equivalent* in their makeup as they both contain legislative, executive, and judicial branches.

equivalent _____ equal, the same _____

9. The science of *bionics,* based upon the study of how the human body works, has led to much-improved artificial limbs.

bionics _____ science that attempts to duplicate actual limbs and movements through mechanical means _____

10. After World War II, only a few of the beautiful *antebellum* buildings were still standing in this historic city.

antebellum _____ before the war, especially the Civil War _____

Learning Challenging Words from Context Clues

1. biopsy (BĪ op sē)—noun

- Pathologists are specialists in studying samples of patients' tissues obtained through *biopsies.*
- Fortunately, the *biopsy* revealed the mole on the patient's arm was harmless.

biopsy is an examination of (a) living tissues (b) medical procedures _____ a _____ .

2. **telepathy** (tə LEP ə thē)—noun

- Though the twin sisters are often separated by many miles, they claim to know what each other is thinking at all times; they obviously believe in *telepathy.*
- Many scientists are skeptical about *telepathy,* but there are some who believe it is possible to communicate with those far away by thoughts only.

telepathy is communicating by using (a) the sense of touch (b) minds only _____ *b* _____ .

3. **autonomy** (ə TON ə mē)—noun

- India received its *autonomy* from Great Britain in 1947.
- The parents permitted their fifteen-year-old daughter a great deal of *autonomy* on most matters, but they did not allow her to babysit on school nights.

autonomy is associated with (a) independence (b) dependence _____ *a* _____ .

4. **euphemism** (U fə miz əm)—noun

- "Senior citizen" is a *euphemism* for "old person."
- The words "false teeth" are not featured in the ad; instead, the *euphemism* "dentures" is used.

euphemism is a word that is thought to be more (a) refined (b) descriptive than a word that is more commonly used _____ *a* _____ .

5. **antediluvian** (AN ti di LOO vē ən)—adjective

- The *antediluvian* period is the time before the Flood mentioned in the book of Genesis in the Old Testament.
- When I was younger, I thought my parents' philosophy for raising children was so old-fashioned that it was *antediluvian,* but I've changed my mind since I've become a parent.

antediluvian is related to (a) complicated times (b) ancient times _____ *b* _____ .

6. **rectify** (REK tə fī)—verb

- Pat attempted to *rectify* his clumsiness by slowing down and treading carefully.
- I must try to *rectify* this dangerous situation before someone else gets hurt.

rectify means to make (a) right (b) excuses _____ *a* _____ .

7. **infidelity** (in fi DEL ə tē)—noun

- The diplomat's *infidelity* to his country led to his arrest for treason.
- *Infidelity* is a leading cause of divorce because it is devastating to be betrayed.

infidelity is (a) foolishness (b) disloyalty _____ *b* _____ .

8. **equivocal** (ē KWIV ə k əl)—adjective

- Apparently, Maria hasn't decided what to do about the matter because she gave me an *equivocal* answer when I asked her.
- I hate to be so *equivocal,* but both jobs appeal to me, so I don't know what to do.

equivocal means (a) indefinite (b) ashamed _____ *a* _____ .

9. **panacea** (PAN ə SĒ ə)—noun

- Unfortunately, there seems to be no *panacea* for ending all poverty in every country.
- One of the candidates for the school board said the *panacea* for improving the community's public schools was simple: Hire excellent teachers.

panacea is a (a) lie (b) cure-all _____ *b* _____ .

10. **syndrome** (SIN drom)—noun

- The *syndrome* for diabetes includes fatigue, loss of weight, and thirstiness.
- The economist warned that the *syndrome* of a recession includes a high rate of unemployment and an unstable stock market.

syndrome is a set of (a) agreements (b) symptoms _____ *b* _____ .

Matching Challenging Words and Definitions

Write each word before its definition.

| biopsy | autonomy | antediluvian | infidelity | panacea |
| telepathy | euphemism | rectify | equivocal | syndrome |

___*panacea*___ **1.** cure for all ills, a universal remedy

___*autonomy*___ **2.** self-direction, independence

___*infidelity*___ **3.** unfaithfulness, treason

___*syndrome*___ **4.** set of symptoms

___*biopsy*___ **5.** examination of tissue from a living subject

___*antediluvian*___ **6.** before the Flood, ancient

___*equivocal*___ **7.** wavering, uncertain, indefinite

___*telepathy*___ **8.** mind reading, extrasensory perception (ESP)

___*rectify*___ **9.** make right, correct

___*euphemism*___ **10.** the substitution of a mild word for one thought to be harsh or offensive

Fill-Ins with Challenging Words

In each space, write the appropriate word from those listed below.

biopsy	autonomy	antediluvian	infidelity	panacea
telepathy	euphemism	rectify	equivocal	syndrome

1. We employees have _____autonomy_____ when it comes to choosing the hours we prefer to work, so that's a big plus, particularly for those of us who are parents.

2. Some of my older relatives believe young men with shoulder-length hair look positively _____antediluvian_____ rather than up-to-date and sophisticated.

3. The _____biopsy_____ revealed the tissue was cancerous, so the doctor prepared herself to give the patient this disturbing news.

4. We were in a(n) _____equivocal_____ state of mind for some time because we couldn't decide whether to paint or wallpaper our apartment.

5. The doctor explained that the _____syndrome_____ for meningitis includes a stiff neck, headache, and fever.

6. Sometimes "antiques" seems to be a(n) _____euphemism_____ for "junk."

7. The political candidate insisted he had been faithful to his ex-wife during their marriage, strongly denying that _____infidelity_____ on his part had led to their divorce.

8. The _____panacea_____ for ridding our city of smog is to ban all vehicles from the downtown area.

9. You may not believe in mental _____telepathy_____, but I have an open mind when it comes to ESP because I've sometimes thought about getting in touch with someone when out of the blue he or she telephones me.

10. I completely botched the job when I tried to install a garbage disposal unit in our kitchen sink, so the only way I knew to _____rectify_____ matters was to call a plumber.

Checking Your Word Power

After selecting your response, put the letter in the space provided.

_____d_____ 1. The *opposite* of **infidelity** is
  a. dedication
  b. talent
  c. crankiness
  d. loyalty

_____a_____ **2.** The *opposite* of **antediluvian** is
  a. modern
  b. stubborn
  c. ambitious
  d. boring

_____c_____ **3.** The *opposite* of **rectify** is
  a. blame
  b. request
  c. harm
  d. fix

_____b_____ **4. Autonomy** suggests
  a. poverty
  b. self-sufficiency
  c. indecency
  d. delicacy

_____d_____ **5. Biopsy** is most closely associated with
  a. engineering
  b. business
  c. law
  d. medicine

_____a_____ **6. Telepathy** is most closely associated with
  a. communication
  b. charity
  c. illness
  d. freedom

_____a_____ **7.** If a person acts in an **equivocal** manner, he or she is acting
  a. uncertainly
  b. confidently
  c. arrogantly
  d. maturely

_____c_____ **8. panacea : rare :: a.** beautiful : desirable
  b. view : occasionally
  c. cure : unusual
  d. noise : frequently

_____a_____ **9. syndrome : related :: a.** cluster : similar
  b. group : unlike
  c. symptoms : unreliable
  d. collection : dependable

_____d_____ **10. euphemism : tactful :: a.** request : impolite
  b. statement : politeness
  c. exclamation : indifference
  d. curse : rude

50   **Part One • Word Parts and Challenging Words**

Completing a Passage

After reading the selection, fill in each space with one of the words listed below.

rectify	panacea	biopsy	equivocal	autonomy
antediluvian	infidelity	syndrome	euphemism	telepathy

LACI

Laci has been a close friend since our middle school days, so I certainly had
_____equivocal_____ feelings about ending our friendship, but I did so because of her
"enchantment" (a[n] ___euphemism___ for obsession) with her BlackBerry. A while
back, we were partners in biology lab conducting a(n) _____biopsy_____ on the nerve
tissues of a frog when Laci whispered to me that she had to go out to the hall for a minute
to make an important call. This "important" call took twenty minutes, and she might as
well have stayed in the lab because everyone, including the instructor, could hear her
loudly talking and laughing about a volleyball game she had played in recently.

Then there was the time Laci and I were getting a bite to eat in the college cafeteria
while discussing what we were going to do for our joint psychology presentation scheduled in two weeks. Suddenly, we heard "Chirp! Chirp! Chirp!" and Laci quickly grabbed
her BlackBerry out of one of her jacket pockets and excitedly said, "I gotta answer this!"
She and her caller, Brianna, then gabbed for a half-hour about whether Brianna should
have her hair cut shorter than she usually did when she went to her hair appointment the
next day. (Big deal!)

There were numerous other times when I felt absolutely irrelevant while Laci,
lovingly cradling her BlackBerry, was yapping away, text-messaging, taking pictures, or
on the Internet. Once, when I was waiting for her to give me a ride to work, she told me
to wait just a second because she just HAD to call her roommate. The "second" she
asked me to wait turned out to be ten minutes, making me late for work, which made my
boss upset with me. But did Laci ever apologize to me? Are you kidding? Of course not.
Soon after she got her BlackBerry, she developed a bad case of "rudeness."

I don't claim to have the gift of ___telepathy___ , but I know Laci thinks I am
___antediluvian___ when it comes to the "modern marvels of technology" like the Black-
Berry because I still prefer to use regular dial telephones and disposable cameras as well
as my trusty outdated desktop computer. But frankly, I've become convinced that cell

phones, especially one like the BlackBerry, produce not only bad manners but also addiction. Don't believe me? Well, I can assure you that Laci demonstrates the __syndrome__ of someone who is addicted. For example, Laci can't seem to help herself—she MUST have her BlackBerry readily accessibly all the time or she gets really antsy. She also lost her job because she was spending too much time talking on her blasted BlackBerry. Furthermore, her studies have gone down the tube because of her infatuation with it. In fact, Laci's __infidelity__ to her responsibilities is negatively impacting all phases of her life, including her once-close friendship with me.

The last straw for me regarding our friendship was when Laci discovered she didn't have her BlackBerry with her when we were shopping at the mall. She went into an absolute panic—as in, she gasped, screamed, and cried—you would have thought she had just lost one of her limbs! I yelled at her, "Get over it, will ya, Laci?" But she kept carrying on like the world was coming to an end! Laci has obviously lost her __autonomy__ because of her BlackBerry dependency.

Has anyone developed a(n) __panacea__ for cell-phone addiction? I hope so, because unless Laci is able to __rectify__ her present "BlackBerry behavior," our friendship will remain a thing of the past.

Panacea—a remedy for all diseases or difficulties:

• The father believed that Windex was a <u>panacea</u> that would solve whatever was troubling anybody in the family.

Origin: 1540–1550 <Greek—*panakeia* < *pan* (all) and *akos* (cure)

Family word: panacean (adj)

Connotation: *positive*—related to remedy

Image to remember: a medicine that claims to cure all your symptoms

Write an original sentence using *panacea*:

_____

_____

_____

MASTERING CONFUSING WORDS | **passed / past**

passed   the past tense of the action verb *pass*:

Blake <u>passed</u> his driver's license on his second attempt.

past   a noun or adjective referring to a previous time:

Owen hasn't received any type of message from his girlfriend for the <u>past</u> month.

Circle the correct answer:

1. I studied the notes I had taken in the <u>passed</u> / <u>past</u>, and they helped me to do well on the exam.

2. When I <u>passed</u> / past Holly in the hall, she gave me a smile.

Write original sentences using these words:

1. **passed:** _____

2. **past:** _____

Learning Word Parts from Context Clues

1. phil

- *Philosophy* is an excellent major for students who love to study wisdom and reasoning.
- People who admire England and revere anything English are known as *anglophiles*.

phil means (a) intelligence (b) love _____ *b* _____ .

2. mal

- *Malicious* gossip has harmed his reputation in the community.
- Thomas Jefferson suffered from migraine headaches, a *malady* that would disable him for days.

mal is associated with (a) harmful (b) mysterious _____ *a* _____ .

3. spec

- I always *inspect* my car before I take a long trip.
- At our college baseball games, the *spectators* are knowledgeable and well mannered.

spec has to do with (a) viewing (b) assisting _____ *a* _____ .

4. omni

- Young children often believe their parents are *omniscient,* but as they grow older, they realize their parents don't know everything after all.
- Dogs seem to be *omnipresent* at any picnic.

omni means (a) large (b) limitless _____ *b* _____ .

5. hyper

- Gail is *hyperactive,* so she enjoys jogging four miles every evening.
- Alex is *hypersensitive,* so be tactful when you offer your suggestions.

hyper means (a) excessive (b) lacking _____ *a* _____ .

6. anti

- The scientist's watch is *antimagnetic,* so its accuracy is unaffected by experiments involving magnets.
- The development of *antibiotics,* because of their effectiveness against harmful bacteria, has contributed significantly to the average life span.

anti means (a) increasing (b) opposing _____*b*_____ .

7. voc, vok

- A *convocation* was called by the college dean to discuss the new graduation requirements.
- The unexpected letter *evoked* memories of her old friend.

voc and **vok** relate to (a) a calling (b) an arrival _____*a*_____ .

8. bi

- The United States *bicentennial* in 1976 celebrated the country's two hundredth anniversary.
- One of my neighbors has been accused of *bigamy;* apparently, his divorce was not finalized before he remarried.

bi means (a) two (b) luxury _____*a*_____ .

9. path

- The newspaper's picture of the *pathetic* puppy brought many offers for adoption.
- The movie was full of *pathos,* and a number of people in the audience cried.

path has to do with (a) imagination (b) feelings _____*b*_____ .

10. ben

- As the result of a generous contribution from an unannounced *benefactor,* our college will be able to complete its building plans.
- Hazel was the *beneficiary* of her aunt's insurance policy, so she can now afford to open a florist shop of her own.

ben means (a) disagreeable (b) favorable _____*b*_____ .

Matching Word Parts and Definitions

Match each definition with the word part it defines.

_____c_____	**1.** phil	**a.** to call; voice
_____j_____	**2.** mal	**b.** good; well
_____e_____	**3.** spec	**c.** to love
_____h_____	**4.** omni	**d.** two
_____g_____	**5.** hyper	**e.** to look
_____i_____	**6.** anti	**f.** feelings
_____a_____	**7.** voc, vok	**g.** over; excessive; beyond what is normal
_____d_____	**8.** bi	**h.** all
_____f_____	**9.** path	**i.** opposite; against
_____b_____	**10.** ben	**j.** bad

Fill-Ins with Word Parts

Select the appropriate word part so the proper word is formed in each sentence.

phil	spec	hyper	voc	path
mal	omni	anti	bi	ben

1. I felt no sym _____path_____ y for the rude young man when he was expelled from the restaurant.

2. Lately, my husband has been _____anti_____ social—he refuses to go anyplace where he might have to mingle with other people.

3. Carlos is pleased with the physical and emotional _____ben_____ efits regular exercise has brought him.

4. The airport is equipped with a(n) _____omni_____ directional device capable of transmitting or receiving signals in all directions.

5. The _____phil_____ anthropist's concern and generosity were deeply appreciated by those left homeless by the fire.

6. Coach Page admits she was _____hyper_____ critical when she first began coaching, but now she offers suggestions in a positive, encouraging way.

7. Sofia is unsure what _____voc_____ ation she should pursue.

8. Unfortunately, a great amount of _____mal_____ ice exists between the couple filing for divorce.

9. Lucia brought _____bi_____ noculars to the game as our seats were high in the grandstand.

10. Turell says that in retro _____spec_____ t, his high school years were some of the happiest years of his life.

Matching Words and Definitions

Use your knowledge of the underlined word parts to match the definitions and words.

_b_	**1.** <u>bi</u>partisan	**a.** to breathe abnormally fast
_g_	**2.** <u>bene</u>diction	**b.** both parties cooperating to achieve a common goal
_i_	**3.** <u>biblio</u>phile	**c.** a serious personality disorder in which a person
_a_	**4.** <u>hyper</u>ventilate	expresses no normal feelings toward others
_j_	**5.** <u>omni</u>bus	**d.** a haunting, disturbing image; a ghost
_c_	**6.** psycho<u>pathy</u>	**e.** to speak badly about; to slander
_f_	**7.** <u>anti</u>dote	**f.** substance that acts against poison
_e_	**8.** <u>mal</u>ign	**g.** a prayer requesting God's blessing
_h_	**9.** <u>re</u>voke	**h.** to call back or to cancel what once was given or said
_d_	**10.** <u>spec</u>ter	**i.** person who loves books
		j. all-encompassing; comprehensive

Writing Your Own Definitions

Write the definitions of the words after noting the underlined word parts and studying the context of the sentences; if you are still uncertain, feel free to consult a dictionary. Typical responses:

1. Cats and dogs are four-footed, but humans are <u>*bipeds*</u>.

bipeds _____two-legged animals_____

2. The doctor diagnosed her injury as a <u>*hyperextension*</u> of her right knee.

hyperextension _____overextension; strain_____

3. Did you get rid of your contact lenses so you could wear those groovy <u>*spectacles*</u>?

spectacles _____eyeglasses_____

4. We were baffled by his <u>*apathetic*</u> response after we told him our exciting news.

apathetic _____lacking enthusiasm or emotion; indifferent_____

5. The player glared <u>*malevolently*</u> at the referee after he was charged with a technical foul.

malevolently _____hatefully; with an "evil" eye; maliciously_____

6. As a result of the <u>*benevolent*</u> acts of many people in the community, a new house was built for the family who had lost their home due to lightning.

benevolent _____kind; charitable_____

7. When it was discovered that the young woman did not actually have a master's degree, the *revocation* of her recent appointment swiftly followed.

revocation _____ the act of taking back or withdrawing _____

8. My neighbors are devoted to *philharmonic* music, so they never miss an opportunity to attend a symphony concert.

philharmonic _____ devoted to music; relating to a symphony orchestra _____

9. The *antiphonal* composition was performed by having the sopranos and altos singing at the front of the church and the tenors and basses responding at the back of the sanctuary.

antiphonal _____ of or like a text sung by responding groups _____

10. The park's *omnifarious* garden contained every type of flower and bush that can grow in this state.

omnifarious _____ of all kinds _____

Learning Challenging Words from Context Clues

1. **philanthropy** (fə LAN thrə pē)—noun
   - As a result of the Webbs' *philanthropy,* the college was able to build a new Student Union.
   - The famous athlete's *philanthropy* included generous financial contributions to the Salvation Army, the YWCA, and the United Way.

   philanthropy has to do with a love of (a) publicity (b) humankind _____ b _____ .

2. **malicious** (mə LISH əs)—adjective
   - A *malicious* rumor began circulating that the defendant had been found innocent because he had bribed a witness to lie for him.
   - The police have just arrested the people responsible for the *malicious* attack on the elderly couple.

   malicious is related to (a) wicked (b) bold _____ a _____ .

3. specter (SPEK tər)—noun

- The swiftly moving fog was like some sort of *specter* one would see in a horror movie.
- A shimmering, blinding figure burst into view, a *specter* that filled us with dread.

specter is similar to a (a) storm (b) ghost _____ *b* _____ .

4. omnipotent (om NIP ə tent)—adjective

- The arrogant supervisor felt she was *omnipotent*, so she was shocked when the company's president took away much of her authority.
- Although the Supreme Court justices may appear to be *omnipotent*, their power is limited by the Constitution.

omnipotent means (a) all-powerful (b) everywhere _____ *a* _____ .

5. hypertension (HĪ pər TEN shən)—noun

- After checking the patient's blood pressure a number of times, the doctor gave the middle-aged man a prescription for his *hypertension*.
- My neighbor is watching her diet and exercising more in an effort to reduce her *hypertension*.

hypertension is (a) lack of muscular strength (b) high blood pressure ___ *b* ___ .

6. antithesis (an TITH ə sis)—noun

- She, fortunately, was the *antithesis* of a spoiled celebrity as she graciously signed autographs, posed for pictures with the children, and stayed to answer the reporters' questions.
- The sales representative first showed me a four-door blue sedan, which was the *antithesis* of what I was looking for, so I told him I wasn't interested in giving the car a test drive.

antithesis means (a) model of (b) opposite of _____ *b* _____ .

7. vociferous (vō SIF ər əs)—adjective

- Our team's hockey fans have the reputation for being rowdy and *vociferous*.
- City council members have heard *vociferous* complaints about the rise in property taxes.

vociferous means (a) adventurous (b) loud _____ *b* _____ .

8. **bilingual** (bī LING gwəl)—adjective

   ■ Sandra's *bilingual* ability was helpful to us all as she was able to speak to the waiter in French and then translate into English what he said.
   ■ One of the requirements for that particular position with the Border Patrol is to be *bilingual* or, to be more specific, to have the ability to speak Spanish and English.

   bilingual is the ability to (a) speak two languages (b) offer sound advice _____a_____ .

9. **empathy** (EM pə thē)—noun

   ■ My *empathy* for my young nephew was genuine because I can distinctly remember how upset I felt when my dog died during my childhood.
   ■ I can generate no *empathy* for the striking ballplayers because they make so much more money than I do.

   empathy is most closely related to (a) impatience (b) sympathy _____b_____ .

10. **benign** (bə NĪN)—adjective

    ■ My ferocious-looking dog actually has a *benign* disposition, so you have nothing to fear from him.
    ■ I thought the food might be too spicy for my tastes, but it actually had a *benign* flavor.

    benign means (a) mild (b) interesting _____a_____ .

Matching Challenging Words and Definitions

Write each word before its definition.

philanthropy	specter	hypertension	vociferous	empathy
malicious	omnipotent	antithesis	bilingual	benign

vociferous	**1.**	noisy, blaring, disruptive
benign	**2.**	harmless, mild, inoffensive
malicious	**3.**	brutal, cruel
antithesis	**4.**	opposite, other extreme
philanthropy	**5.**	helpfulness, generosity, charity
empathy	**6.**	identification with the feelings of another person
omnipotent	**7.**	almighty, all-powerful
bilingual	**8.**	able to speak and/or write two languages
hypertension	**9.**	high blood pressure
specter	**10.**	ghost, spook

Fill-Ins with Challenging Words

In each space, write the appropriate word from those listed below.

philanthropy	specter	hypertension	vociferous	empathy
malicious	omnipotent	antithesis	bilingual	benign

1. What started out as a friendly snowball fight between members of the two fraternities escalated into a(n) _____malicious_____ brawl, resulting in a number of injuries and arrests.

2. Antonio's high-strung personality is the _____antithesis_____ of that of his older brother, who is much more laid-back.

3. The proceeds from the exhibition game were given to a charity; this _____philanthropy_____ on the part of the promoters and players was wildly applauded by those in attendance.

4. The television ad stressed that untreated high blood pressure can lead to heart attacks and strokes, so everyone should be checked for _____hypertension_____ .

5. My boss usually has a calm, _____benign_____ personality, but she becomes extremely upset with her employees if they are late to work or ignore or are indifferent to customers in the store.

6. The _____vociferous_____ complaints of the coach, which could be heard throughout the gym, led to his dismissal from the game.

7. The man quietly responded, "Only God is immortal and _____omnipotent_____ ."

8. I didn't know Julie was _____bilingual_____ until I heard her carry on a long conversation in Italian with her grandparents.

9. Steve has always enjoyed studying history, so he has no _____empathy_____ for those who complain that it is a dry, uninteresting subject.

10. I never believed in ghosts until I saw some type of eerie _____specter_____ late one night when I drove by a graveyard.

Checking Your Word Power

After selecting your response, put the letter in the space provided.

____b____ 1. The *opposite* of **benign** is
    a. nonthreatening
    b. deadly
    c. costly
    d. inexpensive

_____d_____ **2.** The *opposite* of **philanthropy** is
  a. good health
  b. sickness
  c. generosity
  d. stinginess

_____a_____ **3.** The *opposite* of **hypertension** is
  a. low blood pressure
  b. high blood pressure
  c. uncaring
  d. uptight

_____c_____ **4. Empathy** suggests
  a. misunderstanding of
  b. anger within
  c. identification with
  d. nervousness about

_____c_____ **5.** The word most closely associated with **vociferous** is
  a. infection
  b. insecurity
  c. intensity
  d. information

_____d_____ **6. Bilingual** is most closely associated with
  a. mathematics
  b. social sciences
  c. biological sciences
  d. languages

_____a_____ **7.** If a person thinks he or she sees a **specter,** he or she likely feels
  a. frightened
  b. delighted
  c. unconcerned
  d. confident

_____c_____ **8. malicious : vicious :: a.** laughing : crying
  b. rebelling : obeying
  c. kindliness : compassion
  d. loss : tragedy

_____b_____ **9. antithesis : identical :: a.** captivating : interesting
  b. opposite : same
  c. alter : change
  d. seek : search

_____b_____ **10. omnipotent : weak :: a.** weak : feeble
  b. feeble : powerful
  c. powerful : strong
  d. strong : mighty

Completing a Passage

After reading the selection, fill in each space with one of the words listed below.

bilingual	specter	empathy	benign	philanthropy
malicious	vociferous	hypertension	omnipotent	antithesis

CURRENCY FOR THE VISUALLY IMPAIRED

Of the many daily challenges the over 1 million visually impaired citizens of our country face, there is at least one that could be eliminated—dealing with our present currency. Because ones, fives, tens, twenties, and the other denominations of U.S. paper money are of the same size, shape, and feel, it is impossible for the blind to make distinctions among the various bills. This uniformity in our currency, a federal judge ruled in 2006, amounts to discrimination against the visually impaired, and since discrimination is the ___antithesis___ of equality, he ordered the Treasury Department to alter the bills in some manner so that the blind will also have ways of identifying them.

However, some top Treasury officials and others, while expressing ___empathy___ for the plight the blind face regarding this issue, nevertheless made ___vociferous___ objections to the judge's ruling, loudly arguing that it would be much too difficult and expensive to implement the major currency changes necessary to accommodate the visually impaired. These objections bring back the ___specter___ of similar protests made decades ago when some people voiced, often in hurtful, ___malicious___ ways, their disapproval for proposals designed to provide the physically challenged with special parking spots, bathrooms, doors, and ramps. But soon after these proposals were enacted into law, the public seldom had even ___benign___ objections to them as people with wheelchairs, walkers, baby strollers, and the like benefited from these special accommodations. To help those for whom English is a second language, these accommodations are increasingly being identified with ___bilingual___ signs, often made possible by the ___philanthropy___ of individuals and charitable organizations.

The government maintains that to alter currency sizes to accommodate the visually challenged would cost nearly $180 million initially and up to $50 million annually for the necessary new printing plates. However, one need not be ___omnipotent___ to know there are much less expensive ways to accomplish this goal. These methods include the use of Braille dots, foil strips, raised numbers, rounded edges, and punched holes.

Most of the nations in the world have already adopted one or more of the methods mentioned to enable the blind to make currency distinctions; there is simply no need for our government officials to develop ___hypertension___ or other stress-induced ailments to comply with the judge's orders. Our visually challenged citizens deserve to live in a society that is as accessible to them as possible, and changing our currency would be a major contribution toward that objective.

FEATURED WORD: philanthropy

Philanthropy—compassionate concern for others as well as socially useful projects:

- The Harrisons' <u>philanthropy</u> was well known in the community as they donated their time, talents, and money to such worthwhile causes as the local homeless shelter and historical museum.

Origin: 1600–1610 <Latin and Greek—*philanthropia*—love for mankind; *phil* (love) and *anthropos* (mankind)

Family words: philanthropist (n), philanthropic (adj)

Connotation: *positive*—suggests unselfishness

Image to remember: Oprah Winfrey giving money to build a new school

Write an original sentence using *philanthropy*:

_____

_____

_____

MASTERING CONFUSING WORDS | **a / an**

a   Use *a* before words that begin with a consonant sound:

<u>A</u> car was stuck in front of our driveway.

an   Use *an* before words beginning with a vowel (*a, e, i, o, u*) sound:

Mark ate two peanut butter sandwiches and <u>an</u> apple before heading back to his afternoon classes.

Circle the correct answer:

1. Holden is (a) / an part-time UPS driver.

2. One of my uncles drove a / (an) Oldsmobile for years.

Write original sentences using these words:

1. a: _____

2. an: _____

Word Parts

Matching Word Parts and Definitions

Match each underlined word part with its definition.

A

_c_	**1.** <u>pro</u>ponent	**a.**	study of
_e_	**2.** <u>re</u>state	**b.**	to hold
_d_	**3.** <u>inter</u>state	**c.**	in favor of, for
_a_	**4.** psych<u>ology</u>	**d.**	between, among
_b_	**5.** <u>ten</u>ure	**e.**	again

B

_b_	**1.** <u>uni</u>son	**a.**	against
_d_	**2.** <u>sub</u>merge	**b.**	one
_a_	**3.** <u>op</u>ponent	**c.**	person who does something
_e_	**4.** <u>pre</u>view	**d.**	under
_c_	**5.** humor<u>ist</u>	**e.**	before

C

_b_	**1.** <u>stat</u>us	**a.**	person who does something
_e_	**2.** <u>com</u>panion	**b.**	position, standing
_a_	**3.** play<u>er</u>	**c.**	away from
_c_	**4.** <u>de</u>part	**d.**	one
_d_	**5.** <u>mono</u>tonous	**e.**	with

D

_d_	**1.** viol<u>ation</u>	**a.**	over, beyond
_c_	**2.** <u>a</u>typical	**b.**	many
_a_	**3.** <u>super</u>sonic	**c.**	opposite
_e_	**4.** <u>trans</u>continental	**d.**	act of
_b_	**5.** <u>poly</u>gamy	**e.**	across, change to

Fill-Ins with Word Parts

Select the appropriate word part so the proper word is formed in each sentence.

A

> bio   tele   auto   eu   ante

1. Does anyone send _____ _tele_ _____ grams anymore?

2. We saw a number of beautiful _____ _ante_ _____ bellum mansions when we were in Louisiana.

3. I read an excellent _____ *bio* _____ graphy of President Kennedy during the summer.

4. The beautiful _____ *eu* _____ phonic sound soothed us as we awaited the news from the doctor.

5. ATM stands for _____ *auto* _____ matic teller machine.

B

rect   fid   equ   pan   syn

1. Their back deck provides a(n) _____ *pan* _____ oramic view of the Blue Ridge Mountains.

2. The flight cadet was tested to see how quickly she recovered her _____ *equ* _____ ilibrium after being spun around in the capsule for five minutes.

3. Please don't con _____ *fid* _____ e what I told you to anyone.

4. Do you know how to play this music _____ *syn* _____ thesizer? I'd like to blend a number of sounds together when we play our numbers.

5. The teacher's aide helped to cor _____ *rect* _____ the papers, so we got them back at our next class session.

C

bi   ben   phil   hyper   omni

1. The Republicans and Democrats must work in a(n) _____ *bi* _____ partisan way if an effective alternative energy program is to become a reality.

2. A(n) _____ *omni* _____ bus is a term referring to something that is all-encompassing.

3. Karla is certainly a biblio _____ *phil* _____ e as she has loved books ever since she was a small child.

4. A(n) _____ *ben* _____ ediction is a prayer asking for God's blessings.

5. That _____ *hyper* _____ active youngster is certainly a challenge for his parents to control as he has more energy than three kids put together.

D

path   anti   mal   vok   spec

1. To _____ *mal* _____ ign others is to speak badly of them.

2. There were over 40,000 _____ *spec* _____ tators who witnessed the thrilling game.

3. The public health official informed the restaurant owners that she would

re _____vok_____e their license unless they met the sanitation

requirements.

4. The veterinarian assured the dog's owner that the _____anti_____ dote he

administered would soon restore his pet to good health.

5. I felt sym _____path_____ y for the old man, but I didn't have any money

to give him.

E

mis   dis   ob   ir   chron

1. Coach McIntosh seldom gets after the referees, so getting two technical fouls in

one game was highly _____ir_____ regular for him.

2. Patricia is _____dis_____ contented with her job, so she's looking for

other employment.

3. Because of arthritis, my grandfather has had a _____chron_____ ic ache in

his knees for the past eight years.

4. I wasn't surprised that Allen _____ob_____ jected to an increase in the

dues as he likes to hang on to his money.

5. I've worn glasses for only two weeks, but I'm constantly _____mis_____ laying

them; fortunately, though, I've always been able to find them—so far.

F

ible   ex   ism   post   ver

1. When the service was over, Carolyn played a moving cello solo for the

_____post_____ lude.

2. That year, our country _____ex_____ ported more goods than it

imported.

3. Keung had to show his driver's license with his picture on it to

_____ver_____ ify his identity before he was permitted to take

the exam.

4. Katy is fun to be around because she's always full of optim _____ism_____ .

5. Do you really think that would be a sens _____ible_____ thing to do?

Challenging Words

Matching Challenging Words and Definitions

Write each word before its definition.

A

antediluvian	vociferous	antithesis	transition	anthropology
hypertension	benign	syndrome	empathy	

<u>syndrome</u> **1.** set of symptoms

<u>hypertension</u> **2.** high blood pressure

<u>transition</u> **3.** passage from one stage to another

<u>vociferous</u> **4.** loudly disruptive

<u>empathy</u> **5.** identification with the feelings of others

<u>antediluvian</u> **6.** ancient, before the Flood

<u>anthropology</u> **7.** study of the beginnings of humans

<u>benign</u> **8.** harmless, mild

<u>antithesis</u> **9.** opposite, other extreme

B

malicious	equivocal	omnipotent	philanthropy	rectify
infidelity	dissipate	superfluous	autonomy	

<u>rectify</u> **1.** to make right, to correct

<u>superfluous</u> **2.** excessive, unnecessary

<u>malicious</u> **3.** brutal, cruel

<u>autonomy</u> **4.** independence, self-direction

<u>philanthropy</u> **5.** generosity, charity

<u>dissipate</u> **6.** to fade away, to waste away

<u>infidelity</u> **7.** treason, unfaithfulness

<u>omnipotent</u> **8.** all-powerful

<u>equivocal</u> **9.** wavering, uncertain

Completing a Passage

After reading the selection, fill in each space with one of the words listed below.

bilingual   biopsy   obstreperous   specter   subterfuge

When Marco came downstairs for breakfast, Giselle, his wife, said, "My goodness, you startled me! You're so pale you look like some kind of <u>specter</u> from a graveyard!

You'd better see a doctor!" In reality, Marco's complexion looked normal. Giselle's outburst was merely a(n) _____subterfuge_____ masking her concern over an irregular growth on Marco's neck, which she was convinced warranted a(n) _____biopsy_____. Marco had become too angry and _____obstreperous_____ to submit to her earlier pleas for him to see a dermatologist, partly because, she was sure, he was insecure with his English. So on this occasion she added, "I know a doctor you'd feel comfortable with because she's _____bilingual_____."

Unscrambling Words

Unscramble each "word" to discover one you have studied, using the sentence as a clue to the word's identity.

CLUE	SCRAMBLED	UNSCRAMBLED
Example: Here's what happened to them after their adventure ended.	oepeigul	epilogue
1. Cell phones are used everywhere!	rsnviyauell	universally
2. No! No! You don't understand what I mean!	cmruensiots	misconstrue
3. Unfortunately, she didn't become famous until after she died.	symhopsluout	posthumously
4. So what is the relationship between soft drinks and dental cavities?	linootrcear	correlation
5. Look at all those colors streaming from the fireworks!	lrtmoiycophac	polychromatic
6. How'd you know I was coming? Do you have ESP?	pheetytal	telepathy

Analogies

After selecting your response, put the letter before it in the space provided.

_____d_____ 1. **rectify : repair ::** **a.** fix : ruin
  b. invest : withdraw
  c. discourage : modify
  d. restore : mend

_____d_____ 2. **infidelity : loyalty ::** **a.** trustworthy : dependable
  b. inconsistent : erratic
  c. inaccurate : erroneous
  d. disloyalty : reliability

_____c_____ **3. benign : harmless :: a.** harmless : hurtful
b. hurtful : helpful
c. helpful : supportive
d. supportive : helpless

_____a_____ **4. tentative : certain :: a.** positive : negative
b. inquisitive : curious
c. logical : reasonable
d. inability : incapability

_____b_____ **5. culpable : bad :: a.** praiseworthy : bad
b. innocent : good
c. fame : bad
d. inadequacy : good

Mastering Confusing Words

Circle the correct answer.

1. If Judson should (advice / (advise)) me to take the job, I will take his ((advice) / advise).

2. I dripped milk all over the kitchen floor because there was ((a) / an) leak in the milk carton, but I was able to clean up the mess because I had (a / (an)) all-purpose mop.

3. Rocky Marciano, a boxer of the (passed / (past)), is the only undefeated heavyweight champion in the history of boxing; even Muhammad Ali never ((passed) / past) Marciano's 49–0 record.

4. Ariana is trying to (device / (devise)) an effective ((device) / devise) for keeping her cat out of the living room.

5. Her encouraging words, the doctor thought, would ((affect) / effect) her patient in a positive way; at least, that was the (affect / (effect)) she was hoping for.

Crossword Puzzle

Solve the crossword by using the following words.

compliance	precocious	panacea	monomania	stature	euphemism	tentative
interim	debilitate	culpable	unseemly	veracity	replicate	nepotism
extricate	chronic	proclivity	hedonist	apathy	incongruous	

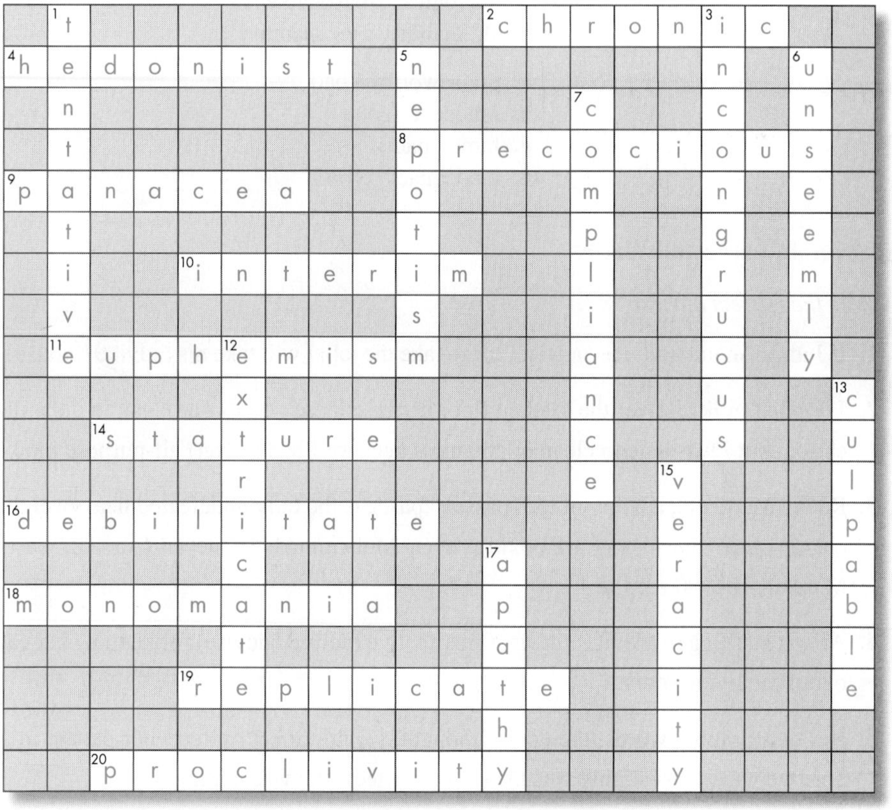

The crossword grid contains the following answers:

ACROSS and DOWN entries filled in:

- 2 (across): chronic
- 4 (across): hedonist
- 8 (across): precocious
- 9 (across): panacea
- 10 (across): interim
- 11 (across): euphemism
- 14 (across): stature
- 16 (across): debilitate
- 18 (across): monomania
- 19 (across): replicate
- 20 (across): proclivity
- 1 (down): tentative
- 3 (down): incongruous
- 5 (down): nepotism
- 6 (down): unseemly
- 7 (down): compliance
- 12 (down): extricate
- 13 (down): culpable
- 15 (down): veracity
- 17 (down): apathy

ACROSS

2. continuous
4. pleasure-seeker
8. advanced ability at an early age
9. cure-all
10. intermission
11. substitute for an offensive word
14. rank
16. to weaken
18. fixation on one thing
19. reproduce, copy
20. tendency

DOWN

1. uncertain, hesitant
3. not in agreement, out of step
5. preference given to relatives
6. inappropriate
7. act of obeying, cooperating
12. free from difficulty
13. responsible for, guilty
15. truth
17. lack of interest

Chapter 6

Learning Word Parts from Context Clues

1. fin

- The project should be _finished_ by the first of October.
- What was the _final_ score?

fin is associated with (a) completion (b) assignment _____ a _____ .

2. geo

- _Geography_ involves the study of the earth's surface, climate, population, and natural resources.
- _Geochemistry_ is the study of the earth's composition and chemical changes.

geo has to do with the (a) universe (b) earth _____ b _____ .

3. bell

- A _rebellion_ erupted in the capital city.
- My enjoyment of the hockey game was undermined by the _bellicose_ behavior of some of the players; their fighting spoiled an otherwise good contest.

bell means (a) war (b) noise _____ a _____ .

4. hydro, hydr

- The first automatic transmissions in cars were called _hydromatics_ because fluids were the key to their operation.
- A _hydraulic_ lift operates by fluid pressure.

hydro and **hydr** are associated with (a) power (b) liquids _____ b _____ .

5. ambi, amphi

- Shawn demonstrated his _ambidexterity_ by writing first with his right hand and then with his left.
- An _amphibian,_ such as a frog, can live on land or in water.

ambi and **amphi** mean (a) highly developed (b) both _____ b _____ .

6. less

- Brigitte is a *fearless* skier.
- It was another beautiful, *cloudless* day in New Mexico.

less means (a) without (b) until _____ *a* _____ .

7. hem

- *Hemoglobin* is the protein matter contained in red blood cells.
- *Hematology* is the medical study of the blood and blood-producing organs.

hem means (a) small (b) blood _____ *b* _____ .

8. intra, intro

- *Intrastate* commerce refers to business transactions within a state.
- *Introverts* are people primarily concerned with their own thoughts and feelings.

intra and **intro** mean (a) modern (b) within _____ *b* _____ .

9. man

- Colin did *manual* work all summer, so he felt fit and strong when he reported for football practice in the fall.
- Her fingernails needed a *manicure*.

man has to do with (a) hands (b) skills _____ *a* _____ .

10. derm, dermis

- The rash only affected the outer layer of skin and was therefore *epidermal*.
- The *ectodermis* is the outer tissue of the embryo, which is the early developmental state of an organism.

derm and **dermis** have to do with (a) growth (b) skin _____ *b* _____ .

Matching Word Parts and Definitions

Match each definition with the word part it defines.

g	**1.** fin	**a.**	blood
h	**2.** geo	**b.**	water; fluids
f	**3.** bell	**c.**	skin
b	**4.** hydro, hydr	**d.**	without
i	**5.** ambi, amphi	**e.**	hand
d	**6.** less	**f.**	war
a	**7.** hem	**g.**	end; limit
j	**8.** intra, intro	**h.**	earth
e	**9.** man	**i.**	both
c	**10.** derm, dermis	**j.**	inside; within

Fill-Ins with Word Parts

Select the appropriate word part so the proper word is formed in each sentence.

fin   bell   amphi   hem   man
geo   hydro   less   intra   derm

1. Athletic contests among students attending the same institution are referred to as ____intra____ mural sports.

2. ____Amphi____ bious planes can land on land or water.

3. All living things are ____fin____ ite; their days are numbered.

4. The patient began to feel immediate relief after the doctor administered a hypo ____derm____ ic injection.

5. ____Hydro____ electric power is generated by water.

6. A heavy discharge of blood is called a(n) ____hem____ orrhage.

7. Citizens are re ____bell____ ing because of the dictator's repression.

8. ____Geo____ logy is concerned with the study of rocks and other aspects of the earth's physical history.

9. He was accused of ____man____ ipulating the records to cover his fraud.

10. Although it was a gray, cheer ____less____ day, Monica was in good spirits.

Matching Words and Definitions

Use your knowledge of the underlined word parts to match the definitions and words.

__f__	**1.** peer<u>less</u>	**a.** the stoppage of bleeding
__d__	**2.** <u>geo</u>thermal	**b.** existing before the U.S. Civil War
__i__	**3.** <u>hydro</u>foil	**c.** handcuffs
__a__	**4.** <u>hem</u>ostasis	**d.** relating to earth's internal heat
__h__	**5.** in<u>fin</u>ite	**e.** skin inflammation
__j__	**6.** <u>intro</u>spection	**f.** having no equals; can't be matched
__b__	**7.** <u>ante</u>bellum	**g.** having more than one possible meaning; uncertain
__g__	**8.** <u>ambi</u>guous	**h.** without ending
__e__	**9.** <u>derm</u>atitis	**i.** winglike boat
__c__	**10.** <u>man</u>acles	**j.** observation of one's own mental processes

Writing Your Own Definitions

Write the definitions of the words after noting the underlined word parts and studying the context of the sentences; if you are still unsure, feel free to consult a dictionary. Typical responses:

1. The director recommended that the rare bird that had just died be taken to the local *taxidermist* so museum visitors would still be able to see what the bird had looked like in real life.

   taxidermist _____ person who stuffs and mounts the skins of dead animals for exhibition _____

2. The beautiful old *manuscript,* written in the 17th century, was in remarkably good condition.

   manuscript _____ book written by hand _____

3. The *intravenous* injection soon relieved the patient's discomfort.

   intravenous _____ delivered into a vein _____

4. Do you have any other fears besides *hemophobia?*

   hemophobia _____ fear of blood _____

5. He remained *heedless* of the advice offered him by his fellow employees, so, as a consequence, he was soon out of a job.

   heedless _____ throwing caution to the wind; ignoring advice; paying no attention _____

6. After being in the scorching sun much of the day, she felt *dehydrated,* so she drank plenty of water when she got home.

   dehydrated _____ depleted of water; feeling weak from thirst _____

7. The child attempted to count the raindrops running down his bedroom window, but they proved to be *infinitesimal,* so he eventually turned his attention to the toys scattered about his room.

   infinitesimal _____ without end; unable to be counted; limitless _____

8. After the *rebellious* crowd was finally quieted, a police officer told the people to disperse or they would be arrested for disturbing the peace.

*re**bell**ious* _____ disobedient; feeling defiant; expressing resistance _____

9. His responses were characteristic of a person who displays both an inward and an outward personality, so he was classified as an *ambivert*.

ambivert _____ person with a balanced personality, having the qualities of both introversion and extroversion _____

10. Most astronomical measurements are *geocentric* because objects in space are usually related to their distance from earth.

geocentric _____ having the earth as the center _____

Learning Challenging Words from Context Clues

1. finale (fə NAL ē)—noun

- When the orchestra finished the *finale* of Beethoven's Ninth Symphony, the audience stood and applauded.
- The Fourth of July celebration's *finale* was highlighted by a spectacular fireworks display.

finale means (a) conclusion (b) prominence _____ a _____ .

2. geopolitics (JĒ ō POL i tiks)—noun

- *Geopolitics* is a major determiner of how countries relate to each other economically.
- An understanding of a nation's *geopolitics* is important because a country's natural resources and location in the world significantly contribute to the living conditions of its people, including the type of government under which they live.

geopolitics involves the study of how (a) biology (b) geography influences international relationships _____ b _____ .

3. belligerent (bə LIJ ər ənt)—adjective, noun

- The police officers finally subdued the screaming, *belligerent* person responsible for the commotion.
- The *belligerent* was charged with disorderly conduct and assault.

belligerent is associated with (a) aggressiveness (b) independence _____ a _____ .

4. **hydrology** (hi DROL ə jē)—noun

- As a civil engineer specializing in the construction and maintenance of dams, Mr. O'Neil is an expert in *hydrology*.
- Irrigation and landscape specialists must be knowledgeable in *hydrology* since water plays such an important part in their work.

hydrology is a science concerned with the study of (a) water (b) plants _____a_____ .

5. **ambivalence** (am BIV ə ləns)—noun

- Austen is experiencing *ambivalence* because he can't decide whether to go to college or to join the Navy.
- Isabella's *ambivalence* about whether to audition for the repertory theater is understandable because of her already demanding college schedule.

ambivalence is associated with (a) sorrow (b) indecision _____b_____ .

6. **dauntless** (DANT lis)—adjective

- The *dauntless* eight-year-old girl jumped off the high diving board.
- The firefighters were recognized for their *dauntless* courage in rescuing the terrified family from their burning home.

dauntless means without (a) planning (b) fear _____b_____ .

7. **hemostat** (HĒ mə STAT)—noun

- The surgeon clamped a *hemostat* on the vein to stop the bleeding.
- The bleeding was slight, so no *hemostat* was needed.

hemostat is a medical instrument used to stop (a) bleeding (b) pain _____a_____ .

8. **introspection** (IN trə SPEK shən)—noun

- After considerable *introspection,* Toby realized he should apologize to Curtis.
- Reena's *introspection* has resulted in a number of beautiful songs.

Introspection is most closely related to (a) boldness (b) self-analysis _____b_____ .

9. **manhandle** (MAN han dəl)—verb

- Our young son soon learned not to *manhandle* the kitten after she scratched him on the arm.
- If you continue to *manhandle* the ladder in that way, you're either going to hurt yourself or break a window.

manhandle means to do something in a (a) rough (b) complex manner _____a_____ .

10. <u>**dermatology**</u> (DUR mə TOL ə jē)—noun

- Teenagers sometimes suffer so much from acne that they have to consult a specialist in *dermatology.*
- According to this article concerned with *dermatology,* sun-tanning booths are unsafe.

dermatology is concerned with (a) psychological problems (b) the skin ___*b*___ .

Matching Challenging Words and Definitions

Write each word before its definition.

| finale | belligerent | ambivalence | hemostat | manhandle |
| geopolitics | hydrology | dauntless | introspection | dermatology |

<u>   finale   </u>   **1.** the final section, end, climax, final event

<u>   dauntless   </u>   **2.** without fear, bold, daring

<u>   dermatology   </u>   **3.** science dealing with the skin and its diseases

<u>   introspection   </u>   **4.** soul-searching, contemplation

<u>   manhandle   </u>   **5.** to do something in a gruff or abusive way

<u>   belligerent   </u>   **6.** aggressively disobedient; person who is hostile and combative

<u>   ambivalence   </u>   **7.** uncertainty, hesitation, doubt, conflicting feelings

<u>   hemostat   </u>   **8.** instrument used to compress bleeding vessels

<u>   hydrology   </u>   **9.** science concerned with the occurrence, circulation, distribution, and properties of water

<u>   geopolitics   </u>   **10.** study of how geography affects relationships among countries

Fill-Ins with Challenging Words

In each space, write the appropriate word from those listed below.

| finale | belligerent | ambivalence | hemostat | manhandle |
| geopolitics | hydrology | dauntless | introspection | dermatology |

1. Despite the driver's rude and <u> belligerent </u> behavior, the state trooper remained calm and respectful.

2. Jason engages in a great deal of <u> introspection </u> every time he thinks about his past.

3. Brooke has finished her basic medical training, and now she plans to specialize in <u> dermatology </u> as she is interested in helping patients with skin cancer and other serious skin diseases.

4. Although Jim weighs only 130 pounds, he is a(n) <u> dauntless </u> hockey player as he's not afraid to slam into much bigger opponents to get to the puck.

5. For the <u> finale </u>, the rock band played a medley of its hits, then left the stage to thunderous applause and cheers.

6. Benjamin is enrolled in a two-year program having to do with golf courses, and one of the classes he's presently taking is ____hydrology____ since water plays such a crucial role in the proper care of a course's fairways and greens.

7. "Geographical factors," the instructor stressed, "must be understood if insight is to be gained on how a nation interacts with other nations, so pay particular attention to matters relating to ____geopolitics____ when this subject enters our discussions."

8. The basketball coach at our small but prestigious college is well known and greatly admired by everyone associated with our school, including players, students, staff, faculty, and administrators, so I can understand his ____ambivalence____ about accepting the pressure-packed coaching offer from a large out-of-state university.

9. The instructor scolded the students after he saw them ____manhandle____ some of the expensive laboratory equipment.

10. The nervous medical student had difficulty clamping the ____hemostat____ on the patient's spurting vein.

Checking Your Word Power

After selecting your response, put the letter in the space provided.

____c____ **1.** The *opposite* of **dauntless** is
   a. tightness
   b. fearless
   c. timid
   d. grouchy

____b____ **2.** The *opposite* of **ambivalence** is
   a. harshness
   b. certainty
   c. accelerate
   d. inspect

____d____ **3.** The *opposite* of **finale** is
   a. demotion
   b. promotion
   c. demonstration
   d. beginning

____a____ **4. Geopolitics** is associated with
   a. foreign policy
   b. national scandal
   c. advanced mathematics
   d. dishonest elections

_____d_____ **5. Manhandle** suggests
      a. precision
      b. distinction
      c. weakness
      d. mistreatment

_____d_____ **6. Hydrology** is associated with
      a. language
      b. psychology
      c. fire
      d. water

_____c_____ **7. Introspection** suggests
      a. popularity
      b. misery
      c. thoughtfulness
      d. extravagance

_____a_____ **8. hemostat : medicine :: a.** chalk : teaching
      b. trombone : talent
      c. radio : advertisements
      d. tire : necessity

_____c_____ **9. belligerent : rival :: a.** unfaithful : patriot
      b. courageous : coward
      c. cooperative : friend
      d. insulting : stranger

_____d_____ **10. dermatology : peculiar :: a.** biology : required
      b. psychology : average
      c. ecology : expected
      d. ophthalmology : odd

Completing a Passage

After reading the selection, fill in each space with one of the words listed below.

finale	geopolitics	belligerent	hydrology	ambivalence
dauntless	hemostat	introspection	manhandle	dermatology

COLLEGE NICKNAMES

Numerous colleges, in an effort to portray how fearsome and _____belligerent_____ their teams are, have nicknames like the Lions, Bulldogs, Wildcats, and Tigers, while others, because of their geographic and economic realities, reflect the influence of a certain amount of _____geopolitics_____, such as the Humpback Whales (University of Alaska, Southeast) and the Hardrockers (South Dakota School of Mines and Technology). On the other hand, the Cedar Crest College Classics, the Rowan College Professors, and the St. Louis College of Pharmacy Eutectic (a word having to do with physical chemistry) appear to have been named by an intellectual holed up in a library. Still other names, including the University of Delaware Blue Hens and the College of Atlantic Black Flies, create laughs, puzzlement, or perhaps _____ambivalence_____. Other nicknames definitely leave most people scratching their heads: What is an Eph (Williams College Ephs), a Saluki (Southern Illinois University Salukis), or a Gorlok (Webster University Gorloks, St. Louis)?

And how would you like to play for a team called the Banana Slugs (University of California, Santa Cruz) or the Bantams (Trinity College in Hartford, Connecticut)? Don't these nicknames suggest that your opponents could easily _____manhandle_____ your team? Of course, that's generally not the case, but such nicknames certainly don't indicate that your team is tough and _____dauntless_____; those who came up with such nicknames should have had a few minutes of _____introspection_____ before branding such names on a school's athletic teams.

There are, though, some unusual nicknames that make sense if you take the time to investigate the history of the institution or the state in which they are located: Boilermakers (Purdue University), Cornhuskers (University of Nebraska), Sooners (University of Oklahoma), Judges (Brandeis University), and Poets (Whittier College) are such examples.

For a(n) _____finale_____, here are suggestions for some team nicknames that probably are not presently being used: for a department of _____dermatology_____ team at a medical school—the Skins; for those handy with a(n) _____hemostat_____ and playing for a College of Surgeons team—the Operators; and, finally, for those playing for a department of _____hydrology_____ at some university—the Well Diggers.

Belligerent—inclined or eager to fight; a person or country engaged in fighting or a war:

- Because of his <u>belligerent</u> attitude toward his classmates, the angry boy was sent to the principal's office.

- The country that was a <u>belligerent</u> in that war is now a peaceful nation.

Origin: 1577 <Latin—*belligerare*—to wage war, *bellum* (war) and *gerera* (to wage) (used as a noun, *belligerent* refers to a party or nation at war, and this use dates from 1811)

Family word: belligerently (adv)

negative—suggests suggests hostility

Image to remember: a baseball manager screaming at an umpire

Write an original sentence using *belligerent*:

_____

_____

MASTERING CONFUSING WORDS quiet / quite / quit

quiet silent, peaceful:

The night was so <u>quiet</u> I could hear the hall clock ticking downstairs.

quite really, entirely:

Courtney is <u>quite</u> concerned about how she did on her zoology test.

quit to stop, to give up:

Colby was so homesick his freshman year that he almost <u>quit</u> college.

Circle the correct answer:

1. Leila never quiet / quite / quit practicing the piece until she could play it perfectly.

2. It was a quiet / quite / quit party, so there were no complaints from the neighbors.

3. Victor had quiet / quite / quit a time on his trip, including having to spend the night sleeping at the airport.

Write original sentences using these words:

1. **quiet:** _____

2. **quite:** _____

3. **quit:** _____

Chapter 7

Learning Word Parts from Context Clues

1. bon, boun

- Simone received a *bonus* for exceeding the yearly sales quota.
- The winners of the contest donated their *bounty* to a number of charities.

bon and **boun** mean (a) beneficial (b) unexpected _____ *a* _____ .

2. multi

- A *multitude* of people were crowded in front of the courthouse.
- It was a *multinational* meeting, with representatives from as far away as Finland and China.

multi means (a) many (b) noisy _____ *a* _____ .

3. hypo

- *Hypothyroidism* is a deficient functioning of the thyroid gland.
- The patient has *hypotension,* the opposite of high blood pressure.

hypo is related to (a) vagueness (b) lack _____ *b* _____ .

4. neo

- The *Neolithic* period in history was the first time farming and certain advanced stone tools were introduced.
- A *neologism* is a new word or phrase.

neo is associated with something that is (a) old-fashioned (b) recent _____ *b* _____ .

5. ful, ous

- A *frightful* tornado carried Dorothy's house away.
- The well water was found to be *poisonous.*

ful and **ous** mean (a) full of (b) changeable _____ *a* _____ .

6. non

- My cousin is a *nonconformist,* so he has trouble with those in authority.
- I'm *nonpartisan,* so I don't care which candidate wins the election.

non means (a) super (b) not _____ *b* _____ .

7. aud

- The *audio* circuits in the television set reproduce the sound.
- The *auditorium* was almost empty although the game was scheduled to begin in fifteen minutes.

aud is related to (a) technology (b) sound _____ *b* _____ .

8. extra, ultra

- It was *extraordinary* for Miami to be so cool in March.
- Our *ultraconservative* senator is opposed to further federal aid for education.

extra and **ultra** mean beyond (a) normal (b) possibility _____ *a* _____ .

9. temp

- *Tempo* refers to the speed at which a musical passage is played.
- Angela was appointed as a *temporary* replacement for Brenda.

temp refers to (a) authority (b) time _____ *b* _____ .

10. ward

- It had been a long, tiring trip, so we were happy to be finally heading *homeward.*
- After resting for a while, the elderly lady hobbled *forward* to the post office.

ward means (a) toward (b) slowly _____ *a* _____ .

Matching Word Parts and Definitions

Match each definition with the word part it defines.

___*b*___	**1.** bon, boun	**a.** full of
___*i*___	**2.** multi	**b.** good
___*g*___	**3.** hypo	**c.** not
___*j*___	**4.** neo	**d.** beyond; extreme
___*a*___	**5.** ful, ous	**e.** toward; in the direction of
___*c*___	**6.** non	**f.** time
___*h*___	**7.** aud	**g.** under; insufficient
___*d*___	**8.** extra, ultra	**h.** hear; listen
___*f*___	**9.** temp	**i.** many
___*e*___	**10.** ward	**j.** new

Fill-Ins with Word Parts

Select the appropriate word part so the proper word is formed in each sentence.

bon   hypo   ous   aud   temp
multi   neo   non   extra   ward

1. The wallpaper is _____*multi*_____ colored, including shades of blue, red, green, and brown.

2. We were able to understand her speech because she explained the basic concepts in plain, _____*non*_____ technical language.

3. My son bought a hide _____*ous*_____ Halloween mask.

4. The Gardners are living _____*temp*_____ orarily in an apartment on Maple Street.

5. The patient was suffering from _____*hypo*_____ calcemia, a deficiency of calcium in the blood.

6. I'm not fond of heights, so I never look down _____*ward*_____ once I climb a ladder.

7. The medical laboratory announced it had developed a(n) _____*neo*_____ mycin, a new antibiotic to fight a variety of infections.

8. Martina won the cash prize, which was a much-needed _____*bon*_____ anza for her.

9. The Olympic Games were a wonderful _____*extra*_____ vaganza to watch.

10. The _____*aud*_____ ience sat in complete silence during the children's concert.

Matching Words and Definitions

Use your knowledge of the underlined word parts to match the definitions and words.

_*c*_	1. <u>temp</u>oral	**a.**	unwilling to take sides or commit oneself; cautious
_*f*_	2. <u>extra</u>curricular	**b.**	deficiency in size; underdeveloped condition
_*a*_	3. <u>non</u>committal	**c.**	concerned with time
_*h*_	4. <u>aud</u>itory	**d.**	reflecting a new interest in or rebirth of old architectural, artistic, or musical styles
_*i*_	5. tumult<u>uous</u>	**e.**	abundant; generous
_*d*_	6. <u>neo</u>classic	**f.**	in addition to or outside of the regular academic offerings
_*b*_	7. <u>hypo</u>plasia	**g.**	facing the direction toward which the wind is blowing
_*j*_	8. <u>multi</u>lingual	**h.**	having to do with sound or hearing
_*g*_	9. lee<u>ward</u>	**i.**	full of violence or noisy commotion
_*e*_	10. <u>boun</u>tiful	**j.**	speaking many languages

Writing Your Own Definitions

Write the definitions of the words after noting the underlined word parts and studying the context of the sentences; if you are still uncertain, feel free to consult a dictionary.
Typical responses:

1. Since his retirement, my grandfather has become a *vorac<u>ious</u>* reader, reading everything from newspapers to novels and from poems to periodicals.

vorac<u>ious</u> _____ ravenous; devouring; enthusiastic; ardent; avid _____

2. What he said was *<u>in</u>audible* to me because of the noisy traffic passing by.

<u>in</u>audible _____ unable to be heard _____

3. The infection had spread to the *<u>hypo</u>dermal* area, so it was fortunate indeed that Anton's friends had finally succeeded in persuading him to go to the emergency room for treatment.

<u>hypo</u>dermal _____ under the skin _____

4. Every time Greg asked about his promised promotion, his boss either changed the subject, pretended he didn't hear, or resorted to some other *<u>tempor</u>izing* tactic.

<u>tempor</u>izing _____ delaying; stalling; procrastinating _____

5. The realtor told us that ours was the only *<u>bona</u>fide* offer made for the property, so she was sure the owners would accept it.

<u>bona</u>fide _____ authentic; genuine; real _____

6. His tendency to *in<u>ward</u>ness* became even more noticeable to his few friends after his girlfriend broke up with him.

in<u>ward</u>ness _____ introversion; shyness _____

7. The teacher often supplemented her lectures with impressive *<u>multi</u>media* presentations.

<u>multi</u>media _____ using a variety of visual and audio displays, such as computer graphics, films, DVDs, audiotapes, brochures _____

8. Stan is known for being a _nonconformist_, so few people were surprised that he showed up at the banquet wearing bib overalls instead of a tuxedo.

   nonconformist _____maverick; misfit; lone wolf; oddball_____

9. Having never been around babies much before, the medical student was pleasantly surprised by how much he enjoyed working in the _neonatal_ section of the hospital.

   neonatal _____relating to new or young babies_____

10. The machine's _ultrasonic_ frequency is well beyond a human's hearing capacity.

    ultrasonic ___having a sound with such a high frequency it's beyond human hearing___

Learning Challenging Words from Context Clues

1. **bounteous** (BOUN tē əs)—adjective

   - All the wheat farmers I've recently talked to are in a happy frame of mind because they expect a _bounteous_ harvest in a couple of weeks.
   - The flood victims expressed their gratitude for the _bounteous_ gifts of food, furniture, appliances, and money from their fellow citizens throughout the country.

   bounteous means (a) beautiful (b) plentiful _____b_____ .

2. **multifaceted** (MUL tə FAS ə tid)—adjective

   - Bradley has _multifaceted_ interests, ranging from Civil War history to kayaking.
   - Arianna's _multifaceted_ acting talent enables her to play many roles.

   multifaceted is related to (a) many (b) impressive _____a_____ .

3. **hypochondria** (HĪ pə KON drē ə)—noun

   - My uncle was usually in good physical health, but his spirits were often low because he worried constantly that he was harboring some serious illness; _hypochondria,_ unfortunately, had plagued him much of his life.
   - The doctor said a significant number of his patients had nothing wrong with them other than depression brought on by their _hypochondria,_ or imaginary illnesses.

   hypochondria is a preoccupation with (a) social approval (b) supposed ailments _____b_____ .

4. **neophyte** (NĒ ə FĪT)—noun

- I had played golf only once before, but, fortunately, my companion was also a *neophyte.*
- Ayo is certainly not a *neophyte* drummer as he's been playing with one band or another since he was in seventh grade.

neophyte means a (a) beginner (b) shy person _____ *a* _____ .

5. **acrimonious** (ak rə MŌ nē əs)—adjective

- I thought my friends were having an *acrimonious* discussion, but I finally realized they were just kidding one another.
- The *acrimonious* shouting was from one of my neighbors who was upset because my dog had made a mess on his lawn.

acrimonious means (a) unreasonable (b) angry _____ *b* _____ .

6. **nondescript** (NON də SKRIPT)—adjective

- Most of the guests were stylishly dressed, but a few were wearing *nondescript* jeans, khakis, and rumpled sweaters or sweatshirts.
- He obviously isn't interested in cars or doesn't make much money because he drives a ten-year-old *nondescript* four-door sedan.

nondescript means (a) colorful (b) dull _____ *b* _____ .

7. **audible** (Ö də bəl)—adjective

- Because Olivia had yelled so much at the game, her voice was barely *audible* when she got home.
- The instructor uses a microphone to make his voice *audible* throughout the large lecture hall.

audible means (a) hearable (b) accented _____ *a* _____ .

8. **extraneous** (ik STRĀ nē əs)—adjective

- One of the committee members continuously made comments having nothing to do with the topic, and his *extraneous* remarks unnecessarily prolonged the meeting.
- The contractor tried to add some *extraneous* charges to his bill, but when I challenged him about their fairness, he agreed to drop them.

extraneous means (a) complicated (b) irrelevant _____ *b* _____ .

9. contemporary (kən TEM pə rer ē)—adjective, noun

- My older brother, a classically trained musician, doesn't care much for *contemporary* music.
- Devon was a *contemporary* of mine in high school, so he must be around twenty-six years old, as I am.

contemporary refers to the (a) present, or of the same time (b) past, or of a different era _____ *a* _____ .

10. wayward (WĀ wərd)—adjective

- The kindergarten teacher at first had difficulty with the *wayward* youngster because he refused to sit down or to participate in any activity.
- One of my relatives' *wayward* way of life has resulted in two failed marriages and the loss of numerous jobs.

wayward means (a) secretive (b) unruly _____ *b* _____ .

Matching Challenging Words and Definitions

Write each word before its definition.

bounteous	hypochondria	acrimonious	audible	contemporary
multifaceted	neophyte	nondescript	extraneous	wayward

nondescript **1.** unremarkable, lacking in distinctive qualities

extraneous **2.** beside the point, irrelevant, unnecessary

multifaceted **3.** many-sided, wide-ranging

acrimonious **4.** harsh, bitter, hostile, angry

audible **5.** capable of being heard

wayward **6.** turning away from what is right and proper; disobedient, contrary, obstinate

hypochondria **7.** a preoccupation with imaginary illnesses

bounteous **8.** plentiful, generous, overflowing, abundant

neophyte **9.** amateur, beginner

contemporary **10.** of the same time or date, or of the here and now

Fill-Ins with Challenging Words

In each space, write the appropriate word from those listed below.

| bounteous | hypochondria | acrimonious | audible | contemporary |
| multifaceted | neophyte | nondescript | extraneous | wayward |

1. We were talking about the importance of Josh getting a date when Isaiah started making _____extraneous_____ remarks about the great time he had had in Las Vegas.

2. I grew up in a(n) _____nondescript_____ housing development, the type you see in almost every city.

3. One of my grandfathers is now wearing hearing aids because normal sounds and conversations were no longer _____audible_____ to him.

4. In my opinion, _____contemporary_____ cars are much better designed and engineered than those of any other time.

5. The employee benefits are indeed _____bounteous_____, so it's no wonder the company has no difficulty filling a position when one does become available.

6. An elderly person well known for his _____hypochondria_____ throughout his life had engraved on his tombstone "*See, I told you I was sick!*"

7. Because he is a(n) _____neophyte_____ in the teaching profession, our instructor was obviously nervous the first couple of weeks of the semester.

8. Their _____wayward_____ son, who had a previous criminal record, was recently sentenced to five years in prison.

9. Flying, I quickly learned, is a(n) _____multifaceted_____ undertaking as there are many things to learn and many skills to master.

10. The chefs were having a(n) _____acrimonious_____ debate over who was to be in charge of the lavish meal.

Checking Your Word Power

After selecting your response, put the letter in the space provided.

_____a_____ 1. The *opposite* of **acrimonious** is
    a. friendly
    b. dangerous
    c. spacious
    d. hostile

_____d_____ 2. The *opposite* of **bounteous** is
    a. ugly
    b. intelligent
    c. stiff
    d. scarce

_____ c _____ **3.** The *opposite* of **nondescript** is
  - **a.** continuous
  - **b.** interfering
  - **c.** unique
  - **d.** ordinary

_____ b _____ **4. Hypochondria** is associated with people who think they are
  - **a.** foolish
  - **b.** sick
  - **c.** disliked
  - **d.** religious

_____ d _____ **5.** Which of the following is likely to be the most **audible**?
  - **a.** memo
  - **b.** gesture
  - **c.** whisper
  - **d.** shout

_____ c _____ **6. Multifaceted** is associated with
  - **a.** expense
  - **b.** simplicity
  - **c.** variety
  - **d.** lying

_____ c _____ **7.** If a person is **wayward,** he or she is likely to be
  - **a.** popular
  - **b.** talented
  - **c.** defiant
  - **d.** friendly

_____ a _____ **8. contemporary : modern ::**
  - **a.** modern : up-to-date
  - **b.** up-to-date : old-fashioned
  - **c.** old-fashioned : current
  - **d.** current : out of style

_____ d _____ **9. extraneous : essential ::**
  - **a.** necessary : required
  - **b.** character : personality
  - **c.** happy : delighted
  - **d.** neat : sloppy

_____ b _____ **10. neophyte : beginner ::**
  - **a.** neighbor : stranger
  - **b.** rookie : trainee
  - **c.** expert : amateur
  - **d.** teacher : student

Completing a Passage

After reading the selection, fill in each space with one of the words listed below.

bounteous	multifaceted	hypochondria	neophyte	acrimonious
nondescript	audible	extraneous	contemporary	wayward

"SOCIAL HOST" LAWS

Albion, seventeen, was a(n) ___multifaceted___ high school junior, a member of the choir, student council, and soccer and track teams. Far from having a(n) ___nondescript___ personality, he was considered quite a unique person because of all of his talents. But when it came to drinking beer, Albion was a(n) ___neophyte___, as he should have been, considering his age. On the other hand, his ___contemporary___, Lucas, had been drinking beer for the past two years, generally in the privacy of his home and with the consent of his parents. One afternoon after track practice, Lucas invited Albion and some other friends over to his house to watch TV and to have some refreshments. With his mother's permission, Lucas got three six-packs of beer out of the basement refrigerator. Lucas and some others then talked a reluctant Albion into sharing a few beers with them. Within an hour, Albion was complaining of feeling sick, but the others laughed at him because Albion was well known for his ___hypochondria___; he loudly moaned of pulled muscles and a sick stomach every time he raced in a meet. However, when he started vomiting and then passed out, Lucas and his mother became alarmed and rushed Albion to the emergency room at the local hospital, where his stomach had to be pumped because of alcohol poisoning.

"Albion" incidents are much too common, even though furnishing alcohol to minors is prohibited in all fifty states; however, because it is a criminal offense, it is often frustratingly difficult to get the necessary burden of proof for a conviction. Consequently, numerous communities and counties throughout this rich, ___bounteous___ nation have been adopting civil ordinances relating to underage drinking. Then if a "furnishing alcohol to a minor" infraction occurs, the violation can be legally dealt with administratively rather than by the court system, saving law authorities a great deal of ___extraneous___ time, energy, and taxpayers' money.

These civil ordinances, referred to as "social host" laws, enable the police to break up home parties and fine parents or other ___wayward___ adults who permit underage drinking $2,500 or more. Even if parents are out of town or unaware of an underage drinking party, they are held responsible; the ordinances indicate they should have known teens might drink illegally at their home. Parents sometimes object to this provision, not only in a clear, _____audible_____ way but also in an angry, _____acrimonious_____ manner, but their objections have not been met with sympathy by the courts.

These "social host" laws should be seriously considered everywhere because alcohol abuse, including binge drinking, is among the leading causes of death among America's youth. Because surveys indicate that a large percentage of underage drinking occurs at house parties, it is hoped that the growth of "social host" laws in communities across the nation will dramatically decrease alcohol-related deaths among teenagers.

FEATURED WORD: neophyte

Neophyte—a beginner:

Pedro was a <u>neophyte</u> when it came to driving in the snow, so he was happy to let Dylan drive.

Origin: 1500s <Latin—*neophytes*—new convert <Greek—*neophytos*—newly planted; *neos* (new) and *phytos* (planted) (*neophyte's* meaning of "one who is new to any subject" was first recorded in 1599)

Connotation: *neutral*—a synonym for beginner

Image to remember: Tiger Woods giving a young boy his first golf lesson

Write an original sentence using *neophyte*:

_____

_____

_____

than   use in comparisons:

The large shopping mall was busier today <u>than</u> it was on Saturday.

then   when, at that time:

After working for a year, Jodi <u>then</u> plans to attend graduate school.

Circle the correct answer:

1. After they went bowling, they <u>than</u> / (<u>then</u>) went to a nearby pizza restaurant.

2. I'd rather finish the job today (<u>than</u>) / <u>then</u> come back tomorrow to do it.

Write original sentences using these words:

1. than: _____

2. then: _____

Chapter 8

Learning Word Parts from Context Clues

1. ann, enn

- Our *annual* family reunion will be in Ohio this year.
- We look forward to our *perennial* flowers blooming every spring.

ann and **enn** mean (a) beautiful (b) year _____ *b* _____ .

2. gram, graph

- We completed the project by following the steps outlined in the *diagram*.
- The television star signed her *autograph* on the restaurant's menu.

gram and **graph** mean (a) writing (b) working _____ *a* _____ .

3. phon

- A specific speech sound is known as a *phoneme*.
- Our old *phonograph* still has an excellent sound.

phon is most closely associated with (a) sound (b) music _____ *a* _____ .

4. mor, mort

- After his serious illness, he realized his *mortality* for the first time.
- Mr. Wolfe, who operates a funeral home on Sixth Street, has been a *mortician* for over forty years.

mor and **mort** are most closely associated with (a) endurance (b) death _____ *b* _____ .

5. pos

- Lucas was promoted to a supervisory *position*.
- During the museum's remodeling, paintings were stored in a *repository*.

pos has to do with (a) leadership (b) location _____ *b* _____ .

6. cap

- Sergio was elected *captain* of the team.
- Madison is the *capital* of Wisconsin.

cap means (a) head (b) fame _____ *a* _____ .

7. dia

- The length of a straight line through the center of a figure is the *diameter.*
- The *diastolic* reading is obtained when the blood is passing through the heart's chambers.

dia means passing (a) through (b) around _____ *a* _____ .

8. ness

- Mr. Hidu enjoys the *quietness* of the early mornings.
- Everybody was enjoying the child's *silliness* except his embarrassed parents.

ness relates to (a) absence of (b) condition of _____ *b* _____ .

9. hetero

- Words having the same spelling but different pronunciations and meanings, such as *lead* (a metal) and *lead* (to conduct), are called *heteronyms.*
- Animals of this type are generally *heterochromatic,* that is, of mixed colors.

hetero refers to (a) difference (b) similarity _____ *a* _____ .

10. homo

- Words having the identical spelling and pronunciation but different meanings, such as *bat* (a club) and *bat* (a flying mammal), are called *homonyms.*
- Animals of this type are generally *homochromatic,* that is, one color.

homo refers to (a) difference (b) similarity _____ *b* _____ .

Matching Word Parts and Definitions

Match each definition with the word part it defines.

f	**1.** ann, enn	**a.** sound
c	**2.** gram, graph	**b.** condition of; capable of
a	**3.** phon	**c.** write
j	**4.** mor, mort	**d.** same; like
h	**5.** pos	**e.** head; chief
e	**6.** cap	**f.** year
i	**7.** dia	**g.** different
b	**8.** ness	**h.** place; location
g	**9.** hetero	**i.** through
d	**10.** homo	**j.** death

Fill-Ins with Word Parts

Select the appropriate word part so the proper word is formed in each sentence.

enn   phon   pos   dia   hetero
graph   mort   cap   ness   homo

1. His stooped _____ *pos* _____ ture is due to a back injury.

2. A(n) _____ *dia* _____ gonal path had been worn in the grass leading from the post office to the bank.

3. Our college will be celebrating its cent _____ *enn* _____ ial this year.

4. Tragically, the injuries the young woman suffered in the accident proved _____ *mort* _____ al; she died a few hours later.

5. The article begins with a(n) _____ *cap* _____ tion that summarizes the major points the author discusses.

6. _____ *Homo* _____ genized milk is made by blending milk and cream.

7. _____ *Phon* _____ ics is a method of teaching reading by having students master the common sounds of letters and letter combinations.

8. Holding religious views contrary to established church doctrines is known as _____ *hetero* _____ doxy.

9. Tamar eventually tired of her boyfriend's moodi _____ *ness* _____, so she broke up with him.

10. The term associated with correct spelling is ortho _____ *graph* _____ y.

Matching Words and Definitions

Use your knowledge of the underlined word parts to match the definitions and words.

_g_	**1.** <u>phon</u>etic	**a.** to place, put, or set
_e_	**2.** haughti<u>ness</u>	**b.** having a common center
_i_	**3.** <u>graph</u>ite	**c.** muscular membrane across the lower part of the chest
_j_	**4.** de<u>cap</u>itate	**d.** funeral room
_b_	**5.** <u>homo</u>centric	**e.** excessive pride and arrogance
_c_	**6.** <u>dia</u>phragm	**f.** occurring twice a year
_d_	**7.** <u>mort</u>uary	**g.** pertaining to speech sounds
_f_	**8.** bi<u>ann</u>ual	**h.** pertaining to the opposite sex
_h_	**9.** <u>hetero</u>sexual	**i.** mineral used for pencil leads
_a_	**10.** <u>pos</u>it	**j.** to cut off the head

Writing Your Own Definitions

Write the definitions of the words after noting the underlined word parts and studying the context of the sentences; if you are still uncertain, feel free to consult a dictionary.
Typical responses:

1. Fred's tendency for *gaudiness* in clothes was very much in evidence as he was wearing orange slacks, a red shirt, a purple tie, green sneakers, and an old-fashioned straw hat.

   gaudiness _____ flashiness; loudness; flamboyance _____

2. Management refused to *capitulate* to the union's demands, so a strike costly to both sides occurred.

   capitulate _____ give in; surrender; yield; concede _____

3. A small white *monogram* on the upper-left side of his blue sweater read "BJs."

   monogram _____ a design with a few letters—usually a person's initials—often sewn on a shirt or sweater _____

4. My aunt's *heterodox* religious views contrasted sharply with those held by all the churches in the community, so she never became a member of any of them.

   heterodox _____ not in agreement with accepted beliefs _____

5. A number of new file cabinets and an impressively large walnut desk were *juxtaposed* against the south wall of his spacious new office.

   juxtaposed _____ placed side by side _____

6. The manager's *diatribe* against the homeplate umpire could be heard throughout the stands.

   diatribe _____ tirade; verbal abuses; bawling out; cursing _____

7. The houses in the new subdivision were attractive, but their *homogeneity* turned me off.

   homogeneity _____ sameness; uniformity _____

8. If the Cubs, White Sox, Bears, Blackhawks, and Bulls would all win championships in the same year, it would certainly be an *annus mirabilis*!

annus mirabilis _____ a year of wonders or miracles _____

9. The state trooper warned the young woman to drive slower and more carefully in such conditions; otherwise, he said, she might discover she wasn't *immortal,* as she apparently assumed she was.

immortal _____ never dying; living forever _____

10. Words such as *great-grate, to-two-too,* and *bare-bear* are *homophones.*

homophones _____ words that sound alike but have different meanings and spellings _____

Learning Challenging Words from Context Clues

1. annuity (ə NOO ə tē)—noun

- Rosa is contributing to a financial plan that will pay her an *annuity* of guaranteed income every month after she retires.
- My grandparents' income is based upon social security payments and an *annuity* they receive four times a year.

annuity refers to financial (a) deductions (b) payments during specific times of the year _____ *b* _____ .

2. graphology (gra FOL ə jē)—noun

- An expert on *graphology* is studying the suspect's handwriting to see if it corresponds to that on the ransom note.
- A *graphology* analysis indicated my friend is a confident, optimistic person, but I'm not convinced handwriting reveals that much about a person's personality.

graphology is concerned with the study of (a) handwriting (b) health _____ *a* _____ .

3. cacophony (kə KOF ə nē)—noun

- The *cacophony* of music, laughter, and shouting next door made sleeping impossible.
- Before the concert began, members of the orchestra tuned their instruments separately, creating a *cacophony* of weird sounds.

cacophony refers to sounds that are (a) harsh (b) pleasant _____ *a* _____ .

4. <u>moribund</u> (MOR ə BUND)—adjective

- My friend's limousine business has been in a *moribund* condition for some time, so I wasn't surprised that he's started bankruptcy proceedings.
- The veterinarian told us she was sorry, but that our dog was in a *moribund* state and would probably die before the day was over.

moribund means near (a) danger (b) death _____ *b* _____ .

5. <u>composure</u> (kəm PŌ zhər)—noun

- The speaker kept his *composure* despite the heckling from some members of the audience.
- After a hectic day at work, Teri regains her *composure* by taking a refreshing shower, listening to some soothing music, drinking herbal tea, and stretching out in a recliner.

composure refers to (a) calmness (b) humor _____ *a* _____ .

6. <u>capricious</u> (kə PRISH əs)—adjective

- My youngest brother is so *capricious* he's likely to do anything that suddenly pops into his head.
- Spring can be *capricious,* with summer temperatures one day and winter ones the next.

capricious means (a) steady (b) erratic _____ *b* _____ .

7. <u>diaphanous</u> (dī AF ə nəs)—adjective

- Nylon is an example of a sheer, *diaphanous* material.
- The new model was obviously self-conscious in her flimsy, *diaphanous* dress.

diaphanous means (a) transparent (b) expensive _____ *a* _____ .

8. <u>blandness</u> (BLAND nəs)—noun

- Alison, known for the *blandness* of her personality in high school, surprised her old classmates at the reunion because of her charming, outgoing manner.
- The *blandness* of the flat, brown countryside made Logan yearn for the lush, green valleys of his home state.

blandness means lacking in (a) simplicity (b) interest _____ *b* _____ .

9. <u>heterogeneous</u> (HET ər ə JĒ nē əs)—adjective

   ■ A *heterogeneous* group of business people, including a laundromat owner, a dog trainer, a beauty salon operator, and a pharmacist, attended the city council meeting on the proposed zoning change.
   ■ Aaron's *heterogeneous* talents, ranging from painting to plumbing, made him the ideal choice for the custodian's job at the summer camp.

   heterogeneous means (a) related (b) unrelated _____ *b* _____ .

10. <u>homogeneous</u> (HO mə JĒ nē əs)—adjective

   ■ One reason we cousins get along so well is because of our *homogeneous* interests as we all love to fish, hunt, hike, and camp.
   ■ The houses along one side of the lake were a *homogeneous* group of A-frames.

   homogeneous means (a) related (b) unrelated _____ *a* _____ .

Matching Challenging Words and Definitions

Write each word before its definition.

annuity	cacophony	composure	diaphanous	heterogeneous
graphology	moribund	capricious	blandness	homogeneous

*homogeneous* **1.** similar, alike, corresponding

*capricious* **2.** impulsive, changeable, flighty, unstable, acting as if one can do anything at any time

*annuity* **3.** money received at specific times of the year

*composure* **4.** calm state of mind, tranquility, poise, self-control

*blandness* **5.** dullness, something boring or indistinct

*graphology* **6.** the study of handwriting

*moribund* **7.** in a dying state, near death

*heterogeneous* **8.** dissimilar, various, unlike

*diaphanous* **9.** transparent, see-through, delicate

*cacophony* **10.** disagreeable sound that is grating, harsh, or unharmonious

Fill-Ins with Challenging Words

In each space, write the appropriate word from those listed below.

annuity	cacophony	composure	diaphanous	heterogeneous
graphology	moribund	capricious	blandness	homogeneous

1. Until the AMTRAK system was developed, passenger trains were practically _____moribund_____ in most states.

2. Heidi suddenly felt like doing something _____capricious_____ , so instead of going to work, she turned her car around and headed for the mall.

3. The soldiers looked so _____homogeneous_____ in their uniforms when they marched by the reviewing stand that Jennifer couldn't pick out her husband.

4. According to experts in _____graphology_____ , people's handwriting reveals a great deal about their character.

5. The racetrack was a(n) _____cacophony_____ of squealing tires, gunning motors, and blaring reports from the stadium's speakers.

6. Brent said his IRA (individual retirement account) will eventually provide him with a(n) _____annuity_____ , guaranteeing him a certain income for life.

7. Although the Eagles trailed throughout most of the game, they kept their _____composure_____ and were able to rally and pull out a victory.

8. We had nothing in common, but despite our _____heterogeneous_____ backgrounds and interests, my new roommate and I became good friends by the end of the semester.

9. Even though it's a(n) _____diaphanous_____ material, gauze is a strong cloth.

10. Some critics panned the movie for its _____blandness_____ , saying the dialogue was boring and the plot predictable.

Checking Your Word Power

After selecting your response, put the letter in the space provided.

_____c_____ 1. The *opposite* of **capricious** is
   a. capable
   b. healthy
   c. predictable
   d. stingy

_____b_____ 2. The *opposite* of **cacophony** is
   a. genuine
   b. melodious
   c. embarrassing
   d. hilarious

_____a_____ **3.** The *opposite* of **composure** is
  a. frantic
  b. confident
  c. secretive
  d. calm

_____b_____ **4. Graphology** is associated with
  a. music
  b. penmanship
  c. swimming
  d. mathematics

_____c_____ **5.** Who would most likely receive an **annuity**?
  a. beginning lawyer
  b. experienced electrician
  c. retired teacher
  d. elected official

_____d_____ **6.** If a person is **heterogeneous,** he or she is likely to be interested in the
  a. stock market
  b. sports world
  c. outdoors
  d. opposite sex

_____a_____ **7.** If a material is **diaphanous,** then it can
  a. be seen through
  b. be purchased at a reasonable price
  c. rarely be made
  d. resist wear

_____d_____ **8. homogeneous : similar :: a.** large : small
                                    b. neighborly : unfriendly
                                    c. attractive : repulsive
                                    d. identical : same

_____c_____ **9. moribund : lively :: a.** winning : joyful
                                    b. sad : depressed
                                    c. inactive : energetic
                                    d. complex : interesting

_____d_____ **10. blandness : vigor :: a.** vigorous : peppy
                                    b. peppy : dynamic
                                    c. dynamic : exciting
                                    d. exciting : dull

Completing a Passage

After reading the selection, fill in each space with one of the words listed below.

homogeneous   annuity   graphology   cacophony   moribund
capricious   diaphanous   blandness   heterogeneous   composure

YOUNG ADULTS AND INSURANCE

Studies confirm that the majority of skateboarders, snowboarders, hang gliders, bungee jumpers, and other thrill seekers are in their teens, twenties, and early thirties. Though __heterogeneous__ in gender, those in this age group are __homogeneous__ in certain traits, including their willingness to take chances; specifically, adults below the age of thirty-five are much more likely to take major risks than people in any other age group. Part of the reason is that everyday routines appear to have a(n) __blandness__ to them that many find intolerable after a while, and even the financial security and personal __composure__ that can result from having a steady, well-paying job soon lose their appeal to a surprisingly large number of young people.

A willingness to take risks can produce an interesting and rewarding life; however, if this lifestyle results in __capricious__ behavior, there can be serious and lifelong consequences.

For example, many young adults pooh-pooh the idea that it is critical that they have adequate medical insurance, especially if they have to buy it themselves. A significant number of these adults, despite the __cacophony__ heard during election years about the need for universal health coverage, are uninsured because they are willing to take the risk that they won't get seriously sick or injured. This is a foolhardy decision, because a serious illness could easily result in a hospital bill of over $100,000; a traumatic injury suffered in a car accident could exceed $750,000. It doesn't take experts to read thin, __diaphanous__ tea leaves or to analyze a person's writing (that is, use __graphology__) to know that if either of the above misfortunes happens to the uninsured, he or she will likely be spending the rest of his or her days, even when he or she is __moribund__, trying to pay off his or her medical bills.

Sure, it's important for young adults to invest in a(n) __annuity__ for retirement purposes, but securing adequate medical coverage should be their top priority; willingness to take risks has its place, but not when it comes to this matter.

Capricious—characterized by acting on an impulse, on the spur of the moment, or on a whim:

- Jack was in a <u>capricious</u> mood when he suddenly jumped on top of the table and began singing at the top of his lungs.

Origin: 1667 <French—*caprice*—whim <Italian—*capriccio*—a shivering; probably from *capro* (goat) referring to frisking, but another theory connects "capricious" to *capo* (head) + *riccio* (curl, frizzled) <Latin *ericius* ("hedgehog," hair standing on end like a hedgehog). The use of "capricious" was first attested in 1594.

Family words: caprice (n), capriciousness (n), capriciously (adv)

Connotation: generally considered *negative*, but can also be a *neutral* word as it is linked to unpredictable

Image to remember: a fully clothed man suddenly jumping into a swimming pool

Write an original sentence using *capricious*:

_____

_____

_____

their   possessive pronoun meaning "belongs to them":

I believe <u>their</u> house is located on Brighton Avenue.

there   points out something or refers to a location or place:

<u>There</u> is the car Zachary hopes to buy someday.

Roxana is standing over <u>there</u> by the newsstand.

they're   a contraction standing for "they are":

I think <u>they're</u> planning to go to the theater with us.

Circle the correct answer:

1. The car parked over their / (there) / they're by the fire hydrant has a parking ticket tucked under one of its windshield wipers.

2. Did you know that (their) / there / they're coach used to play for Penn State?

3. When their / there / (they're) here visiting us, please make them feel welcome.

Write original sentences using these words:

1. **their:** _____

2. **there:** _____

3. **they're:** _____

Learning Word Parts from Context Clues

1. contra, contro, counter

- She *contradicted* what Juanita had told me.
- The *controversy* was about who was responsible for paying the bill.
- Our team made several successful *counterattacks,* finally winning the game in the closing minutes of the fourth quarter.

contra, contro, and **counter** mean (a) against (b) support _____*a*_____ .

2. psych

- *Psychosis* is a general term to indicate a severe mental disorder or disease.
- A *psychosomatic* problem is a physical disorder caused by the mind or emotions.

psych refers to the (a) body (b) mind _____*b*_____ .

3. semi

- A *semicolon* (;) is part colon and part comma.
- We arranged our chairs in a *semicircle,* but after more people arrived, we made a complete circle.

semi means (a) complete (b) half _____*b*_____ .

4. dic

- Sanjay's *diction* was influenced by his childhood years in England.
- Mr. Reed's *dictation* was concerned with the sales campaign.

dic has to do with (a) talk (b) intelligence _____*a*_____ .

5. meter, metr

- A *barometer* measures atmospheric pressure.
- *Trigonometry* is a branch of mathematics concerned with the calculations of sides and angles of triangles.

meter and **metr** have to do with (a) measuring (b) solving _____*a*_____ .

6. terr

- This area is the best farming *territory* in the entire state.
- Firm, solid land is sometimes referred to as *terra firma*.

terr is associated with (a) wealth (b) land _____ *b* _____ .

7. anthrop

- *Anthropology* involves the study of the origins, beliefs, and cultural developments of humankind.
- *Anthropomorphic* means attributing human forms and characteristics to things not human.

anthrop is associated with (a) humans (b) beliefs _____ *a* _____ .

8. fore

- The weather *forecast* indicates that snow is on its way.
- No one can *foretell* what the nation's economy will be like during the upcoming year.

fore refers to the (a) past (b) future _____ *b* _____ .

9. se

- Ms. Artesani's photographs were *selected* for first prize.
- South Carolina became the first state to *secede* from the Union.

se means (a) apart from (b) awarded to _____ *a* _____ .

10. therm

- Jason set the *thermostat* to 62 degrees.
- The *thermometer* indicated the temperature was below freezing, but it didn't seem that cold.

therm means (a) technical (b) heat _____ *b* _____ .

Matching Word Parts and Definitions

Match each definition with the word part it defines.

_e_	**1.** contra, contro, counter	**a.**	measure
_c_	**2.** psych	**b.**	heat
_h_	**3.** semi	**c.**	mind; spirit
_f_	**4.** dic	**d.**	human
_a_	**5.** meter, metr	**e.**	opposed to
_j_	**6.** terr	**f.**	say; tell
_d_	**7.** anthrop	**g.**	before
_g_	**8.** fore	**h.**	half of
_i_	**9.** se	**i.**	apart from; away
_b_	**10.** therm	**j.**	earth

Fill-Ins with Word Parts

Select the appropriate word part so the proper word is formed in each sentence.

counter	semi	meter	anthrop	se
psych	dic	terr	fore	therm

1. A _____*dic*_____ tator exercises absolute control; his or her word becomes the law of the land.

2. A _____*terr*_____ ace is a strip of land with steep sides.

3. _____*Therm*_____ odynamics is concerned with the relationships between heat and the mechanical energy of work.

4. Seth longed for the _____*se*_____ clusion of his country home after experiencing the hustle and bustle of the city.

5. _____*Psych*_____ oanalysis is concerned with the relationship between the conscious and unconscious minds.

6. It was a _____*fore*_____ gone conclusion they would marry soon after graduation.

7. _____*Anthrop*_____ oids are animals, such as apes, that resemble humans.

8. People included in this study were examined _____*semi*_____ annually, in January and July.

9. Smoking is certainly _____*counter*_____ productive to your otherwise good health practices.

10. A hygro _____*meter*_____ measures the water content in the atmosphere.

Matching Words and Definitions

Use your knowledge of the underlined word parts to match the definitions and words.

_i_	**1.** semi<u>spheric</u>	**a.** official pronouncement, saying
_f_	**2.** <u>psycho</u>genic	**b.** separate, set apart
_j_	**3.** gravi<u>meter</u>	**c.** stubborn, disobedient, opposite, clashing
_h_	**4.** <u>terra</u>rium	**d.** pertaining to heat or temperature
_a_	**5.** <u>dict</u>um	**e.** association of human characteristics with nonhuman beings or things
_g_	**6.** <u>fore</u>shadow	**f.** originating in the mind
_c_	**7.** <u>contra</u>ry	**g.** to show or indicate beforehand
_d_	**8.** <u>therm</u>al	**h.** a glass case containing land animals and plants
_b_	**9.** <u>se</u>gregate	**i.** shaped like half of a round figure
_e_	**10.** <u>anthropo</u>morph<u>ism</u>	**j.** instrument used to measure gravity

Writing Your Own Definitions

Write the definitions of the words after noting the underlined word parts and studying the context of the sentences; if you are still uncertain, feel free to consult a dictionary.
Typical responses:

1. At times, Mr. McPherson reluctantly used a computer to write short messages, but he still preferred to use his old-fashioned *<u>dict</u>aphone* for letters.

   <u>dict</u>aphone apparatus that records and reproduces dictation for transcription

2. Beth finally decided to write her term paper on *<u>anthropo</u>genesis* because she thought learning about the beginning and development of humankind would be interesting.

   <u>anthropo</u>genesis the scientific study of the origins and development of humans

3. The veteran sergeant decided to *<u>contra</u>vene* the newly commissioned lieutenant's order because he knew the order would actually result in trouble for him, the lieutenant, and the troops under their command.

   <u>contra</u>vene oppose; contradict; nullify

4. Her outstanding athletic success in high school provided her with a *<u>fore</u>taste* of the fame that could await her in college.

   <u>fore</u>taste sample; advance indication

5. Sheila Walker, M.D., has always been interested in the mental and emotional health of people, so she has decided to specialize in *psychiatry*.

psychiatry _branch of medicine dealing with mental and emotional disorders_

6. The *secretion* from the gland was causing the condition.

secretion _a substance that is generated and separates from cells or bodily fluids_

7. After he got back from his week's jaunt, Todd checked his motorcycle's *odometer*, which showed he had traveled 2,011 miles.

odometer _instrument measuring miles traveled_

8. On the first day of class, our professor asked, "So what do you good people think *thermochemistry* will be about?"

thermochemistry _chemistry of heat and heat-associated reactions_

9. The victim was found *semiconscious* sprawled underneath a ladder.

semiconscious _partially awake; not completely aware_

10. Actually, dolphins, porpoises, whales, and sharks are not considered *terrestrial* animals because they live in water.

terrestrial _having to do with the earth or land_

Learning Challenging Words from Context Clues

1. contraband (KON trə BAND)—noun

- The Border Patrol arrested the pair for trying to sneak *contraband,* including stolen jewelry, into the country.
- Among the major duties of the Coast Guard is to seize all ships carrying any type of *contraband,* such as banned drugs, near our shores.

contraband refers to trade and items that are (a) priceless (b) illegal ___b___ .

2. <u>psychedelic</u> (SĪ kə DEL ik)—adjective

- Members of the rock band were wearing *psychedelic* short-sleeve shirts containing splashes of purple, blue, yellow, red, orange, and green.
- The artist who painted this *psychedelic* picture must have been hallucinating as all the people and objects in it are badly distorted.

psychedelic describes perceptions that are (a) wild (b) dignified _____*a*_____ .

Rock star Jimi Hendrix created *psychedelic* effects in his music through the use of guitar feedback and distortion. *(Michael Ochs Archives/Getty Images)*

3. **semicentennial** (SEM ē sen TEN ē əl)—noun

- Westlake High School will celebrate its *semicentennial* this fall, and as part of the festivities, the graduates of fifty years ago will be especially honored.
- In recognition of its *semicentennial* in our community, one of our local radio stations is giving away fifty dollars to each of the first fifty listeners who call the station for the next two days.

semicentennial is a (a) 50th (b) 100th anniversary _____ *a* _____ .

4. **malediction** (MAL ə DIK shən)—noun

- Suddenly, the angry politician shouted a *malediction* at the journalists; a few minutes later, he calmed down and apologized for his remark.
- In a number of fairy tales, a witch mutters a *malediction* to cast a spell on her unsuspecting victim.

malediction is a (a) promise or secret (b) curse or threat _____ *b* _____ .

5. **altimeter** (al TIM ə tər)—noun

- The pilot of the small plane checked the *altimeter* on the instrument panel to make sure she had sufficient altitude to clear the approaching mountain range.
- The weather balloon contains an *altimeter* among its instruments so the height above sea level can be checked in various parts of the country.

altimeter is an instrument used to measure (a) altitude (b) a variety of weather conditions _____ *a* _____ .

6. **terrain** (tə RĀN)—noun

- Much of the *terrain* of western Washington is mountainous.
- The scientist is convinced part of the planet's *terrain* contains water, indicating to him that some form of life may exist there.

terrain refers to (a) outer space (b) land _____ *b* _____ .

7. **misanthrope** (MIS ən THRŌP)—noun

- He really seems to hate everybody; has he always been a *misanthrope*?
- The crazed tyrant became a *misanthrope,* despising everyone, including members of his own family.

misanthrope is a person who (a) hates (b) misunderstands others _____ *a* _____ .

8. <u>foreboding</u> (fôr BŌ ding)—noun

   ■ Matthew had a *foreboding* he wouldn't be happy living in the apartment he had verbally agreed to rent, so he called the apartment manager to tell him he had changed his mind.
   ■ Megan's *foreboding* about going to class turned out to be justified as the instructor gave a surprise test for which she was completely unprepared.

   foreboding is (a) an uneasy feeling about the future (b) an immature response _____ *a* _____.

9. <u>sedition</u> (si DISH ən)—noun

   ■ After years of turmoil, the colonists finally declared their independence from Great Britain, but the British authorities took forceful steps in a futile attempt to stop the *sedition*.
   ■ The dictator, fearing *sedition,* ordered the military to arrest the rioters and to enforce an 8:00 P.M. curfew for all citizens.

   sedition is a (a) strike (b) rebellion _____ *b* _____.

10. <u>hypothermia</u> (HĪ pə THUR mē ə)—noun

   ■ Although the crew members were rescued from the icy sea within minutes of their ship's capsize, they all suffered from *hypothermia*.
   ■ After I got home from sledding one frigid day in January, I couldn't stop shivering because of *hypothermia,* so Dad wrapped me in a couple of blankets and Mom had me drink a couple of cups of hot chocolate.

   hypothermia is a body temperature that is (a) above (b) below _____ *b* _____ normal.

Matching Challenging Words and Definitions

Write each word before its definition.

contraband	semicentennial	altimeter	misanthrope	sedition
psychedelic	malediction	terrain	foreboding	hypothermia

malediction   **1.** curse, damning, threat, insult, slander

misanthrope   **2.** hater of humankind

contraband   **3.** smuggled goods, goods prohibited in trade

sedition   **4.** incitement of public disorder against the government, rebellion, riot

semicentennial   **5.** fiftieth anniversary

terrain   **6.** plot of land with reference to its natural features

hypothermia   **7.** below normal body temperature

psychedelic   **8.** describes distorted images or exaggerated representations

foreboding   **9.** a strong inner certainty of a future misfortune, an omen

altimeter   **10.** instrument used to measure altitude

Fill-Ins with Challenging Words

In each space, write the appropriate word from those listed below.

| contraband | semicentennial | altimeter | misanthrope | sedition |
| psychedelic | malediction | terrain | foreboding | hypothermia |

1. The wealthy man, considered a(n) _____misanthrope_____ because of the nasty way he treated people throughout his life, left his entire fortune to various charitable causes.

2. After we refused to give money to the young beggar, he shouted a(n) _____malediction_____ at us as we walked away.

3. When the phone rang around one in the morning, I had a(n) _____foreboding_____ I was about to receive some bad news, but, fortunately, I was wrong.

4. The plane's _____altimeter_____ indicated we had quickly reached a height of nearly 7,000 feet.

5. The _____psychedelic_____ picture looked like the artist had simply thrown buckets of red, purple, yellow, and black paint on the canvas.

6. Iowa, one of the leading agricultural states, has some of the richest _____terrain_____ in the nation.

7. A popular rebel leader was arrested and accused of _____sedition_____ by leaders of the central government.

8. Canadian customs officials checked our car, packages, and luggage for _____contraband_____ before waving us on our way.

9. When we go ice fishing, we make sure we wear sufficient winter clothes and have a source of heat as there is always a danger of _____hypothermia_____ because of the freezing temperatures and frigid wind.

10. The _____semicentennial_____ anniversary of the Youth Center in our small community will be celebrated by special events throughout the year.

Checking Your Word Power

After selecting your response, put the letter in the space provided.

_____a_____ 1. The *opposite* of a **malediction** is a
   a. blessing
   b. triumph
   c. defeat
   d. curse

_____d_____ **2.** The *opposite* of **sedition** is
   a. laughter
   b. reward
   c. transfer
   d. loyalty

_____c_____ **3.** The *opposite* of **psychedelic** is
   a. unhealthy
   b. colorful
   c. realistic
   d. disturbing

_____b_____ **4.** An **altimeter** is an instrument used to measure
   a. precipitation
   b. altitude
   c. relative humidity
   d. wind velocity

_____b_____ **5.** **Semicentennial** is associated with the number
   a. twenty-five
   b. fifty
   c. seventy-five
   d. one hundred

_____a_____ **6.** **Contraband** is associated with goods obtained by
   a. illegal means
   b. trading
   c. credit
   d. cash

_____d_____ **7.** If a person is a **misanthrope,** he or she is likely to
   a. enjoy entertaining
   b. enjoy family reunions
   c. dislike exercise
   d. dislike social gatherings

_____c_____ **8.** **terrain: earth:: a.** earth : sky
   b. sky : ocean
   c. ocean : sea
   d. sea : sun

_____a_____ **9.** **hypothermia : hyperthermia :: a.** low : high
   b. cold : frigid
   c. hot : torrid
   d. normal : average

_____d_____ **10.** **foreboding : uneasiness :: a.** warning : relaxation
   b. announcement : indifference
   c. caution : promptness
   d. suspicion : worry

Completing a Passage

After reading the selection, fill in each space with one of the words listed below.

contraband	psychedelic	semicentennial	malediction	altimeter
terrain	misanthrope	foreboding	sedition	hypothermia

FACTS ABOUT ANTS

If ants had "humanlike" feelings, you might think each one was a ___misanthrope___

because they cause so much damage to people's yards, trees, and homes every year, but

before you pronounce a ___malediction___ against them, keep in mind that ants also play

an important role in nature. For example, ant nests, which can be found under practically

any ___terrain___, have numerous openings and tunnels, and these passageways

enable air and moisture to nourish the roots of plants. In addition, seed-eating ants

remove seeds from plants and transfer them to their underground storage chambers,

scattering seeds in the process. Ants also feed on other insects, both living and dead,

helping to control insect populations and contributing to the recycling of organic matter.

And ants are a major source of food for birds, insects, and a variety of animals, includ-

ing the weird-looking armadillos and aardvarks.

Here are some other interesting facts about ants:

- Except for the frozen Arctic and Antarctic, the coldest mountaintops, and a few
  islands, ants thrive the world over, including in deserts, swamps, and the trop-
  ics, where they are the most abundant; some species of ants live so high up in
  trees or other lofty elevations that an ___altimeter___ is almost needed to
  measure the altitude.

- There are over 11,000 species of ants.

- Both the smaller male ants and the larger queen ants have wings, but the queen
  ants shed their wings after starting a new colony by themselves, and the male
  ants die soon after breeding with a queen.

- The life span of most species of ants is usually less than six months, though
  some queen ants have been known to live for several years. (Obviously, then,
  ants never live long enough to celebrate a golden, or ___semicentennial___,
  anniversary of a colony's existence.)

- If we could run as fast for our size as ants can for theirs, we could run as fast as
  racehorses.

- Ants can lift twenty times their own body weight, and they work in teams to move extremely heavy things.

- Ants' combined weight is greater than the combined weight of all humans.

- Ants have the largest brains of all insects; in fact, according to some scientists, an ant's brain may possess a processing power similar to that of a computer.

- In one scientific study, in which the ants looked rather _psychedelic_ because their backs were painted in various colored dots, findings indicated that each group of ants performed distinct tasks: the orange-dotted ants took care of the young, the yellow-dotted ants concentrated on cleaning the colony's nest, and the green-dotted ants left the nest to look for food.

- If a worker ant finds a good source for food, it leaves a trail of scent so that the other ants in the colony can find the food; the scent also enables the worker ant to find its way back to the colony.

- Ants display remarkable engineering skills; for example, they tunnel from two directions and meet exactly midway, and they build underground chambers within the colony for storing food, some of which is _contraband_ they have stolen from other colonies. They also build underground chambers that maintain a steady temperature regardless of what the temperature is on the out-side, so they never suffer from either too much heat (hyperthermia) or too much cold (_hypothermia_).

- Ants' various behaviors are influenced by their senses and information stored within their nervous systems, which seems to provide them with a feeling of _foreboding_ when their territory is about to be invaded by other ants. Within a colony's population, however, there is generally no type of _sedition_ , as ants live in a highly organized and cooperative society.

Misanthrope—one who hates humankind:

- We concluded that our waiter was a <u>misanthrope</u> because he was rude to everyone, including children and the elderly.

Origin: 1563 <Greek—*misanthropos*—hating mankind; *misein* (to hate) and *anthropos* (mankind)

Family words: misanthropist (n), misanthropic (adj), misanthropically (adv), misanthropy (n)

Connotation: *negative*—used for a person who is antisocial, uncaring, and cruel to others

Image to remember: a hermit

Write an original sentence using *misanthrope*:

_____

_____

_____

MASTERING CONFUSING WORDS	principal / principle

principal   the chief or main one; also refers to a school administrator:

The principal reason Stacy wants to be a social worker is so she can help people.
Chandler is working on his master's degree so he will be qualified to be an elementary school principal.

principle   rule or standard:

Attending every class is a good principle for college students to remember.
Putting 10 percent of his earnings in a savings account is a principle my brother has always followed, even when he was a newspaper carrier.

Circle the correct answer:

1. The principal / principle at the high school I attended was well liked by all the students.

2. Being considerate of other people's feelings is an excellent principal / principle to follow.

3. What was the principal / principle reason you dropped out of choir?

Write original sentences using these words:

1. **principal:** _____

2. **principle:** _____

Learning Word Parts from Context Clues

1. aster, astro

- *Asters* are flowers having petals varying from white or pink to blue that radiate around a yellow disk.
- John Glenn was among the first American *astronauts*.

aster and **astro** mean (a) modern (b) star _____ *b* _____ .

2. peri

- Damara is not sure of the exact *perimeter* of the property her family owns, but she knows it embraces nearly 250 acres.
- The commander ordered the *periscope* raised so he could get a complete view of the submarine's surroundings.

peri means (a) around (b) wandering _____ *a* _____ .

3. cred

- Monique is honest, so I know she'll be a *credible* witness.
- Have you ever subscribed to any particular religious *credo*?

cred is associated with (a) trust (b) deceit _____ *a* _____ .

4. em, en

- Do you have confidence in the lawyers who have been *empowered* to negotiate a new employee's contract?
- The coach *encouraged* Tiffany to try out for the team.

em and **en** mean (a) outside (b) put into _____ *b* _____ .

5. itis

- Ali is ill with *bronchitis*.
- The doctor prescribed aspirin for the patient's *arthritis*.

itis means (a) itch (b) inflammation _____ *b* _____ .

6. macro, magn

- The entire universe is sometimes referred to as a *macrocosm.*
- Ellen was able to read the fine print by using a *magnifying* glass.

macro and **magn** mean (a) big (b) special _____ a _____ .

7. the

- *Theology* is concerned with the study of God and religion.
- An *atheist* is a person who doesn't believe in the existence of God.

the relates to (a) discussion (b) God _____ b _____ .

8. pseud

- *Astrology* is a *pseudoscience,* so you may be foolish to believe in it.
- A *pseudocode* is an unrelated or false program code for a particular computer's hardware.

pseud is (a) impressive (b) false _____ b _____ .

9. vid, vis

- The class was shown a *video* about the Everglades.
- Although some things are *invisible,* they nevertheless exist.

vid and **vis** are associated with (a) sight (b) play _____ a _____ .

10. gen

- A motel he built fifteen years ago became the *genesis* of his financial success.
- The child was operated on to correct a *congenital* problem with her spine.

gen relates to (a) honesty (b) beginning _____ b _____ .

Matching Word Parts and Definitions

Match each definition with the word part it defines.

d	**1.** aster, astro	**a.** large; great
h	**2.** peri	**b.** believe; trust
b	**3.** cred	**c.** birth; beginning
e	**4.** em, en	**d.** star
i	**5.** itis	**e.** put into
a	**6.** macro, magn	**f.** false
j	**7.** the	**g.** to see
f	**8.** pseud	**h.** around
g	**9.** vid, vis	**i.** inflammation
c	**10.** gen	**j.** God

Fill-Ins with Word Parts

Select the appropriate word part so the proper word is formed in each sentence.

astro	cred	itis	the	vis
peri	en	magn	pseud	gen

1. Can you en _____ *vis* _____ ion what you'll be doing five years from now?

2. Congress _____ *en* _____ acted the bill into law last month.

3. _____ *Astro* _____ nomy, often called the science of the stars, also includes the study of planets, meteors, and other objects in the universe.

4. _____ *The* _____ ocracy is a form of government led by officials who claim to be guided by God.

5. A(n) _____ *magn* _____ ificent cathedral covered the entire block.

6. A mineral that looks identical to another one but doesn't actually contain the same composition is called a(n) _____ *pseud* _____ omorph.

7. The _____ *cred* _____ ibility of the applicant suffered when it was discovered he had exaggerated his scholastic achievements.

8. _____ *Gen* _____ esis is the first book of the Bible.

9. _____ *Peri* _____ phrasis is a roundabout way of speaking.

10. Sharon's headaches are caused by sinus _____ *itis* _____ .

Matching Words and Definitions

Use your knowledge of the underlined word parts to match the definitions and words.

__*g*__	**1.** <u>peri</u>phery	**a.** skeptical, unbelieving
__*i*__	**2.** gast<u>ritis</u>	**b.** to increase to a higher degree
__*f*__	**3.** <u>macro</u>phage	**c.** to produce, cause, or give birth to
__*e*__	**4.** <u>vis</u>ta	**d.** study of the physical matter of heavenly masses
__*h*__	**5.** <u>pseudo</u>intellectual	**e.** field of view; landscape
__*a*__	**6.** <u>in</u>credulous	**f.** large one-celled animal
__*j*__	**7.** <u>the</u>ism	**g.** the outer boundary
__*c*__	**8.** <u>en</u>gender	**h.** person who fakes being well informed about scholarly matters
__*d*__	**9.** <u>astro</u>physics	**i.** inflammation of the stomach
__*b*__	**10.** <u>en</u>hance	**j.** belief in the existence of God or gods

Writing Your Own Definitions

Write the definitions of the words after noting the underlined word parts and studying the context of the sentences; if you are still uncertain, feel free to consult a dictionary.
Typical responses:

1. Diana put an <u>asterisk</u> beside the names of the people she intended to notify about the meeting.

   <u>asterisk</u> _____ star-shaped figure _____

2. Vincent's remarks, I thought, were interesting, but <u>peripheral</u> at best to the main issue being discussed.

   <u>peripheral</u> _____ relating to outer edges; distantly related; of minor relevance _____

3. Mike's young, <u>credulous</u> sister believed him when he said Spiderman was spinning a web around the entire shopping mall.

   <u>credulous</u> _____ believing too readily; gullible _____

4. Age and illness have <u>embrittled</u> her bones to such an extent that she has to use a walker or a wheelchair to move around in her apartment.

   <u>embrittled</u> _____ made brittle; made weak and easy to break or snap _____

5. The concert is canceled because the lead singer has <u>laryngitis</u>.

   <u>laryngitis</u> _____ inflammation of the throat or larynx _____

6. The Barton family's <u>magnanimity</u> enabled the college to build a much needed new music building.

   <u>magnanimity</u> _____ generosity; charitableness _____

7. Although they are engaged in a variety of activities throughout the day, the monks' lives are unquestionably <u>theocentric</u>.

   <u>theocentric</u> _____ centered on God _____

8. These ancient writings, supposedly written by various biblical characters, are considered by most scholars to be <u>pseudepigrapha</u>.

   <u>pseudepigrapha</u> _____ false writings, especially about biblical people _____

9. Leonardo da Vinci, who lived in the 15th century, is a noted painter, sculptor, architect, and engineer; he is also considered a *visionary* as he <u>fore</u>saw the development of the airplane centuries before it actually occurred.

visionary _____ having foresight; seeing into the future; imaginative _____

10. Samantha is finding her course in *genetics* fascinating because of what she is learning about how hereditary factors influence human development.

genetics _____ science concerned with the study of genes or heredity _____

Learning Challenging Words from Context Clues

1. <u>astronautics</u> (AS trə NOT iks)—noun

- Hideki received a bachelor's degree in physics last spring, and he is beginning a master's degree in *astronautics* this fall as he's hoping to eventually get a job with NASA (National Aeronautics and Space Administration).
- Some of the *astronautics* courses are offered by the astronomy department.

astronautics is the science concerned with space (a) below the earth's atmosphere (b) beyond the earth's atmosphere _____ b _____ .

2. <u>peripatetic</u> (PER ə pə TET ik)—adjective

- The Dearborns are the most *peripatetic* people I know as they've traveled throughout the world, including Australia, New Zealand, Germany, and Brazil.
- Of all the military branches, the Navy probably offers the most *peripatetic* opportunities as its ships sail on all the oceans.

peripatetic has to do with being (a) well traveled (b) well off _____ a _____ .

3. <u>credence</u> (KRĒD əns)—noun

- The discovery of primitive tools, weapons, and pottery provides *credence* to the long-held belief that this small New Mexico town was once the home of a prehistoric people.
- The sportswriter asked the athletic director if there was any *credence* in the rumor that the basketball coach had been asked to resign.

credence has to do with (a) controversy (b) trust _____ b _____ .

4. **embroil** (em BROIL)—verb

   - Amy's grandparents said they didn't want to *embroil* themselves in a family dispute when Amy asked them to help persuade her parents to buy her a car.
   - Don't *embroil* me in the conversation if it has anything to do with money, politics, or religion.

   embroil means to involve in a (a) conflict (b) surprise _____ *a* _____ .

5. **neuritis** (noo RĪ tis)—noun

   - Esperanza is taking medicine for the *neuritis* she has in one of her elbows.
   - Ian has *neuritis* in his neck as a result of a field hockey injury.

   neuritis refers to a (a) nerve inflammation (b) muscle strain _____ *a* _____ .

6. **magnanimous** (mag NAN ə məs)—adjective

   - A wealthy couple's *magnanimous* gift provided most of the funding for the new science building.
   - The announcer on public television said the station's broadcasts were made possible by the *magnanimous* support of its listeners.

   magnanimous means (a) mysterious (b) generous _____ *b* _____ .

7. **monotheism** (MON ə thē IZ əm)—noun

   - The ancient Greeks believed in many gods, not in *monotheism*.
   - Which civilizations were among the first to follow *monotheism* rather than the worship of many gods?

   monotheism is the (a) belief in one God (b) belief in no God _____ *a* _____ .

8. **pseudonym** (SOOD ə nim)—noun

   - The author Samuel Clemens used the *pseudonym* Mark Twain.
   - The movie star used a *pseudonym* while she was a patient at the hospital so she and the hospital staff wouldn't be besieged by the media.

   pseudonym refers to a (a) false name (b) hidden meaning _____ *a* _____ .

9. **vis-à-vis** (VĒz ə VĒ)—preposition, adverb

   - Don't you realize a dog requires more care *vis-à-vis* a cat?
   - *Vis-à-vis* your report, I found it interesting as well as comprehensive.

   vis-à-vis means (a) difficult or troublesome (b) in relation to or relating to _____ *b* _____ .

Jay-Z is the *pseudonym* of rapper Shawn Carter. *(AP Photo/Gary He)*

10. ge̱neric (jə NER ik)—adjective

- Acetaminophen is the *generic* name for Tylenol and many other nonaspirin pain relievers.

- Mrs. Healy saved money by asking her doctor to prescribe a *generic* medicated skin cream rather than one with a brand name.

generic means (a) specific (b) general _____ *b* _____ .

Matching Challenging Words and Definitions

Write each word before its definition.

| astronautics | credence | neuritis | monotheism | vis-à-vis |
| peripatetic | embroil | magnanimous | pseudonym | generic |

vis-à-vis **1.** compared with or regarding

magnanimous **2.** charitable, generous, merciful, liberal

peripatetic **3.** walking, traveling about, roving

generic **4.** descriptive of an entire class

embroil **5.** to involve in a struggle, to bring into a conflict

monotheism **6.** belief in one God

neuritis **7.** inflammation of a nerve

astronautics **8.** the science of travel beyond the earth's atmosphere

pseudonym **9.** false name, pen name, name used by someone to conceal his or her true identity

credence **10.** belief, trust, trustworthiness

Fill-Ins with Challenging Words

In each space, write the appropriate word from those listed below.

| astronautics | credence | neuritis | monotheism | vis-à-vis |
| peripatetic | embroil | magnanimous | pseudonym | generic |

1. My anthropology instructor stated that there are still cultures in the world today whose religion involves the worship of many gods, so _monotheism_ is not the center of all religious beliefs.

2. I wasn't going to pay that much for sneakers just because they were a brand name, so, instead, I bought a less expensive _generic_ pair.

3. She's told so many versions of what happened that her story lacks _credence_ , as far as I'm concerned.

4. "George Eliot" was the _pseudonym_ the author Mary Ann Evans (1819–1890) used because it was difficult for a woman to have her writings published under her own name in the 19th century.

5. The coach is worried about the inexperience of his players _vis-à-vis_ those on the other team.

6. Fortunately, the nagging _neuritis_ I had been suffering from in my left shoulder went away after a couple of weeks of taking aspirin.

7. _Astronautics_ became a popular field of study when the Space Age dawned in the early 1960s.

8. My _____ peripatetic _____ friend arrived from England, stayed with me for a couple of days, then took a flight to Finland.

9. Casey is a considerate and _____ magnanimous _____ young man, so I'm not surprised he's such a generous contributor to the hospital's fundraising efforts.

10. I really didn't want to _____ embroil _____ myself in my sister and her husband's argument, but before I knew it, I was right in the middle of their heated debate.

Checking Your Word Power

After selecting your response, put the letter in the space provided.

_____ b _____ **1.** The *opposite* of **magnanimous** is
    a. simple
    b. stingy
    c. quiet
    d. bored

_____ d _____ **2.** The *opposite* of **embroil** is to
    a. engage
    b. participate
    c. correct
    d. prohibit

_____ a _____ **3.** The *opposite* of **generic** is
    a. special
    b. common
    c. happy
    d. sad

_____ c _____ **4. Vis-à-vis** often suggests
    a. abundance
    b. survival
    c. comparison
    d. embarrassment

_____ a _____ **5. Peripatetic** is associated with
    a. travel
    b. competition
    c. praise
    d. deception

_____ b _____ **6. Monotheism** is associated with the belief in
    a. no God
    b. one God
    c. many gods
    d. evolution

_____d_____ **7.** A person interested in **astronautics** would be most likely to be interested in
  a. oceanography
  b. law
  c. architecture
  d. astronomy

_____c_____ **8. credence : true ::** **a.** disturbance : quiet
  b. send : arrive
  c. reliance : authentic
  d. dependable : unreliable

_____a_____ **9. neuritis : inflammation ::** **a.** flu : fever
  b. headache : migraine
  c. pneumonia : breathing
  d. arthritis : joints

_____c_____ **10. pseudonym : alias ::** **a.** synonym : antonym
  b. public : private
  c. courage : bravery
  d. deceive : restrict

Completing a Passage

After reading the selection, fill in each space with one of the words listed below.

astronautics	peripatetic	credence	embroil	neuritis
magnanimous	monotheism	pseudonym	vis-à-vis	generic

THE CASE FOR LIBERAL ARTS

High school seniors intending to attend college are often surprised to learn that many employers look favorably upon liberal-arts graduates. These employers maintain that college graduates should be grounded in broad knowledge, ethical reasoning, social responsibility, speaking and writing skills, and problem-solving abilities; a major in liberal arts, they have found, often provides the best opportunity to acquire such competencies. For example, the chief executive officer of a business involved in the study of the earth's atmosphere recently said, "Yes, we are interested in hiring graduates in ___astronautics___ , but it's equally important, if not more so, that they excel in communication and social skills. Our employees with a solid college background in liberal arts generally do."

Another employer went so far as to say, "___Vis-à-vis___ technical and people skills, both are important, but my top priority in hiring is finding college graduates who have strong problem-solving and social skills." Her comments give ___credence___ to the importance of good critical-thinking and interpersonal skills, skills that a liberal-arts major has many opportunities to develop.

Most employers don't want to ___embroil___ themselves in arguments as to the specific liberal-arts courses college students should take, but they are ___magnanimous___ in both their financial support and praise for community colleges, universities, and private colleges that insist that all students, regardless of their major, receive a solid foundation in liberal arts.

But what is meant by liberal arts? Unlike ___monotheism___ (a belief in one God), which has a restricted meaning, *liberal arts* is a ___generic___ term applying to a wide array of courses, ranging from history and literature to art and music. A ___peripatetic___ person traveling from one campus to another across the country would discover a great deal of inconsistency in the designation of liberal-arts courses. For example, on some campuses, women's studies and journalism are considered liberal-arts courses, but on others they are not. One university president, who used the ___pseudonym___ "Jackie Jones" rather than her actual name, and who insisted that the name of her university not be revealed because of the controversy on her campus regarding what courses should be included under liberal arts, said that she had actually developed ___neuritis___ in her back from sitting through hours of arguments about this matter, including over whether courses in fashion design and geology should or should not be included among the liberal arts.

While there may not be agreement on what specific courses should be designated liberal arts, the term *liberal arts* itself has always meant to indicate studies that provide general knowledge, communication abilities (reading, speaking, listening, writing), and intellectual skills (critical thinking and reasoning), as opposed to more specialized vocational or scientific skills.

Despite the confusion and even controversy that surround the liberal arts, there is general agreement among education, business, and professional people that a major in the liberal arts is worth serious consideration because of the personal enrichment and career enhancement possibilities such a major provides.

Vis-à-vis—face to face, or compared to/contrasted with:

- Eleanor suddenly found herself <u>vis-à-vis</u> with an angry police officer.
- Because oil prices continue to skyrocket, people are interested in alternative fuels like ethanol <u>vis-à-vis</u> gasoline.

Origin: 1753 <French—*vis-à-vis*—face to face; *vis* (face)

Family word: visage (a noun referring to the features and expression of the face or to the appearance of something)

Connotation: *neutral*—a French word meaning face to face, compared to, or contrasted with

Image to remember: two people staring at each other face to face

Write an original sentence using *vis-à-vis*:

_____

_____

_____

personal concerned with private matters:

My brother never shared his <u>personal</u> feelings with me about not making the team, but I could tell by just looking at his face that he was extremely disappointed.

personnel a group of people working for the same organization or on the same team:

The bank <u>personnel</u> gave a farewell party for the retiring branch manager.

People in the community were optimistic that the local high school team would do well this season because most of the <u>personnel</u> on the squad had gained a lot of valuable experience last year.

Circle the correct answer:

1. Kelsey is looking for a part-time job on campus, so I told her where the college's <u>personal / personnel</u> office is located.

2. Reggie made a <u>personal / personnel</u> pledge to himself that he would improve his grades this semester.

3. The platoon's <u>personal / personnel</u> included people from nine different states.

Write original sentences using these words:

1. **personal:** _____

2. **personnel:** _____

REVIEW TEST, CHAPTERS 6–10

Word Parts

Matching Word Parts and Definitions

Match each underlined word part with its definition.

A

_b_	**1.** rebellion	**a.**	large
_e_	**2.** intrastate	**b.**	war
_c_	**3.** perimeter	**c.**	around
_a_	**4.** magnify	**d.**	sight
_d_	**5.** video	**e.**	within

B

_d_	**1.** hydraulic	**a.**	star
_e_	**2.** hemoglobin	**b.**	inflammation
_a_	**3.** astronaut	**c.**	beginning
_b_	**4.** bronchitis	**d.**	liquids
_c_	**5.** genesis	**e.**	blood

C

_d_	**1.** geography	**a.**	without
_a_	**2.** cloudless	**b.**	put into
_e_	**3.** epidermis	**c.**	false
_b_	**4.** empower	**d.**	earth
_c_	**5.** pseudoscience	**e.**	skin

D

_d_	**1.** final	**a.**	trust
_e_	**2.** amphibian	**b.**	hand
_b_	**3.** manacles	**c.**	God
_a_	**4.** credible	**d.**	completion
_c_	**5.** theology	**e.**	both

Fill-Ins with Word Parts

Select the appropriate word part so the proper word is formed in each sentence.

A

boun   extra   cap   se   contra

1. Concord is the _____*cap*_____ ital city of New Hampshire.

2. The Andersons were elated because the _____*boun*_____ tiful harvest enabled them to pay off their mortgage.

3. The cottage was hard to find because it was located on a(n)

_____ *se* _____ cluded part of the lake.

4. The Super Bowl always features a(n) _____ *extra* _____ vaganza show during halftime.

5. I'm sorry to _____ *contra* _____ dict you, but you're flat-out wrong.

B

neo   ous   dia   psych   anthrop

1. There were four nurses working in the _____ *neo* _____ natal section of the hospital.

2. A term referring to matters originating in the mind is _____ *psych* _____ ogenic.

3. _____ *Anthrop* _____ ology involves the study of humankind's origin, behavior, and cultural development.

4. The circle was large, with the _____ *dia* _____ meter measuring 36 feet.

5. The victori _____ *ous* _____ candidate and his supporters celebrated for hours after the election results were in.

C

non   aud   ness   fore   therm

1. Eli broke one of his _____ *fore* _____ arms when he fell from a ladder.

2. The quiet _____ *ness* _____ of the dormitory was unusual for a Saturday evening.

3. Would you please explain to me in _____ *non* _____ -technical terms how that gadget works?

4. We were sitting so far back in the auditorium that the speaker was barely

_____ *aud* _____ ible to us even though he was using a microphone.

5. I turned up the _____ *therm* _____ ostat because the house was chilly.

D

pos   temp   hetero   homo   mort

1. Can't _____ *hetero* _____ sexual refer either to both sexes or to the opposite sex?

2. And can't _____ *homo* _____ sexual refer either to one or to the same sex?

3. I _____ *temp* _____ porarily rented a car while mine was getting repaired.

4. Do members of that religious faith believe that all people possess an

im _____ *mort* _____ al spirit?

5. Terrell was recently promoted to one of the top managerial _____ *pos* _____ itions in the company.

E

multi   terr   ward   dia   semi

1. The next day, we continued driving south _____ward_____ toward the Florida Keys.

2. Our small apartment consisted of a _____multi_____ purpose room where we studied, ate, watched TV, and slept.

3. The unusual ring was highlighted by several glittering _____semi_____ precious stones.

4. The team's gold warm-up jerseys had two black _____dia_____ gonal stripes running across the front.

5. I didn't realize that Tennessee's _____terr_____ ain was so hilly and mountainous.

F

hypo   ann   phon   dic   meter

1. Unfortunately, the choir's poor _____dic_____ tion on several of the songs made it difficult for the audience to understand what words were being sung.

2. Kurt knew he was becoming _____hypo_____ thermic because of his daylong exposure to the bitter cold, so he was relieved to see the lodge come into view.

3. An ancient _____phon_____ ograph, with some old records on top of it, was featured in the antique store's front window.

4. The baro _____meter_____ has been falling for the last several hours, so I suspect we'll have a storm before nightfall.

5. Shasta passed her _____ann_____ ual medical exam with flying colors.

Challenging Words

Write each word before its definition.

A

Matching Challenging Words and Definitions

acrimonious   manhandle   cacophony   contemporary   neophyte
finale   moribund   bounteous   ambivalence

_____finale_____ **1.** the end, the last section

___manhandle___ **2.** perform in a rough, abusive manner

__ambivalence__ **3.** uncertainty, hesitation

contemporary **4.** of the same time period, of the here and now

___neophyte___ **5.** amateur, beginner

__acrimonious__ **6.** bitter, hostile, angry, disagreeable

___moribund___ **7.** near death, dying

__cacophony__ **8.** harsh, unpleasant sound

__bounteous__ **9.** plentiful, abundant

B

foreboding   magnanimous   misanthrope   peripatetic   graphology
capricious   generic   malediction   monotheism

__graphology__ **1.** the study of handwriting

__misanthrope__ **2.** hater of humankind

__malediction__ **3.** curse, threat

__foreboding__ **4.** feeling of doom, omen

__peripatetic__ **5.** walking about, roving

__monotheism__ **6.** belief in one god

magnanimous **7.** generous, charitable

___generic___ **8.** descriptive of an entire class

__capricious__ **9.** impulsive, changeable

Completing a Passage

After reading the selection, fill in each space with one of the words listed below.

embroil   altimeter   terrain   sedition   astronautics

Lance has always been fascinated with space travel, so he plans to get a degree in

___astronautics___ someday. As a youngster, he often daydreamed about blasting off from earth in a spacecraft, and when the ___altimeter___ indicated he was 200,000 miles out in space, he would guide his spacecraft to an imaginary planet he had christened Patcheroon, named after his beloved dog Patch. When he would land on the mountainous ___terrain___ of Patcheroon, he would generally ___embroil___ himself in a war between the loyal Patcheroonies and some invading aliens, who would try to stir up ___sedition___ among discontented Patcheroonies against their government. Lance, though, was always a magnificent hero in helping the loyal Patcheroonies win the key battles, thus saving Patcheroon from an evil invasion—at least until the next time his imagination took flight.

Unscrambling Words

Unscramble each "word" to discover one you have studied, using the sentence as a clue to the word's identity.

CLUE	SCRAMBLED	UNSCRAMBLED
Example: You'll be sorry if you try to smuggle those goods across the border.	aaconbtrdn	contraband
1. He knows something about this subject because he's the superintendent at the dam.	dlhooyygr	_hydrology_
2. When I was troubled with acne, I saw a specialist in this field.	dyegromoatl	_dermatology_
3. She is utterly fearless!	ntsedlasu	_dauntless_
4. He indulges in a lot of self-analysis.	trinnootipsec	_introspection_
5. I think I have a deadly disease!	porchanyhodi	_hypochondria_

Analogies

After selecting your response, put the letter in the space provided.

____b____ 1. **pseudonym : alias ::** **a.** deceive : contribute
           b. courage : bravery
           c. rough : smooth
           d. brilliant : hazy

____c____ 2. **credence : false ::** **a.** quiet : silence
           b. water : thirst
           c. sickness : well
           d. immobile : stationary

_____d_____ **3. blandness : peppy :: a.** peppy : vigorous
b. vigorous : energetic
c. energetic : lively
d. liveliness : boring

_____a_____ **4. extraneous : essential :: a.** unnecessary : required
b. joyous : delighted
c. sloppy : messy
d. costly : expensive

_____c_____ **5. belligerent : rival :: a.** unfaithful : friend
b. courageous : coward
c. cooperative : friend
d. compliment : enemy

Mastering Confusing Words

Circle the correct answer.

1. I wish Carla would (quiet / quit / quite) snapping her gum because it's (quiet / quit / quite) annoying, and it also disturbs the (quiet / quit / quite) I need when I'm studying.

2. Rather (than / then) going home for the summer, I'm going to work on the campus maintenance crew.

3. While my brother and his wife are (there / their / they're) visiting my parents, (there / their / they're) going to shop for a new car because (there / their / they're) present one has over 160,000 miles on it.

4. My brother-in-law is the (principal / principle) of Oakton High School.

5. One (principal / principle) he insists on is that teachers, students, and staff treat each other with respect.

6. The (personal / personnel) at his school is a nice mixture of veteran and new teachers.

7. His (personal / personnel) advice to me was to consider majoring in mathematics and education so that I can teach high school math after I graduate.

Crossword Puzzle

Solve the crossword by using the following words.

geopolitics	multifaceted	nondescript	wayward	annuity	psychedelic
semicentennial	hypothermia	neuritis	vis-à-vis	composure	diaphanous
heterogeneous	homogeneous	audible	hemostat	generic	

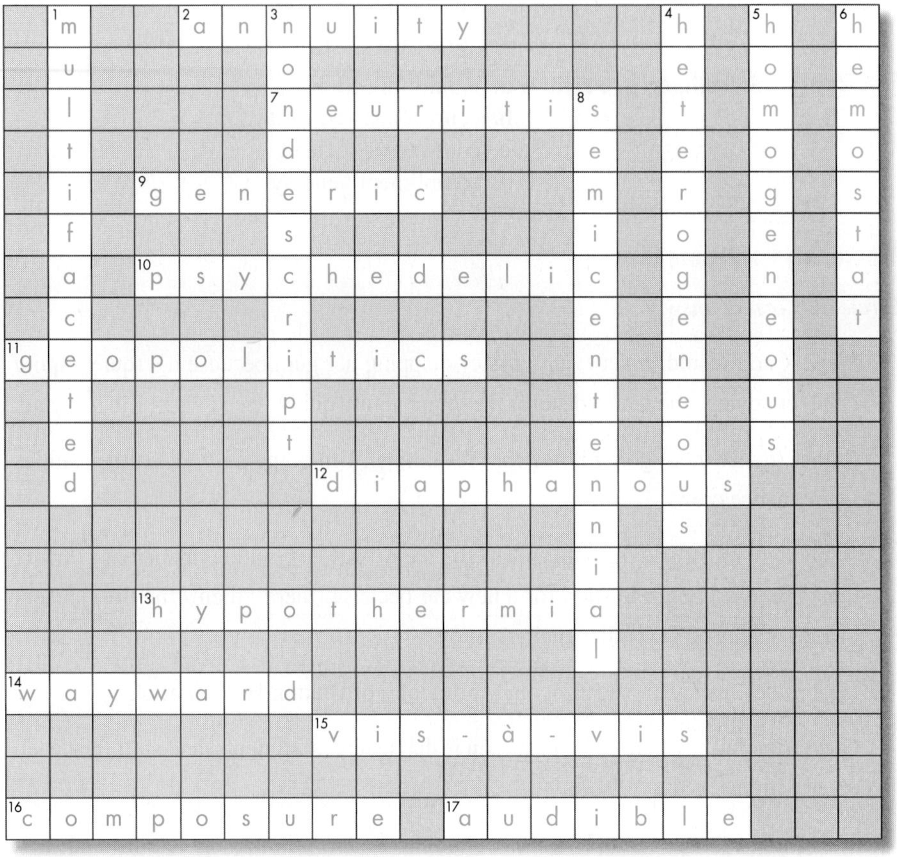

ACROSS

2. payments throughout the year
7. inflammation of a nerve
9. general, descriptive of an entire group
10. describes distorted images or representations
11. geography's effects on relations among nations
12. transparent, delicate
13. below-normal body temperature
14. unruly, deviating from normal
15. face to face
16. calmness
17. capable of being heard

DOWN

1. many-sided, wide-ranging
3. unremarkable, lacking distinctiveness
4. dissimilar, unrelated
5. similar, related
6. instrument to stop bleeding
8. fiftieth anniversary

Learning Word Parts from Context Clues

1. ped, pod

- *Pedestrians* were waiting patiently for the *Walk* sign to appear.
- My feet have been bothering me, so I've made an appointment with a *podiatrist*.

ped and **pod** mean (a) foot (b) person _____ *a* _____ .

2. micro

- After I focused the *microscope,* I could see the bacteria on the slide.
- A *micrometer* is equal in length to one-millionth of a meter.

micro means extremely (a) small (b) complex _____ *a* _____ .

3. scrib, scrip

- I *scribbled* down a list of groceries I needed to buy, then hurried to the store.
- Aaron added a *postscript* to his letter telling me of his recent promotion.

scrib and **scrip** are associated with (a) memory (b) writing _____ *b* _____ .

4. port

- Laptop computers, of course, have the advantage of being *portable*.
- *Exports* are goods shipped out of a country.

port is associated with (a) weight (b) movement _____ *b* _____ .

5. arch

- A *monarchy* is a form of government headed by one person, such as a king or queen.
- Kathy's uncle was recently appointed *archbishop* in the Houston area, so he'll be in charge of many churches, priests, and parishioners.

arch means (a) chief (b) high _____ *a* _____ .

6. cent

- A *centennial* celebration takes place after one hundred years.
- A *centigrade* thermometer's scale ranges from zero to one hundred degrees.

cent means (a) large (b) one hundred _____ *b* _____ .

7. ven, vent

- The _convention_ brought together educational specialists from throughout the nation.
- The _advent_ of the holiday season brought ever-increasing crowds to the nearby malls.

ven and **vent** mean to (a) speak (b) come _____ _b_ _____ .

8. cide

- The murder was made to look like a _suicide_.
- A police's _homicide_ division has the responsibility of investigating murders.

cide means to (a) kill (b) seek _____ _a_ _____ .

9. poten

- The doctor prescribed a _potent_ medicine in an effort to cure the infection.
- Jessica has the _potential_ of becoming the most influential person on the board of supervisors.

poten is associated with (a) price (b) power _____ _b_ _____ .

10. leg

- Kirk is seeking _legal_ advice in an effort to regain his former property.
- The state _legislature_ is the branch of government having the responsibility for making laws.

leg is related to (a) law (b) expense _____ _a_ _____ .

Matching Word Parts and Definitions

Match each definition with the word part it defines.

_f_	**1.** ped, pod	**a.** hundred
_d_	**2.** micro	**b.** carry
_j_	**3.** scrib, scrip	**c.** come; go
_b_	**4.** port	**d.** extremely small
_h_	**5.** arch	**e.** law
_a_	**6.** cent	**f.** foot
_c_	**7.** ven, vent	**g.** possessing strength; powerful
_i_	**8.** cide	**h.** chief; ruler
_g_	**9.** poten	**i.** killing of
_e_	**10.** leg	**j.** writing

Fill-Ins with Word Parts

Select the appropriate word part so the proper word is formed in each sentence.

ped	scrip	arch	ven	poten
micro	port	cent	cide	leg

1. In the vault, we found an old manu ___scrip___ t containing the town's history up to the early 1900s.

2. A(n) ___cent___ ipede doesn't really have one hundred legs, does it?

3. A(n) ___micro___ be is a very small living organism.

4. It was the most important athletic e ___ven___ t in our school's history, so everyone came to the game.

5. When I was growing up, there were a few kids I didn't get along with, but my ___arch___ enemy was a bully by the name of Tommy the Terrible.

6. After his supervisors stripped him of his authority, the manager felt worthless and im ___poten___ t.

7. After Tanya had a(n) ___ped___ icure, her feet, toes, and nails looked and felt much better.

8. It's il ___leg___ al to park on this side of the street; didn't you know that?

9. Patri ___cide___ is the killing of one's father.

10. During the summer, I worked as a ___port___ er at a summer resort; some of the suitcases and baggage I carried must have weighed a ton.

Matching Words and Definitions

Use your knowledge of the underlined word parts to match the definitions and words.

_c_	1. <u>arch</u>ives	a. instrument that measures walking distance
_d_	2. pre<u>scrip</u>tion	b. person possessing great power and authority
_h_	3. <u>leg</u>itimate	c. where chief or important documents are kept
_g_	4. <u>micro</u>fiche	d. written instruction for a specific medicine
_j_	5. <u>port</u>folio	e. to come together for an official or public purpose
_i_	6. <u>cent</u>urion	f. killing of a brother or a relative
_a_	7. <u>ped</u>ometer	g. sheet of film containing numerous pages in reduced form on one frame
_f_	8. fratri<u>cide</u>	h. lawful, proper
_b_	9. <u>poten</u>tate	i. commander of a group of one hundred soldiers in ancient Rome
_e_	10. con<u>ven</u>e	j. a carrying case for holding papers and notebooks

Writing Your Own Definitions

Write the definitions of the words after noting the underlined word parts and studying the context of the sentences; if you are still uncertain, feel free to consult a dictionary.
Typical responses:

1. After the band played, the candidate quickly stepped up to the *po<u>dium</u>* and addressed the cheering crowd.

po<u>dium</u> _____ elevated platform where a speaker stands _____

2. My boss is frustrating to work for because she tends to *<u>micro</u>manage* even the smallest details of everything I do.

<u>micro</u>manage _____ to manage with too much attention to minor details _____

3. The *in<u>script</u>ion* on the monument included the dates 1941–1945.

in<u>script</u>ion _____ something written; etched or engraved writing _____

4. The *im<u>port</u>ation* of foreign cars into the United States began in earnest in the early 1970s.

im<u>port</u>ation _____ the act of bringing into the country _____

5. After the central government collapsed, *<u>anarch</u>y* reigned until the military restored order.

<u>anarch</u>y _____ chaos; state in which no one is in charge _____

6. A *<u>centi</u>meter* is a unit of length equal to what part of a *<u>meter</u>*?

<u>centi</u>meter _____ one-hundredth of a meter _____

7. The teacher was gratified to see two older students *<u>inter</u>vene* to settle the playground dispute between a number of third and fourth graders.

<u>inter</u>vene _____ to step in to settle differences; umpire; reconcile _____

8. A powerful *germi<u>cide</u>* is used to keep this room in sterile condition.

germi<u>cide</u> _____ something that kills germs _____

9. The _potency_ of the police force was increased by the hiring of a dozen new officers.

potency _____ the condition of possessing strength and power _____

10. Our community college's _paralegal_ program has a well-deserved excellent reputation throughout this part of the state.

paralegal _____ relating to specialized training in law so that a person can assist an attorney _____

Learning Challenging Words from Context Clues

1. podiatry (pō DĪ ə trē)—noun

- Randy developed some foot problems after line dancing for over three hours one evening, so he's getting an appointment with a doctor of _podiatry_.
- Students of _podiatry_ must take a number of anatomy and physiology courses, particularly those involving the feet.

podiatry is the study and treatment of (a) foot ailments (b) muscle strains _____ a _____ .

2. microbiology (MĪ krō bī OL ə jē)—noun

- Before I took _microbiology_ to study bacteria and other small organisms, I had a general biology course.
- Because she plans to go to medical school, Shelly is taking a course in _microbiology_ to become familiar with using a microscope as well as to learn about the structure and function of microscopic life that can help or hinder health.

microbiology is a science devoted to the study of (a) plant life (b) extremely small organisms _____ b _____ .

3. proscribe (prō SKRĪB)—verb

- As a result of the recent vandalism that has taken place in our state parks, the governor has written a directive that will _proscribe_ entry to the parks after 7:00 P.M.
- I'll have to read the details about this diet carefully because if it does _proscribe_ meat, eggs, and dairy products as you maintain, then I know it's not a diet I could stay with for very long.

proscribe means to (a) prohibit (b) prescribe _____ a _____ .

4. <u>portage</u> (POR tij)—noun, verb

- We had to *portage* our canoes over a mile before the river became navigable again.
- The climbers had to *portage* all of their supplies to the base of the mountain before nightfall.

portage means to (a) repair (b) carry _____*b*_____ .

5. <u>archetype</u> (AR ki TĪP)—noun

- A textile factory in Lowell, Massachusetts, was the *archetype* of similar factories built throughout New England in the 1800s.
- Humphrey Bogart is the *archetype* of the hard-bitten detective that has been the hero in countless movies since the 1940s.

archetype refers to (a) the original model (b) a bad example _____*a*_____ .

6. <u>centenarian</u> (SEN tə NAR ē ən)—noun

- This article says that life expectancy may be one hundred before too many years pass; can you imagine yourself being a *centenarian*?
- Although many friends and a number of relatives passed away when she was in her eighties and nineties, Mrs. Russell, now a *centenarian,* has kept her interest in life as well as her marvelous sense of humor.

centenarian is a person who is (a) an active senior citizen (b) one hundred years old _____*b*_____ .

7. <u>convene</u> (kən VEN)—verb

- Lawyers for both parties will *convene* this morning to see if a settlement can be reached before the matter reaches the court.
- Those interested in auditioning for the play should *convene* at the performing arts building tomorrow evening at 7:30.

convene means to (a) discuss thoroughly (b) meet together _____*b*_____ .

8. <u>genocide</u> (JEN ə SĪD)—noun

- The shocking report accuses the top leaders of that country of plotting to murder all members of an opposition party, a *genocide* that must be prevented.
- The old science fiction movie I saw on TV the other night was about a planet of evil people, the Puxacrotons, who attempt *genocide* against all the people living on the other planets so that they, the Puxacrotons, could rule the entire galaxy.

genocide is the (a) extermination (b) organization _____*a*_____ of a particular group of people.

Long-lived actor and comedian George Burns died in 1996, shortly after achieving *centenarian* status. (© Bettman/ CORBIS)

9. potency (PŌT ən sē)—noun

- According to the label on the bottle, the *potency* of these vitamins expired two months ago, so I guess I'll throw this bottle away and buy a new one.
- The coach cautioned his players not to underestimate the *potency* of their next opponent, that it was a team capable of beating anyone in the conference.

potency is related to (a) conduct (b) strength _____ *b* _____ .

10. legacy (LEG ə sē)—noun

- The wealthy widow left her entire *legacy,* which includes numerous properties and investments, to her two nieces.
- The *legacy* I received from my grandparents is to work hard and to value family and friends above everything else.

legacy is similar to (a) an inheritance (b) a lesson _____ *a* _____ .

Matching Challenging Words and Definitions

Write each word before its definition.

podiatry	proscribe	archetype	convene	potency
microbiology	portage	centenarian	genocide	legacy

__centenarian__   **1.** a person who has reached the age of one hundred

__legacy__   **2.** money or property left legally to someone, anything handed down from the past

__portage__   **3.** act of carrying, the carrying of boats or goods overland from one navigable water to another

__microbiology__   **4.** science concerned with the study of extremely small organisms

__genocide__   **5.** systematic killing of a particular large group of people

__podiatry__   **6.** study and treatment of foot ailments

__potency__   **7.** vigor, powerfulness, strength, force

__archetype__   **8.** chief or original model after which other things are patterned

__proscribe__   **9.** to prohibit, ban, or banish

__convene__   **10.** to come together, to assemble, to meet

Fill-Ins with Challenging Words

In each space, write the appropriate word from those listed below.

podiatry	proscribe	archetype	convene	potency
microbiology	portage	centenarian	genocide	legacy

1. Our new manager announced she will _____proscribe_____ the wearing of jeans to work starting next week because she thinks jeans are too informal for office apparel.

2. Many scholars agree that Hitler's prolonged _____genocide_____ of the Jews in Germany and elsewhere in Europe was unquestionably the evilest act of the 20th century.

3. According to the museum guide, this 1975 computer became the _____archetype_____ for the generation of computers that followed.

4. All committee members are urged to attend the meeting, which will _____convene_____ at 4:00 P.M. on Wednesday.

5. The _____ legacy _____ the young couple received from one of their relatives enabled them to start their own business.

6. Mr. Pratt recently became the fourth _____ centenarian _____ in our community as there are three other people living here who are one hundred or more.

7. My _____ microbiology _____ course includes a four-hour lab that meets on Thursday afternoons; that's a long time to stare through a microscope at little critters, don't you think?

8. Casey and Brook decided to canoe a different lake from us even though it meant they had to _____ portage _____ their canoe, life jackets, and other materials for nearly three miles.

9. The _____ potency _____ of the anesthesia soon had the patient in a deep sleep.

10. Two offices on the first floor will be assigned to doctors of _____ podiatry _____ so patients with foot problems will not have to walk so far.

Checking Your Word Power

After selecting your response, put the letter in the space provided.

____d____ 1. The *opposite* of **potency** is
     a. energy
     b. anxiety
     c. remainder
     d. weakness

____a____ 2. Someone who would be the *opposite* of an **archetype** would be a
     a. follower
     b. leader
     c. debater
     d. peacemaker

____c____ 3. The *opposite* of a **legacy** is something that is
     a. despised
     b. adored
     c. held back
     d. passed on

____b____ 4. **Podiatry** is most closely associated with the
     a. head
     b. feet
     c. back
     d. abdomen

_____a_____ **5. Genocide** is most closely associated with
   a. tragedy
   b. triumph
   c. wealth
   d. poverty

_____d_____ **6.** A student majoring in **microbiology** is likely to be most interested in
   a. journalism
   b. history
   c. literature
   d. science

_____c_____ **7.** A person who is a **centenarian** is definitely
   a. rich
   b. healthy
   c. old
   d. humorous

_____b_____ **8. portage : carry :: a.** moist : dry
   b. grip : hold
   c. start : postpone
   d. move : drop

_____b_____ **9. proscribe : permit :: a.** permit : allow
   b. allow : outlaw
   c. outlaw : prohibit
   d. prohibit : ban

_____d_____ **10. convene : meet :: a.** convince : doubt
   b. generalize : specify
   c. corrupt : purify
   d. meet : gather

Completing a Passage

After reading the selection, fill in each space with one of the words listed below.

podiatry	proscribe	archetype	convene	potency
microbiology	portage	centenarian	genocide	legacy

NEWSPAPER HEADLINES

After <u>CAREFULLY</u> reading through these actual headlines that have appeared in newspapers across the nation, do you think the writers should have (1) paid more attention in their journalism classes, (2) done a better job of proofreading, or (3) become comedy writers?

SOMETHING WENT WRONG IN JET CRASH, EXPERT SAYS

Really? Should we ____*convene*____ more experts to see what they think?

SHOT OFF WOMAN'S LEG HELPS NICKLAUS TO 66

Well, let's hope her toes are all right; otherwise, she'll need to consult an expert in ____*podiatry*____.

FARMER BILL DIES IN THE HOUSE

Poor guy. I wonder what kind of ____*legacy*____ he left his family.

DEER KILLS 17,000

Why, slaying a population of that size is ____*genocide*____! Let's put that animal on trial.

MAN STRUCK BY LIGHTNING FACES BATTERY CHARGE

He claims he has much more energy and ____*potency*____ now; in fact, he thinks he'll live to be a ____*centenarian*____!

KIDS MAKE NUTRITIOUS SNACKS

If we are to believe the latest findings from the world of ____*microbiology*____ and other fields of science.

SAFETY EXPERTS SAY SCHOOL BUS PASSENGERS SHOULD BE BELTED

My goodness, don't they know laws ____*proscribe*____ this type of punishment?

TWO SOVIET SHIPS COLLIDE, ONE DIES

Did they have to ____*portage*____ the other ship across land because of serious injuries?

BAN ON SOLICITING DEAD IN TROTWOOD

This ban should serve as the ____archetype____ for similar bans for communities across the country! I'm not sure those people would have been much help anyway.

LOCAL HIGH SCHOOL DROPOUTS CUT IN HALF

Too bad, but they *were* told they would regret dropping out of school someday.

FEATURED WORD: genocide

Genocide—the deliberate and methodical killing of a racial, political, or cultural group:

- In 1994, two militia groups in Rwanda began a <u>genocide</u> against other people in the country that resulted in the death of at least 500,000 people by July.

Origin: 1944 <Greek—*genos* (race, kind) and *cide*, from Latin *cidere* (kill); apparently coined in a book referring to the Nazis

Family words: genocidal (adj), genocidally (adv)

Connotation: *negative*—used for the systematic extermination of an entire group of people

Image to remember: the movies *Hotel Rwanda, Schindler's List,* and *The Pianist*

Write an original sentence using *genocide:*

_____

_____

_____

shone   the past tense of the verb *shine*:

Many city lights <u>shone</u> brightly as our plane flew over Topeka.

shown   the past tense of the verb *show*:

What film was <u>shown</u> in your literature class yesterday?

Circle the correct answer:

1. Taylor was <u>shone /</u>(shown) pictures of his friend's wedding.

2. The sun (shone)<u>/ shown</u> in the morning, but the sky was cloudy in the afternoon.

Write original sentences using these words:

1. **shone:** _____

2. **shown:** _____

Learning Word Parts from Context Clues

1. sol

- There was no one else around, so after I tired of watching TV, I played a couple of games of *solitaire*.
- For as far as I could see, the area was barren, lifeless, *desolate*.

sol means (a) alone (b) challenging _____ *a* _____ .

2. polis, urb

- *Indianapolis* is the largest city in Indiana.
- Over 4 million people live in this *urban* area.

polis and **urb** mean (a) liveliness (b) city _____ *b* _____ .

3. ish

- A *Danish* ship was unloading cargo at one of the piers.
- I apologized to my girlfriend for acting so *childish* over the unimportant matter.

ish means (a) empty of (b) descriptive of _____ *b* _____ .

4. ly

- Samira is a *friendly*, considerate person.
- The child said *firmly*, "No! I won't go to bed!"

ly refers to how something is (a) done (b) imagined _____ *a* _____ .

5. age, ance, ence, ship

- The *foliage* this fall was spectacular.
- Tomas is a good mechanic, so he's able to do his own *maintenance* for his car.
- After moving into her apartment, Clare enjoyed having more *independence*.
- My *penmanship* has never been good, so I write with a computer whenever possible.

age, ance, ence, and **ship** relate to (a) description or quality (b) nature or product
_____ *a* _____ .

6. tract

- The telephone kept *distracting* him from his work.
- I was relieved when the *extraction* of my tooth was over.

tract is related to (a) attract or pull (b) noise or pain _____a_____ .

7. circum

- Do you know whether the *circumference* of a basketball is over twelve inches?
- *Circumlocution* is unnecessarily wordy and indirect language.

circum means (a) around (b) through _____a_____ .

8. onym

- *Antonyms* are words with opposite meanings, such as *large* and *small*.
- Someone slipped an *anonymous* note under my windshield wiper telling me I should "learn how to park a car."

onym refers to (a) experiences (b) words _____b_____ .

9. photo

- The flash *photography* blinded me for a few moments.
- The *photosphere* is the visible shining surface of the sun.

photo means (a) scenic (b) light _____b_____ .

10. dem

- *Democracy* is a form of government in which people elect their leaders.
- An *epidemic* is a disease that spreads widely and quickly among people.

dem refers to (a) people (b) vicinity _____a_____ .

Matching Word Parts and Definitions

Match each definition with the word part it defines.

_g_ **1.** sol	**a.** done in the manner of
_c_ **2.** polis, urb	**b.** draw; pull
_j_ **3.** ish	**c.** city
_a_ **4.** ly	**d.** name; word
_h_ **5.** age, ance, ence, ship	**e.** light
_b_ **6.** tract	**f.** people
_i_ **7.** circum	**g.** alone
_d_ **8.** onym	**h.** condition, state, or quality of
_e_ **9.** photo	**i.** around
_f_ **10.** dem	**j.** descriptive or characteristic of

Fill-Ins with Word Parts

Select the appropriate word part so the proper word is formed in each sentence.

sol	ish	ship	circum	photo
urb	ly	tract	onym	dem

1. My old high-school friend hadn't lost any of his boy _____ish_____ charm.

2. The cold weather had caused the door's opening to con _____tract_____ , which allowed the wind to come whistling in.

3. _____Dem_____ otic refers to the common people.

4. Syn _____onym_____ s are words with similar meanings, such as *scary* and *frightening*.

5. The police were absolute _____ly_____ flabbergasted by the startling developments.

6. Magellan was the first explorer to _____circum_____ navigate the world, wasn't he?

7. Keith enjoys the peace and _____sol_____ itude of fishing whenever he gets the chance.

8. At first, any Americans feared the presidency would turn into a dictator _____ship_____ .

9. When I was in college, my professors would sometimes distribute _____photo_____ copies of their lectures.

10. Elisa is sophisticated and _____urb_____ ane from having such wonderful cultural experiences in New York City.

Matching Words and Definitions

Use your knowledge of the underlined word parts to match the definitions and words.

___c___	**1.** <u>urb</u>anite	**a.** surgical instrument used to draw back tissue from an incision
___i___	**2.** peev<u>ish</u>	**b.** briefly and to the point; concisely
___e___	**3.** impu<u>dence</u>	**c.** a city dweller
___j___	**4.** <u>circum</u>vent	**d.** the measurement of the intensity of light
___h___	**5.** <u>sol</u>idarity	**e.** disrespect; rudeness
___d___	**6.** <u>photo</u>metry	**f.** false name
___a___	**7.** re<u>tract</u>or	**g.** the statistical study of human population
___g___	**8.** <u>dem</u>ography	**h.** union among a group of people arising from common interests or responsibilities
___b___	**9.** succinct<u>ly</u>	**i.** annoyed; resentful
___f___	**10.** pseud<u>onym</u>	**j.** to go around or to avoid a problem

Writing Your Own Definitions

Write the definitions of the words after noting the underlined word parts and studying the context of the sentences; if you are still uncertain, feel free to consult a dictionary.
Typical responses:

1. Cristina said she was <u>sole</u>ly responsible for the accident, so we were not to blame anybody else.

   <u>sole</u>ly _____ alone; singly _____

2. Do you enjoy being an <u>urban</u>ite, or would you rather live in the country?

   <u>urban</u>ite _____ city dweller _____

3. Many families and friends seem rather *clann<u>ish</u>* in this small community, don't you think?

   clann<u>ish</u> _____ maintaining a close relationship that others are not encouraged to join; cliquish; exclusive _____

4. I felt *blatant<u>ly</u>* out of place eating in the posh restaurant because I was wearing an old pair of jeans, a sweatshirt, and sneakers.

   blatant<u>ly</u> _____ glaringly; flagrantly; notoriously _____

5. It was a happy day indeed when I was finally able to send the final <u>remitt</u>ance owed on my car.

   <u>remitt</u>ance _____ sum of money sent or submitted _____

6. I had never gone horseback riding before, but fortunately my horse was <u>tractable</u>, so I was able to relax and have a good time.

   <u>tractable</u> _____ easily managed _____

7. Do you know of an alternate route we could take to <u>circumvent</u> having to drive through the city?

   <u>circumvent</u> _____ avoid, go around _____

8. In this simple code, each letter is <u>*synonymous*</u> to its numerical order in the alphabet, so "A" is equal to "1," "B" is equal to "2," and so on.

synonymous _____ equivalent in meaning _____

9. Did you know this machine was powered by *photoelectric* cells?

photoelectric _____ relating to electric effects caused by light _____

10. The flu was so *pandemic* during January that the schools, malls, and other places were closed for a number of days.

pandemic _____ widespread; everywhere _____

Learning Challenging Words from Context Clues

1. <u>**soliloquy**</u> (sə LIL ə kwē)—noun

   ■ While one of the actors was on the stage alone giving a *soliloquy* during the play *Our American Cousin,* John Wilkes Booth shot President Lincoln.
   ■ Some of the guys were watching TV and a couple were playing a spirited game of Ping-Pong; Scott, on the other hand, was staring out the window and muttering a *soliloquy* about the beauty of falling snow.

   soliloquy is the act of (a) being silly (b) speaking to oneself _____ b _____ .

2. <u>**megalopolis**</u> (MEG ə LOP ə lis)—noun

   ■ Dallas, Fort Worth, and Denton, Texas, have become so densely populated that the area is now considered a *megalopolis*.
   ■ In Minnesota, Minneapolis, St. Paul, and their nearby communities make up another *megalopolis*.

   megalopolis refers to a region consisting of several (a) large adjoining cities (b) competing governments _____ a _____ .

3. <u>**fetish**</u> (FET ish)—noun

   ■ My roommate has such a *fetish* for getting good grades that he studies until after midnight every night, including weekends.
   ■ My sister-in-law must have a *fetish* for earrings as I know she must have over one hundred pairs.

   fetish is (a) an extreme attraction to (b) a perplexing opposition to _____ a _____ .

4. **ostensibly** (o STEN sə blē)—adverb

- My son *ostensibly* borrowed the car to go to the library, but I found out later he had actually gone to his girlfriend's house.
- *Ostensibly,* Fred wears a baseball cap all the time to look "cool," but I think the real reason is to hide his thinning hair.

ostensibly means (a) impressively (b) supposedly _____ *b* _____ .

5. **abeyance** (ə BĀY əns)—noun

- Title to the estate was in *abeyance* while legal authorities were consulted.
- According to Luke, all promotions are in *abeyance* until business improves.

abeyance is a temporary (a) problem (b) suspension _____ *b* _____ .

6. **retraction** (ri TRAK shən)—noun

- The paper admitted the information printed in yesterday's paper about one of the candidates for mayor was wrong, so the paper contained an appropriate *retraction* today.
- The singer threatened to sue the TV show's producer if the producer didn't issue a *retraction* about her being difficult to work with.

retraction is a (a) taking back of (b) twisting of certain information _____ *a* _____ .

7. **circumspect** (SUR kəm SPEKT)—adjective

- Be sure to be *circumspect* when you mention your complaint to him because he's sensitive to any type of criticism.
- She is *circumspect* in conducting her public, professional, and private life, so there's never been any type of scandal associated with her.

circumspect is being (a) quiet (b) cautious _____ *b* _____ .

8. **acronym** (AK rə nim)—noun

- The *acronym* for "self-contained underwater breathing apparatus" is SCUBA.
- The *acronym* for "situation normal all fouled up" is SNAFU.

acronym is a word formed from (a) the first letters in a group of words (b) using one's imagination _____ *a* _____ .

9. **photosynthesis** (FOH tə SIN thə sis)—noun

- Of course, sunlight is necessary for *photosynthesis* to occur in plants so the plants can have nourishment.
- Chlorophyll, carbon dioxide, and water are also necessary for *photosynthesis* to take place.

photosynthesis refers to plants (a) reproducing themselves (b) making food for themselves _____ *b* _____ .

Plants like this Lady's Mantle survive through the process of *photosynthesis*.　(© Dency Kane/Beateworks/Corbis)

10. **demagogue** (DEM ə gog)—noun

- Many historians consider the late Senator Joseph McCarthy, who served in the Senate in the 1950s, a *demagogue* because he convinced thousands of people that the federal government was full of communists.
- She is a dangerous *demagogue* because many people believe her when she insists all the major television networks are controlled by people whose chief objective is to undermine the morality of our young people.

demagogue is a person who seeks power by appealing to people's (a) fears (b) generosity _____ *a* _____ .

Matching Challenging Words and Definitions

Write each word before its definition.

soliloquy	fetish	abeyance	circumspect	photosynthesis
megalopolis	ostensibly	retraction	acronym	demagogue

retraction **1.** the taking back of a statement, opinion, or promise

megalopolis **2.** an outsize city; an urban area consisting of several large, adjoining cities

acronym **3.** a word formed from the initial letters of a group of words

demagogue **4.** a person who attempts to gain power and influence by appealing to people's fears and other emotions

soliloquy **5.** the act of speaking to oneself

ostensibly **6.** supposedly, apparently, done in a manner to deceive

photosynthesis **7.** the process by which plants form food

fetish **8.** any object or idea abnormally adored, compulsion

circumspect **9.** careful, proper, wisely cautious, using good judgment

abeyance **10.** postponement, temporary suspension, waiting period, delay

Fill-Ins with Challenging Words

In each space, write the appropriate word from those listed below.

soliloquy	fetish	abeyance	circumspect	photosynthesis
megalopolis	ostensibly	retraction	acronym	demagogue

1. Brian was _____*ostensibly*_____ my pal, but it eventually became apparent he was more interested in being "friends" with my gorgeous cousin than he was in being "friends" with me.

2. NATO is a(n) _____*acronym*_____ for North Atlantic Treaty Organization.

3. Although the editor was confident the information in the article was correct, he decided to print a(n) _____*retraction*_____ rather than risk a libel suit.

4. When he is alone, doesn't Hamlet whisper a remorseful _____*soliloquy*_____ after the tragic deed is done?

5. Sarah's boss said he would hold her job in _____*abeyance*_____ while she completes her eight weeks of basic training in the Air National Guard.

6. Some sociologists predict that Denver, Colorado Springs, Boulder, and Fort Collins will be a(n) _____*megalopolis*_____ within a couple of decades because of the continuing rapid population growth in that area of the country.

7. Mr. Aoki said that although it's known that sunlight, carbon dioxide, water, and chlorophyll are involved in the process of ____photosynthesis____ that takes place in plants, the process is still not fully understood.

8. Marcela was dying to meet the attractive young man who sat near her in class, but her ____circumspect____ behavior did not give her away.

9. One of the candidates is nothing more than a(n) ____demagogue____ in my opinion because he maintains the national economy, including the Social Security system, would collapse unless he and other members of his party were elected to Congress.

10. I love anything chocolate, so I'm one of the millions of people who have a(n) ____fetish____ for this delicious food; in fact, I once saw someone wearing a sweatshirt that said, "Hand over your chocolate and no one will get hurt."

Checking Your Word Power

After selecting your response, put the letter in the space provided.

____d____ **1.** The *opposite* of **circumspect** is
   a. quiet
   b. funny
   c. kind
   d. careless

____b____ **2.** The *opposite* of a **megalopolis** is a
   a. city bordered by other large cities
   b. region of sparsely populated villages
   c. metropolitan area with a population of 4 million
   d. sprawling community with high real estate taxes

____a____ **3.** The *opposite* of a **soliloquy** is
   a. a discussion on stage between two actors
   b. talking to oneself on stage
   c. a plea for help over television
   d. praying silently in church

____c____ **4.** The person who would be most likely to know the most about **photosynthesis** would be an expert on
   a. insects
   b. microbes
   c. plants
   d. animals

____a____ **5.** A **retraction** is most likely to sound
   a. apologetic
   b. angry
   c. accusing
   d. arrogant

_____b_____ **6.** Which of the following is an **acronym**?
  a. TELEVISION
  b. NASA
  c. FORD
  d. MICHIGAN

_____c_____ **7.** A **demagogue** is most likely to be
  a. wealthy
  b. poor
  c. bold
  d. shy

_____a_____ **8. fetish : fixation :: a.** fixation : compulsion
  b. compulsion : unthinking
  c. unthinking : habit
  d. habit : impulsive

_____c_____ **9. abeyance : temporary :: a.** costly : inexpensive
  b. violence : delay
  c. postponement : suspension
  d. position: permanent

_____a_____ **10. ostensibly : insincerity :: a.** supposedly : phoniness
  b. flashy : sincerity
  c. honesty : insensitivity
  d. importantly : foolishness

Completing a Passage

After reading the selection, fill in each space with one of the words listed below.

soliloquy	fetish	abeyance	circumspect	photosynthesis
megalopolis	ostensibly	retraction	acronym	demagogue

The *Sultana* Tragedy

In April 1865, the Civil War finally ended, but the nation's sorrow continued. On April 14, President Abraham Lincoln was assassinated, causing unprecedented mourning throughout the country. Then on April 27, the steamship *Sultana*, carrying over 2,000 Union soldiers back to their homes in the North, exploded on the Mississippi River not far from Memphis, Tennessee. Though the exact death toll is not known, respected and ____circumspect____ historians put the figure at 1,700, making the *Sultana* the greatest maritime disaster in United States history.

In Vicksburg, Mississippi, a few days after the war ended, over 2,200 Union soldiers crowded aboard the *Sultana*, which ____ostensibly____ was large enough to carry that many passengers, but in truth was built to carry less than 400. After leaving Vicksburg, the *Sultana* struggled against the strong currents of the Mississippi River as it steamed toward Memphis. As it was planting season and many of the soldiers came from rural areas, it is speculated that some of them, while strolling *Sultana's* deck and observing the farms bordering the river, likely were discussing _photosynthesis_ (though not by that technical name) and other factors involved in growing crops.

The *Sultana* finally made it to Memphis. This city and the nearby towns were certainly not a ___megalopolis___ by any means, but the area was important to the river's traffic. After a short ___abeyance___ in Memphis, the *Sultana* continued on its way.

Just north of Memphis, however, the steamboat's overheated and overworked boilers suddenly exploded. Hundreds of soldiers were killed instantly while others were blown or jumped into the river's cold water. The *Sultana* quickly became engulfed in flames and began to sink. Today most captains have a ___fetish___ about having a sufficient number of life jackets aboard their ships, but the *Sultana* had none. Many of the soldiers in the water could not swim, and others were too badly injured to do so; still others couldn't swim because they were too weak after being prisoners of war for a long period of time.

The fire aboard the *Sultana* was spotted in Memphis, and rescue boats were immediately dispatched to the scene. Although many soldiers were saved, bodies continued to be found months later downriver, and many bodies were never recovered. Of the approximately 500 survivors transported to hospitals in Memphis, more than half of them soon died from burns or exposure.

None of those that did survive ever became a ___demagogue___ who tried to gain fame and fortune by appealing to people's sympathies. The survivors did, however, meet every year on April 27 until 1928, when there were only four still alive.

Even though this was the biggest shipping catastrophe in United States history, there have been no movies made, songs composed, or plays written containing a heartfelt ___soliloquy___ about the *Sultana*. Even most history books through the years have failed to mention the disaster, though one noted historian, Stephen Ambrose, wrote an article entitled "Remembering *Sultana*" for the May 2001 issue of *National Geographic*. Another lesser-known historian committed himself to writing a book about the tragedy, but he submitted a ___retraction___ of the commitment later because of his failing health.

In 1982—though no ___acronym___ , such as "USSS" (United States Ship *Sultana*), was discovered on any of the planks—investigators uncovered charred wooden planks and timbers under 32 feet of water near Memphis that they were convinced were the remains of the ill-fated *Sultana*.

Occurring just days after the bloody conflict ended, the 1,700 soldiers who lost their lives in the *Sultana* disaster were additional victims of the tragic Civil War.

FEATURED WORD: demagogue

Demagogue—a leader who obtains power through impassioned appeals to people's fears and prejudices:

- The <u>demagogue</u> shouted that if he weren't re-elected mayor, the city would soon lack adequate police and fire protection.

Origin: 1648 <Greek—*demagogos*—leader of the people; *demos* (people) and *agogos* (leader); considered a negative term since it was first used in ancient Athens

Family words: demagogic (adj), demagogism (n), demagoguery (n), demagogy (n)

Connotation: *negative*—refers to an unethical person who resorts to lies, exaggerations, slander, fear-mongering, or similar behaviors in an effort to gain power

Image to remember: a dictator

Write an original sentence using *demagogue*:

_____

_____

_____

hole   an empty area:

Darn it, I have a <u>hole</u> in my favorite sweater.

whole   complete, entire:

Darcy painted the <u>whole</u> apartment by herself over the weekend.

Circle the correct answer:

1. My car has a (hole) / whole in the muffler, so it roars like a wounded lion.

2. The <u>hole</u> / (whole) room was so crowded with people I couldn't have fallen down if I had wanted to.

Write original sentences using these words:

1. **hole:** _____

2. **whole:** _____

Learning Word Parts from Context Clues

1. ac

- The *acrid* smell of the fireworks lingered long after the spectacular event was over.
- Michelle's coolness under stress, as well as her *acumen* at determining which patients needed treatment first and what that treatment should be, made her an ideal emergency room doctor.

ac means (a) attractive; appealing (b) bitterly sharp; quickly aware _____ *b* _____ .

2. dys

- Major difficulty in recognizing and comprehending written words is known as *dyslexia*.
- Apparently, the patient's episodes of heart *dysrhythmia* were due to the blood pressure medicine he was taking.

dys is associated with something (a) educational (b) abnormal _____ *b* _____ .

3. err

- The shortstop's throwing *error* allowed the runner on third to score.
- My cousin's *errant* behavior was becoming increasingly common, so all of us were worried about her.

err means (a) costly; rare (b) to slip up; to stray from normal _____ *b* _____ .

4. medi

- An administrator from the school system and a representative from the post office department were selected to *mediate* the unusual dispute between the school custodians and the mail carriers.
- In high school, I was a *mediocre* student, finishing 64th in a graduating class of 128.

medi relates to the (a) middle (b) situation _____ *a* _____ .

5. be

- All of us loved our third-grade teacher because she never *belittled* us if we made a mistake or even if we misbehaved.
- He thought he had *bedazzled* his date with his charm and tales of his many accomplishments, but she never would go out with him again.

be is a prefix meaning (a) to be (b) to reverse   *a*   .

6. claim, clam

- When Ryder discovered someone had dented his car while it was parked in the parking lot, he *exclaimed*, "Who in the heck did this? I wish I could get my hands on that cowardly jerk!"
- The winning contestant's *exclamation* of delight echoed throughout the auditorium.

claim, clam means to (a) shout (b) object   *a*   .

7. greg

- The church's *congregation* had slowly declined over the years.
- The cattle were *segregated* based upon their breed.

greg is related to (a) groups (b) sizes   *a*   .

8. al

- "*Parental* advice," the young man said, "is usually good advice, don't you think?"
- His *denial* of any wrongdoing was not convincing.

al means (a) one who does (b) having the quality of   *b*   .

9. ic

- The movie has *fantastic* special effects.
- We felt *sympathetic* when we learned about all of their troubles, so we decided to help them out.

ic means (a) having the characteristic of (b) more than one   *a*   .

10. ize

- Can you *harmonize* with me on this song?
- To make sure you don't *plagiarize*, cite all the sources you use to write your paper.

ize means (a) to do away with (b) to bring about   *b*   .

Matching Word Parts and Definitions

Match each definition with the word part it defines.

_e_	**1.** ac	**a.** middle
_f_	**2.** dys	**b.** shout; cry out
_j_	**3.** err	**c.** to bring about
_a_	**4.** medi	**d.** to be
_d_	**5.** be	**e.** bitterly sharp; insightful
_b_	**6.** claim, clam	**f.** abnormal; impaired; faulty
_h_	**7.** greg	**g.** having the characteristic of
_g or i_	**8.** al	**h.** crowd; groups
_g or i_	**9.** ic	**i.** having the quality of
_c_	**10.** ize	**j.** to blunder; to stray from normal

Fill-Ins with Word Parts

Select the appropriate word part so the proper word is formed in each sentence.

ac	err	be	greg	ic
dys	medi	claim	al	ize

1. The laboratory supervisor cautioned the students to be particularly careful when working with the _____ *ac* _____ id because of possible burns to the skin or the eyes.

2. My egocentr _____ *ic* _____ co-worker talks constantly about himself, and it's driving me nuts.

3. We decided to _____ *be* _____ friend the stray little kitten after she purred softly when we held her.

4. As is true of many people in my small town, I often synchron _____ *ize* _____ my watch with the blowing of the factory's noon whistle.

5. My roommate's refus _____ *al* _____ to loan me his car for a couple of hours took me by complete surprise.

6. Indigestion, or _____ *dys* _____ pepsia, is usually not a cause for alarm.

7. Deliberately giving the police officer _____ *err* _____ oneous information got the speeding motorist into even more trouble.

8. Both sides have agreed to the hiring of a(n) _____ *medi* _____ ator in an effort to try to settle their long-standing dispute.

9. The principal pro _____ *claim* _____ ed Friday as "Dress-Up Day."

10. Club members will con _____ *greg* _____ ate at the hotel's banquet hall for their next meeting.

Matching Words and Definitions

Use your knowledge of the underlined word parts to match the definitions and words.

_f_	**1.** majes*tic*	**a.** having no fixed course; wandering
_h_	**2.** *acri*mony	**b.** decorated; adorned
_i_	**3.** jeopard*ize*	**c.** one who meets with others to worship
_b_	**4.** *be*decked	**d.** insane; excessively excited or upset
_g_	**5.** *dys*pnea	**e.** located in the middle
_d_	**6.** mania*cal*	**f.** dignified; noble; kingly; magnificent
_j_	**7.** ac*claim*	**g.** difficulty breathing
_a_	**8.** *err*atic	**h.** hostility; resentment; anger
_e_	**9.** *med*ian	**i.** to put into danger
_c_	**10.** con*greg*ant	**j.** praise; fame; applause

Writing Your Own Definitions

Write the definitions of the words after noting the underlined word parts and studying the context of the sentences; if you are still unsure, feel free to consult a dictionary. Typical responses:

1. We proofread the document a number of times before sending it to the printer, so we were disappointed to discover that there is at least one *erratum* in the bound copy.

   erratum ____ an error in writing or printing ____

2. Despite the graduation last spring of a number of key instrumentalists, the director was determined that the band would maintain its reputation for excellence and not slip into *mediocrity* as some people seemed to think it would.

   mediocrity ____ the state of being ordinary, average, or so-so ____

3. The judge ruled in favor of the *claimant*, awarding her $100,000.

   claimant ____ person making a claim or complaint; person who is suing ____

4. As individuals, not everyone had distinguished himself or herself, but as an *aggregate*, their accomplishments were impressive.

   aggregate ____ total; whole ____

5. Don't you think the store owner would have more customers if he didn't have such an _acerbic_ personality?

acerbic _____ sour; bitter; sarcastic; sharp and unpleasant _____

6. The sales staff at the antique store even used an _archaic_ cash register.

archaic _____ old; ancient; out of style _____

7. Look, I know you don't like me and hope that I don't win, so don't _patronize_ me with your expressions of "good luck" and "best wishes."

patronize ____ to act insincerely; to be condescending; to be snooty or scornful ____

8. It was frustrating when my math teacher said, "Why can't you solve these problems? They shouldn't _befuddle_ you."

befuddle _____ confuse; puzzle; fluster _____

9. According to this source, the _autumnal equinox_ always occurs during the third week in September.

autumnal equinox _____ the beginning of autumn, when day and night are of equal length _____

10. From all accounts that I've either heard or read, she grew up in a _dysfunctional_ family; nevertheless, she is reported to be well adjusted and successful in everything she has undertaken.

dysfunctional _____ abnormal or impaired; not operating appropriately _____

Learning Challenging Words from Context Clues

1. **exacerbate** (ig ZAS ər bāt)—verb

   ■ Hot, humid weather like we've been having lately tends to _exacerbate_ his breathing problems, so he stays inside his air-conditioned apartment.
   ■ The road construction scheduled to begin next week will no doubt _exacerbate_ the traffic congestion already existing on this route.

   exacerbate means to (a) worsen (b) soothe _____ a _____ .

2. **dystrophy** (DIS trə fē)—noun

- The annual fall telethon has raised millions of dollars to find a cure for muscular *dystrophy,* a serious disease involving the wasting away of muscles.
- Rescued after nine days of floating in a raft, the young pilot was pale, thin, uncoordinated, and so weak he was unable to stand; such *dystrophy,* the doctors said, was basically due to malnutrition.

dystrophy is usually associated with the (a) kidney (b) muscles _____*b*_____ .

3. **aberration** (ab ə RĀ shən)—noun

- I assure you that my uncle's temper tantrum yesterday was an *aberration* as generally he's a pleasant person to be around.
- It is India's dry season, so today's heavy rainfall was an *aberration.*

aberration is always (a) bad (b) unexpected _____*b*_____ .

4. **medieval** (med Ē vəl)—adjective

- "I mean," Shalini exclaimed, "it's like *medieval* for our principal to insist that we have four chaperones for the dance and that the dance must end at 11:00 P.M.! It's like totally insane!"
- The *medieval* period, also known as the Middle Ages, dates from 500 to 1500.

medieval can mean (a) outdated (b) inadequacy _____*a*_____ .

5. **bereft** (bə REFT)—adjective

- Despite arriving in the United States *bereft* of money, friends, and jobs, countless immigrants have succeeded in making important contributions to the country.
- Until my cousin learned to control his temper, he was almost *bereft* of friends.

bereft indicates a (a) lack (b) bias _____*a*_____ .

6. **clamorous** (KLAM ər əs)—adjective

- The loud music, the shouting and dancing people, and the clanking dishes and glasses made for a wild and *clamorous* wedding reception.
- The magician waited patiently for the *clamorous* children to settle down before beginning his show.

clamorous is associated with (a) hubbub (b) quiet _____*a*_____ .

7. **gregarious** (gri GAR ē əs)—adjective

- Initially, Kendon had a difficult time adjusting to college because he's not *gregarious* among strangers.
- Jaimie is so *gregarious* and thoughtful that everyone knows and likes her.

gregarious means (a) sociable (b) generous _____*a*_____ .

Many castles, such as Raglan Castle, were built during the *medieval* age. *(David Lyons/Alamy)*

8. <u>colloquial</u> (kə LŌ kwē əl)—adjective

- The disk jockey's folksy, *colloquial* speaking style won him a loyal audience over the years.
- My political science professor presents her lectures in a relaxed manner using *colloquial* rather than elaborate language.

colloquial refers to language that is (a) impressive (b) commonly used _____*b*_____ .

9. <u>sophomoric</u> (sof ə MOR ik)—adjective

- A few members of my dorm still enjoy short-sheeting beds, removing light bulbs from the hallways, spraying shaving cream all over the bathrooms, and other such *sophomoric* pranks; I wish they'd grow up.
- After gaining a smattering of knowledge and experience, there are always a few medical students who become rather *sophomoric* in attitude and behavior, convinced they now know as much or more than their professors.

sophomoric is associated with (a) immaturity (b) sorrow _____*a*_____ .

10. ostracize (OS trə sīz)—verb

- Unfortunately, at my high school, the "in" group would *ostracize* others simply because they didn't wear the "right" clothes.
- A month or two after their wedding, one influential church member wanted to *ostracize* the couple after he learned that both had previously been married and divorced.

ostracize means to (a) flatter (b) snub _____b_____ .

Matching Challenging Words and Definitions

Write each word before its definition.

| exacerbate | dystrophy | aberration | medieval | bereft |
| clamorous | gregarious | colloquial | sophomoric | ostracize |

___gregarious___ **1.** seeking and enjoying the company of others

___exacerbate___ **2.** to make a condition worse

___sophomoric___ **3.** exhibiting immaturity; impressed with one's knowledge when, in fact, it is limited

___medieval___ **4.** old-fashioned; belonging to the Middle Ages

___bereft___ **5.** lacking or deprived of something

___dystrophy___ **6.** wasting away of muscles and nerves

___colloquial___ **7.** characteristic of everyday language

___ostracize___ **8.** to exclude from a group

___aberration___ **9.** deviation from what is proper or expected; irregularity

___clamorous___ **10.** continuously noisy

Fill-Ins with Challenging Words

In each space, write the appropriate word from those listed below.

| exacerbate | dystrophy | aberration | medieval | bereft |
| clamorous | gregarious | colloquial | sophomoric | ostracize |

1. Summer's business slump proved to be a temporary _____aberration_____ as sales returned to normal in early fall.

2. I may be _____medieval_____, but I still believe wedding guests should wear suits and dresses, not jeans and slacks.

3. When you speak to them, use _____colloquial_____ language; don't try to impress them with fancy, high-sounding words.

4. Children _____*bereft*_____ of parental love are often insecure.

5. Salvatore is a popular waiter because of his _____*gregarious*_____ nature as his customers appreciate his pleasant chatter and friendliness.

6. Those snobs _____*ostracize*_____ anyone who isn't as rich as they are.

7. Because of some type of _____*dystrophy*_____ , he had a difficult time walking without some type of assistance.

8. You will certainly _____*exacerbate*_____ your sprained ankle if you attempt to play basketball today.

9. As part of the initiation process, candidates used to have to sing their school songs, howl like wolves, recite the names of the presidents, and do other such _____*sophomoric*_____ stunts, but, fortunately, those juvenile requirements were abolished over a decade ago.

10. The party became so wild and _____*clamorous*_____ that the police had to be called to break it up.

Checking Your Word Power

After selecting your response, put the letter in the space provided.

_____*c*_____ 1. The opposite of **gregarious** is
   a. polite
   b. curious
   c. shy
   d. friendly

_____*d*_____ 2. The *opposite* of **bereft** is
   a. painful
   b. panicky
   c. peppy
   d. plentiful

_____*a*_____ 3. The *opposite* of **clamorous** is
   a. quiet
   b. exciting
   c. sadly
   d. noisily

_____*d*_____ 4. **Colloquial** is associated with language that is
   a. regrettable
   b. vague
   c. necessary
   d. conversational

_____c_____ **5. Dystrophy** is associated with
- **a.** finances
- **b.** security
- **c.** disease
- **d.** crime

_____a_____ **6.** If a person is said to be **medieval,** he or she is considered
- **a.** old-fashioned
- **b.** gallant
- **c.** brilliant
- **d.** progressive

_____b_____ **7.** An **aberration** would certainly be
- **a.** expensive
- **b.** unexpected
- **c.** praiseworthy
- **d.** worthless

_____c_____ **8. sophomoric : sophisticated :: a.** handsome : attractive
- **b.** curious : inquisitive
- **c.** immature : knowledgeable
- **d.** honorable : ethical

_____a_____ **9. exacerbate : worsen :: a.** worsen : aggravate
- **b.** aggravate : soothe
- **c.** soothe : disturb
- **d.** disturb : worship

_____d_____ **10. ostracize : include :: a.** shun : banish
- **b.** outburst : eruption
- **c.** recognize : identify
- **d.** expel : embrace

Completing a Passage

After reading the selection, fill in each space with one of the words listed below.

| exacerbated | dystrophy | aberration | medieval | bereft |
| clamorous | gregarious | colloquial | sophomoric | ostracized |

HATFIELDS AND MCCOYS

Though romanticized in legend and folklore, the story of the Hatfield and McCoy feud is actually a long and tragic one. In the mid-1800s, the head of the Hatfield clan was William Anderson "Devil Anse" Hatfield, and the head of the McCoy clan was Randolph, known as "Old Randall," McCoy. The Hatfields and McCoys lived on opposite sides of the Tug River that ran between the mountainous border of Kentucky and

West Virginia. For a number of years, the families were on friendly terms, even inter-marrying. Then the Civil War (1861–1865) erupted.

Except for one ___aberration___, Asa McCoy, members of both families sympa-thized with the South. However, Asa McCoy joined the Union troops and served for a year before being discharged after he broke a leg, resulting in ___dystrophy___ in that limb.

After Asa returned to his Appalachian home in Kentucky, he was approached by Jim Vance, a relative of the Hatfields. Vance warned Asa in the unique ___colloquial___ lan-guage of that region that a group of Confederate supporters, included members of the Hatfield clan, would soon be "visiting him." Fearing for his life, Asa hid in a cave, but he was soon found and shot to death, setting the stage for a feud reminiscent of the ___medieval___ feuds of 500–1500.

Relations between the Hatfields and McCoys remained tense but without further bloodshed for a time; then in 1878, Old Randall McCoy and Floyd Hatfield got into a bitter quarrel over a pig. A trial was held in an effort to determine the lawful owner. The verdict hinged on Old Randall's nephew, Bill Staton, who, no doubt to the surprise of many people, testified that Floyd Hatfield was the rightful owner of the pig. A few months later, Bill Staton was shot to death by Paris and Sam McCoy.

Star-crossed lovers from the clans then became involved in the long and deadly feud. Old Randall McCoy had an attractive and ___gregarious___ daughter, Roseanna, who enjoyed social get-togethers. At one of these noisy, ___clamorous___ events, she met Johnse Hatfield, who was attractive but rather ___sophomoric___, apparently believing he was wiser and more mature than he actually was. Nevertheless, Roseanna fell in love with Johnse, and she became pregnant. She assumed that she and Johnse would marry. However, her brothers kidnapped Johnse, saying they were going to take him "to jail." Roseanna knew better, so she rode to "Devil Anse" Hatfield's home to tell him what had happened. "Devil Anse" quickly got his sons and some neighbors, and they succeeded in rescuing Johnse before he suffered any harm from the McCoy brothers. Johnse, though, never returned to Roseanna, even after she gave birth to their daughter, Sarah Elizabeth, who died in infancy. Johnse added to Roseanna's mis-ery by marrying her sixteen-year-old cousin, Nancy McCoy. Roseanna was now ___ostracized___ by both her family and the Hatfields. ___Bereft___ of family and friends, Roseanna broke down emotionally and physically, dying before she was thirty years old.

The tragedies continued as three of Old Randall's sons ___exacerbated___ the feud by murdering Ellison Hatfield, stabbing him twenty-six times, then shooting him in the back. The Hatfields retaliated by capturing the three McCoy brothers and then killing them. The Hatfields also broke into the home of Mary McCoy Daniels, whipped Mary and her daughter, and later shot to death Jeff McCoy, Mary's brother.

The Hatfield-McCoy feud, which started in 1863 with the death of Asa McCoy, finally ended in 1888 after eight Hatfields were found guilty of murder, with one of them being publicly hanged and seven sentenced to life imprisonment. However, an indication that the feud was truly over occurred in June 2000, when the Hatfields and McCoys held a joint reunion in Pikeville, Kentucky.

FEATURED WORD: sophomoric

Sophomoric—(1) characteristic of a sophomore; (2) intellectually smug; immature:

- The young man tried to impress the panel members by asking what he thought were thought-provoking questions, but they were actually <u>sophomoric</u> inquiries, causing all of the members to smile and a number of them to laugh.

Origin: 1688 <Greek—*sophos* (wise) and *moros* (foolish, dull)
Family words: sophomorical (adj), sophomorically (adv)
Connotation: *negative*—describes a person who exhibits great immaturity and lack of judgment
Image to remember: a prankster

Write an original sentence using *sophomoric*:

_____

_____

_____

conscience   a person's sense of right and wrong:

My <u>conscience</u> bothered me until I finally paid back the money I had borrowed from Shannon a couple of months ago.

conscious   being awake, alert, aware:

The patient was <u>conscious</u> about an hour after the surgery was completed.

Are you <u>conscious</u> of the fact that we have a biology test tomorrow?

Circle the correct answer:

1. Trish suddenly became <u>conscience</u> / <u>conscious</u> of the fact that her remarks had upset her friend, so she apologized.

2. His <u>conscience</u> / <u>conscious</u> told him not to argue with the police officer, so he didn't.

Write original sentences using these words:

1. **conscience:** _____

2. **conscious:** _____

Learning Challenging Words from Context Clues

1. **alienation** (āl yə NĀ shən)—noun

   - President Woodrow Wilson's fervent hope was that the League of Nations formed after World War I would end the *alienation* that had traditionally existed among many of the European countries.
   - After the Bergs became acquainted with more people in the community, their feelings of *alienation* began to vanish.

   alienation suggests (a) affection (b) isolation _____*b*_____ .

2. **collateral** (kə LAT ə rəl)—noun

   - To obtain financing for their purchase of the motel, the Eddicotts used their lumber business as *collateral.*
   - Milo plans to use his pickup truck as *collateral* to secure a bank loan.

   collateral refers to a (a) bonus (b) pledge _____*b*_____ .

3. **deleterious** (del i TER ē əs)—adjective

   - Felicia's inattention to her car's basic maintenance needs had *deleterious* consequences later on.
   - According to this article, unrestricted television watching can have a number of *deleterious* effects on children, including social isolation and poor physical condition.

   deleterious means (a) harmful (b) unknown _____*a*_____ .

4. **felicitous** (fə LIS ə təs)—adjective

   - The timing of the money's arrival was so *felicitous* that Jenna now believes in miracles.
   - The veterinarian's *felicitous* words helped to comfort the little girl over the loss of her beloved dog.

   felicitous means (a) well timed; well chosen (b) out of order; out of date __*a*__ .

5. **hypothetical** (hī pə THET i kəl)—adjective

  - Brendan could give only a *hypothetical* explanation as to why the construction boss hired him for the summer, but he believes it's because he has experience driving heavy trucks.
  - I realize this is a *hypothetical* question, but do you think if our team were to finish the season undefeated that Coach LaPointe would receive a college coaching offer?

hypothetical is associated with (a) sarcasm (b) guessing _____ *b* _____ .

6. **immutable** (i MYOO tə bəl)—adjective

  - My uncle, a farmer, is an *immutable* pessimist when he discusses the weather. For example, if the sun is shining, he's sure a drought is beginning; if it's raining, he's sure his crops will be washed away.
  - One of nature's *immutable* laws is that having to do with inertia, that is, an object's natural resistance to any change in its motion.

immutable means (a) changeless (b) unreasonable _____ *a* _____ .

7. **impeccable** (im PEK ə bəl)—adjective

  - The lovely home was *impeccable* throughout—even the basement was spotlessly clean.
  - James's old Pontiac is still in *impeccable* condition, so I suspect it's worth a lot of money.

impeccable means (a) flashy (b) flawless _____ *b* _____ .

8. **impunity** (im PŪ nə tē)—noun

  - Because his folks were such good friends with the local police chief, Rusty apparently thought he could ignore with *impunity* the town's posted speed limits. However, he learned differently when he was slapped with a $400 fine for speeding.
  - To their regret, three of the players learned they couldn't break training rules with *impunity* as the coach dismissed them from the team.

impunity means freedom from (a) penalty (b) passion _____ *a* _____ .

9. **gullible** (GUL ə bəl)—adjective

  - Advertisers for cold remedies must believe most people are *gullible,* given the exaggerated claims made in their television commercials.
  - Loraine, my young children are *gullible,* so don't tell them any stories about this old house of yours being haunted, okay?

gullible means easily (a) entertained (b) fooled _____ *b* _____ .

10. **trepidation** (trep ə DĀ shən)—noun

- Sydney approached her first flying lesson with *trepidation,* but afterward she was so thrilled she couldn't wait for her next lesson.
- Most people have feelings of *trepidation* when they are told they need to undergo hospital tests.

trepidation is (a) fear (b) shyness _____ *a* _____ .

Matching Challenging Words and Definitions

Write each word before its definition.

| alienation | deleterious | hypothetical | impeccable | gullible |
| collateral | felicitous | immutable | impunity | trepidation |

deleterious   **1.** destructive, harmful

hypothetical   **2.** forming a reasonable opinion but without sufficient evidence or proof

impeccable   **3.** perfect, flawless, unblemished

alienation   **4.** separation due to hostility or suspicion, isolation

gullible   **5.** easily deceived, trustful

felicitous   **6.** appropriate, timely

trepidation   **7.** fear, terror, alarm

collateral   **8.** security pledged in return for a loan

impunity   **9.** freedom from punishment, exemption

immutable   **10.** permanent, changeless

Fill-Ins with Challenging Words

In each space, write the appropriate word from those listed below.

| alienation | deleterious | hypothetical | impeccable | gullible |
| collateral | felicitous | immutable | impunity | trepidation |

1. Erin used her house as _____ *collateral* _____ for a loan to expand her jewelry store.

2. Because these old coins are in _____ *impeccable* _____ condition, they are worth much more than their face value.

3. Ironically, change is one of life's _____ *immutable* _____ laws.

4. Kindergarten helps children learn they must consider the effects of their acts on others, that they can't behave with _____ *impunity* _____ .

5. Carrie eventually realized she should stop dwelling on her disappointment about not receiving the promotion because her preoccupation with this matter was having a(n) _____deleterious_____ effect on her emotional state as well as on her family.

6. Rob is so _____gullible_____ he actually believed me when I told him I was offered a movie contract even though I've never even been in a school play.

7. Kwan's _____felicitous_____ arrival with the car saved me from being late to work.

8. My _____hypothetical_____ reasoning as to why Imogene broke up with Clint is that she has a crush on somebody else, but I'm just guessing.

9. The _____alienation_____ and suspicion initially existing between the two neighbors gradually dissolved as they became better acquainted.

10. Despite his _____trepidation_____ about flying, a fear that developed four years ago when he had flown during a severe thunderstorm, Eddie was determined to fly to California to visit his friend.

Checking Your Word Power

After selecting your response, put the letter in the space provided.

___d___ 1. **Alienation** suggests
    a. movement
    b. participation
    c. harmony
    d. division

___a___ 2. The opposite of **impeccable** is
    a. imperfect
    b. impossible
    c. impatient
    d. immovable

___d___ 3. The word most closely associated with **collateral** is
    a. pleasure
    b. pity
    c. popularity
    d. promise

___a___ 4. **Impunity** suggests
    a. exception
    b. hastiness
    c. weakness
    d. disapproval

_____c_____ **5.** Who is likely to be the most **gullible**?
a. angry parent
b. experienced lawyer
c. young child
d. senior citizen

_____b_____ **6.** A **hypothetical** conclusion is always
a. accurate
b. uncertain
c. acceptable
d. unpopular

_____d_____ **7.** The word most closely associated with **deleterious** is
a. health
b. beauty
c. success
d. ruin

_____a_____ **8. felicitous : unfortunate :: a.** boring : inspiring
b. graceful : skillful
c. impatient : restless
d. honest: trustworthy

_____b_____ **9. trepidation : trembling :: a.** frightening : giggling
b. fear : shaking
c. dread : encouraging
d. foolishness : threatening

_____c_____ **10. immutable : changeable :: a.** changeable : adjustable
b. adjustable : flexible
c. flexible : rigid
d. rigid : unyielding

Completing a Passage

After reading the selection, fill in each space with one of the words listed below.

deleterious	hypothetical	impeccable	alienation	gullible
felicitous	trepidation	collateral	impunity	immutable

CELEBRITY WORSHIP

Are you interested in the lives of celebrities? Using ___hypothetical___ reasoning, I'd say the answer is "yes," as studies indicate that people from six to sixty generally are. Of course, the degree of interest varies. Most people have only a passing interest because they are so involved in their own activities and relationships that they have little time or energy to devote major attention to "star watching." However, for some people, being engrossed with the lives of celebrities results in ___alienation___ from families and friends. Such obsessed worshipers seem compelled to learn every scrap of information they can about their favorite celebrity, devouring magazines, newspapers, blogs, and other Internet sites, many of which are far from ___impeccable___ sources. For example, many bloggers appear to believe they can, with absolute ___impunity___, write anything they want about celebrities, and ___gullible___ fans will believe it, even when the "information" is so absurd that most two-year-olds would know better.

Unfortunately, there are also a few mentally unbalanced individuals who identify so strongly with their idol that they become stalkers. A few years ago, a man from the Midwest borrowed thousands of dollars from a bank, using his house as ___collateral___, so that he could move to Los Angeles to be near his "only love," a popular television actress. The actress naturally became filled with ___trepidation___ as she began to see this man hanging around outside her apartment day and night. It was ___felicitous___ that the security personnel at the apartment complex had also become aware of this stalker's presence, and with their help, she secured a court order banning the man from not only the apartment complex area but also from the studio lot where she worked. The man soon moved back to the Midwest, much to the relief of the actress.

For a minority of people, then, celebrity worship can be ___deleterious___ to their emotional and mental health; however, for most people, it's a welcome diversion from their regular routines. In addition, psychologists say it's also an ___immutable___ fact that admiring accomplished people and having appropriate idols can inspire us to strive toward our life's goals. Celebrity worship, then, like most things in life, is fine if not taken to the extreme—and if the celebrities are actually worthy role models.

Hypothetical—derived from *hypothesis*, an assumption taken to be true for the purpose of argument or investigation:

- So, Jason, let me ask you a <u>hypothetical</u> question: If you were on a long car trip without a spare tire, what would you do if you had a flat 100 miles from nowhere?

Origin: 1588 <Greek—*hypothesis*; *hypo* (under) and *thesis* (a placing, proposition)

Family words: hypothesis (n), hypothesize (v), hypothetical (adj), hypothetically (adv)

Connotation: *positive* or *neutral*—often reflects the positive use of speculation, logical reasoning, and imagination

Image to remember: a police officer speculating as to what caused a car accident

Write an original sentence using *hypothetical*:

_____

_____

_____

weather   atmospheric conditions:

April <u>weather</u> in the Midwest is unpredictable, with chilly rains one day and sunny, summerlike temperatures the next.

whether   means "if":

I don't know <u>whether</u> Joss is coming with us, do you?

Circle the correct answer:

1. I can't remember weather /(whether) Kinsey or Serena is the oldest daughter in the family.

2. During the summer, what's the (weather)/ whether like in Arkansas?

Write original sentences using these words:

1. **weather:** _____

2. **whether:** _____

Learning Challenging Words from Context Clues

1. **de<u>bac</u>le** (də BA kəl)—noun

   ■ Our high-school class reunion turned out to be a *debacle* because someone had failed to mail all the invitations so less than thirty people showed up; the restaurant manager had reserved the banquet room for the wrong evening; and the band knew few of the popular songs of our graduation year.

   ■ Gordon threw his arms up in the air and laughingly complained that his grand plan for redecorating his apartment was quickly turning into a *debacle*. He said the wallpaper started coming off after he painted over it, and the carpet store had sent over a ghastly purple rug instead of the pale blue one he had ordered.

   debacle is related to a (a) crime (b) disaster _____ b _____ .

2. **de<u>pri</u>vation** (dep rə VĀ shən)—noun

   ■ Warren's salary boost finally enabled him and his family to live comfortably and not suffer any basic *deprivation,* such as the inadequate housing they had once experienced.

   ■ Unfortunately, when my dad lost his job, we endured one *deprivation* after another, including the loss of our home, car, and medical insurance.

   deprivation is related to (a) embarrassment (b) hardship _____ b _____ .

3. **garr<u>ulous</u>** (GAR ə ləs)—adjective

   ■ My sister is one of the most *garrulous* persons I know; she has such a gift for gab that I told her she should become a politician.

   ■ Ramon is seldom *garrulous,* but when he does have something to say, he's generally worth listening to.

   garrulous means (a) wordy (b) intelligent _____ a _____ .

4. **meti<u>culous</u>** (mə TIK yə ləs)—adjective

   ■ My brother takes *meticulous* care of his new Chevrolet, driving it in only good weather and constantly polishing it.

   ■ A team of government accountants was conducting a *meticulous* investigation of the company's financial records.

   meticulous means extremely (a) thorough (b) suspicious _____ a _____ .

5. nebulous (NEB yə ləs)—adjective

- My grandparents' retirement plans are still in the *nebulous* stage, but they have talked about spending the winter months in Florida.
- Brianna's *nebulous* ideas about how to correct the computer problem finally crystallized into a clear solution.

nebulous means (a) unclear (b) exciting _____ a _____ .

6. sagacious (sə GĀ shəs)—adjective

- Due to their stockbroker's *sagacious* advice over the years, my in-laws are financially comfortable today.
- Jada is not only well informed about the details of the project, but she's also *sagacious* when it comes to the engineering procedures that will be used.

sagacious means (a) courageous (b) wise _____ b _____ .

7. specious (SPĒ shəs)—adjective

- Based upon the information contained in his resume, the personnel director felt the applicant had given *specious* responses to some of her questions, so she recommended he not be hired.
- My tennis opponent told me he was just an average player, a *specious* statement because I knew he had been among the top finishers in several tournaments in our area.

specious means (a) modest (b) misleading _____ b _____ .

8. redundant (ri DUN dənt)—adjective

- Erika said the professor of her criminal law class had been *redundant* today as he had previously lectured on the rights of the accused.
- I know I'm being *redundant,* but if you want to buy my car, be sure to call me by 5:30 this evening.

redundant refers to unnecessary (a) abruptness (b) repetition _____ b _____ .

9. repudiate (rē PŪ dē āt)—verb

- I not only disagree with you, but I'm also sure Pam will *repudiate* your claim that this is an unfriendly neighborhood in which to live.
- The senator is confident her voting record will *repudiate* her opponent's charge that she is no friend of the environment.

repudiate means to (a) contradict (b) confirm _____ a _____ .

10. **viable** (VĪ ə bəl)—adjective

- Because of the unexpectedly high estimates from several carpenters, the Baylors decided the only *viable* choice for them was to remodel their old house themselves.
- Mr. Francis's law enforcement background made him a *viable* candidate for the sheriff's position.

viable means (a) surprising (b) practical _____ *b* _____ .

Matching Challenging Words and Definitions

Write each word before its definition.

debacle	deprivation	garrulous	meticulous	nebulous
sagacious	specious	redundant	repudiate	viable

repudiate	**1.**	to deny, to reject as untrue or unjust
viable	**2.**	practical, workable, capable of succeeding
meticulous	**3.**	precise, particular, thorough, exacting
debacle	**4.**	complete failure, disaster
garrulous	**5.**	talkative, wordy
deprivation	**6.**	a lack of the usual comforts and necessities of life, a hardship
specious	**7.**	false, misleading
redundant	**8.**	unnecessarily repetitious, excessive
sagacious	**9.**	intelligent, clever, wise
nebulous	**10.**	hazy, vague, indistinct, incomplete

Fill-Ins with Challenging Words

In each space, write the appropriate word from those listed below.

debacle	deprivation	garrulous	meticulous	nebulous
sagacious	specious	redundant	repudiate	viable

1. Trey is often so _____ *garrulous* _____ it's virtually impossible to get a word in edgewise.

2. The pharmaceutical company had to _____ *repudiate* _____ its advertising claim regarding the healing power of its new arthritis medicine because research studies clearly indicate the medicine isn't effective.

3. Although my grandmother never had the opportunity to go to college, she's the most _____ *sagacious* _____ person I know, so I seek her advice whenever I have a problem.

4. Engineers say the only _____ *viable* _____ solution for preventing floods in this part of the state is to construct a series of dams.

5. Our double date turned into a(n) _____debacle_____ because after our car broke down, we arrived too late to attend the concert, so the other couple ended up pouting the rest of the evening.

6. Alex said the major _____deprivation_____ he experienced as an only child was a lack of companionship.

7. Isn't it _____redundant_____ to say someone is a "rich" millionaire?

8. Archaeologists have been conducting _____meticulous_____ excavations in the Middle East for many years in an effort not to damage anything they might uncover.

9. Some people believe car salespeople often make _____specious_____ statements when trying to make a sale, but I've found them to be honest in their conversations with me.

10. If the film had a major point, it was too _____nebulous_____ for me to figure out.

Checking Your Word Power

After selecting your response, put the letter in the space provided.

_____b_____ **1.** The *opposite* of **sagacious** is
  a. interesting
  b. foolish
  c. expensive
  d. ill

_____a_____ **2.** The *opposite* of **specious** is
  a. honest
  b. common
  c. noisy
  d. sharp

_____c_____ **3.** The *opposite* of **viable** is
  a. impatience
  b. impressive
  c. impractical
  d. impolite

_____d_____ **4.** A **meticulous** person is
  a. unfaithful
  b. colorful
  c. dull
  d. thorough

_____b_____ **5.** A **garrulous** person is certainly *not*
  a. opinionated
  b. brief
  c. weak
  d. popular

_____b_____ **6. Deprivation** suggests
   a. elegance
   b. poverty
   c. sensitivity
   d. defiance

_____d_____ **7.** If the person talking to you was being **redundant,** you would probably feel
   a. confused
   b. fascinated
   c. encouraged
   d. bored

_____c_____ **8. nebulous : cloudy :: a.** dark : pale
   b. vague : plain
   c. hazy : fuzzy
   d. bright : gloomy

_____a_____ **9. repudiate : evil :: a.** embrace : good
   b. deny : virtue
   c. commit : crime
   d. support : wickedness

_____b_____ **10. debacle : commotion :: a.** failure : triumph
   b. success : celebration
   c. riot : ceremony
   d. victory : disturbance

Completing a Passage

After reading the selection, fill in each space with one of the words listed below.

debacle	deprivation	garrulous	meticulous	nebulous
sagacious	specious	redundant	repudiate	viable

I'M BACK!

Though the actual number of adults ranging in age from twenty to thirty-four who move back to live with their parents remains somewhat ____nebulous____, most sociologists believe the figure to be at least 18 million, which is approximately one-third of those falling into that age group. Careful, ____meticulous____ research reveals the intriguing finding that households in the higher income brackets are significantly more likely to have adult children living at home than those in the lower income brackets. Another interesting discovery that has remained more or less constant the past several years is that slightly over half of those about to graduate from college indicate they will be moving back home to live with their parents. Should, then, their college education be considered a _____debacle_____ of some sort? According to our most respected and _____sagacious_____ social analysts, the answer is an emphatic "No!" Then why do so many college graduates and other young adults appear to _____repudiate_____ the opportunity to live on their own? Actually, to assume that all these college graduates are willingly denying themselves such an opportunity would be _____specious_____ reasoning, as there are a variety of valid reasons why they are again living at home.

For example, one friendly and _____garrulous_____ recent graduate talked at some length about why he and a number of his classmates had moved back home after graduation. In his case, he had moved back home so he could more quickly pay off his college debts. He also said that three of his classmates had moved back home because they had not been successful so far in finding jobs. Two other classmates, though employed, chose to live at home because they realized the only way they could afford an apartment in the trendy suburban area close to where they worked was to give up many of the comforts they were accustomed to, an unreasonable _____deprivation_____, at least in their minds. Another classmate intended to go to graduate school, and living at home was the only _____viable_____ way she could afford to do so.

It would be _____redundant_____ to repeat the results of other studies because they largely reveal similar findings relating to why young adults move back home. However, others do mention that some people move back home to prepare for their marriages while others do so because of divorce. Regardless of the reasons, studies reveal that most parents are happy to have their children living with them again—particularly if it's only temporary.

Sagacious—describes someone who is keenly insightful and wise:

- The judge was <u>sagacious</u>, fair, and even-tempered.

Origin: 1540–1550 <Latin—*sagax* (wise) and *ous* (full of)

Family words: sagaciously (adv), sagaciousness (n), sagacity (n)

Connotation: *positive*—associated with wisdom and excellent judgment

Image to remember: Albert Einstein

Write an original sentence using *sagacious*:

_____

_____

_____

MASTERING CONFUSING WORDS | **complement / compliment**

complement something that completes or brings to perfection:

Asante's three-point shooting ability serves to <u>complement</u> the scoring ability of the back-court players.

compliment to praise:

Did you <u>compliment</u> Asante for his good game?

Circle the correct answer:

1. I would like to <u>complement</u> /(compliment) all of you for volunteering to clean the park this first day of spring.

2. Do you think paint or wallpaper would best (complement)/ compliment the furniture in this room?

Write original sentences using these words:

1. **complement:** _____

2. **compliment:** _____

Learning Challenging Words from Context Clues

1. catharsis (kə THAR sis)—noun

- Attending basketball games is a *catharsis* for Elliot because he's able to rid himself of stress by cheering for his favorite team.
- As a *catharsis* for her anger and disappointment, Julia took a long, brisk walk.

catharsis is most related to a (a) cleansing (b) saving _____*a*_____ .

2. dearth (DURTH)—noun

- There was a *dearth* of applicants for the city manager's position, so the city council is going to re-advertise the position.
- A *dearth* of hometown fans at the important game was a disappointment to the coaches, players, and cheerleaders as many of the bleachers were empty.

dearth is associated with (a) insufficiency (b) inactivity _____*a*_____ .

3. guile (GĪL)—noun

- Are you suggesting the charges against the defendant were dismissed because of her lawyer's *guile* rather than because of her innocence?
- The reporter's *guile* gained him entrance to the celebrities' wedding.

guile is most related to (a) logic (b) trickery _____*b*_____ .

4. lethargy (LETH ər jē)—noun

- Lying around all day watching television leads to *lethargy,* not vitality.
- Tasha's *lethargy* the past few days is due to her recent bout with the flu.

lethargy is most related to (a) outbursts of anger (b) the blahs _____*b*_____ .

5. affinity (ə FIN ə tē)—noun

- Dillon's lifelong *affinity* for sports led to a coaching career.
- Emily's *affinity* for dancing was apparent the first time she stepped onto a dance floor.

affinity refers to (a) an inclination for (b) a confusion about _____*a*_____ .

6. affluence (AF loo əns)—noun

- The Donaldsons used much of their *affluence,* which they acquired through shrewd investments, in many worthwhile ways, including generous donations to numerous charities.
- The large, luxurious homes and spacious, well-tended lawns made it obvious that people of considerable *affluence* lived in this area.

affluence refers to (a) influence (b) wealth _____ *b* _____ .

7. dichotomy (dī KOT ə mē)—noun

- Some parents, unfortunately, seem to believe a *dichotomy* exists between love and discipline when it comes to raising their children; however, according to most child psychologists, love and discipline go together.
- There is often a *dichotomy* between a business's stated policies and its daily practices.

dichotomy refers to a (a) complex arrangement (b) division into two parts __ *b* __ .

8. enigma (ə NIG mə)—noun

- The reason Lee Harvey Oswald assassinated President John F. Kennedy is an *enigma* that will probably never be solved.
- It's an *enigma* to their friends as to why the couple broke up because they seem perfect for each other.

enigma is a (a) mystery (b) mistake _____ *a* _____ .

9. banal (bə NAL or BĀ nəl)—adjective

- The romance novel lacked originality in all respects as it contained typical characters, *banal* dialogue, and a predictable plot.
- Jarret often goes home on the weekends because he thinks most of the campus activities going on then are juvenile and *banal.*

banal means (a) difficult (b) boring _____ *b* _____ .

10. clandestine (clan DES tən)—adjective

- Unknown to the public and coaching staff, the team owner and general manager had a series of *clandestine* meetings before deciding to make the controversial trade.
- A rebellious group of leaders made a *clandestine* plan to overthrow the government.

clandestine describes something done (a) publicly (b) secretly _____ *b* _____ .

Spies like the character of James Bond are masters of *clandestine* behavior.
(© Bettmann/ Corbis)

Matching Challenging Words and Definitions

Write each word before its definition.

catharsis	guile	affinity	dichotomy	banal
dearth	lethargy	affluence	enigma	clandestine

_____*banal*_____ **1.** common, lacking originality, stale, boring

_____*guile*_____ **2.** deceit, trickery

_____*enigma*_____ **3.** puzzle, mystery

lethargy   **4.** sluggishness, a lack of energy

clandestine   **5.** done in secrecy, hidden

dichotomy   **6.** division into two parts, a split

catharsis   **7.** discharge of pent-up emotions, a cleansing

affinity   **8.** a natural liking or ability for, an attraction to

dearth   **9.** lack, scarcity, insufficiency

affluence   **10.** wealth, riches, prosperity

Fill-Ins with Challenging Words

In each space, write the appropriate word from those listed below.

catharsis	guile	affinity	dichotomy	banal
dearth	lethargy	affluence	enigma	clandestine

1. A punching bag in his basement serves as a(n) _____catharsis_____ for Jerry, so whenever he gets tense or angry, he heads downstairs to flail away it.

2. Nick, after sprawling on the couch for a couple of weeks after school got out, eventually overcame his _____lethargy_____ and went looking for a job.

3. He decided to move to Omaha because of a(n) _____dearth_____ of employment opportunities in his small hometown.

4. My obnoxious uncle bragged that his recent business success was due to his "exceptional cleverness," which most people, including me, would call _____guile_____ , not "exceptional cleverness."

5. The newspaper editorial accused the school board of holding _____clandestine_____ rather than public meetings about the proposed school budget.

6. Actually, most people in the community know there is a(n) _____dichotomy_____ among the board members because six members favor the proposed budget while the other six members oppose it.

7. In certain social situations when people don't know each other too well, they will often talk about the weather or other _____banal_____ subjects just to make conversation.

8. Alfred Hitchcock's films, such as _Rear Window_, always contain a(n) _____enigma_____ that most moviegoers find intriguing to try to unravel.

9. Despite his lifelong _____affinity_____ for candy, desserts, and other sweets, Jay has never been overweight.

10. A person must be of considerable _____affluence_____ to buy a Midwestern farm.

Checking Your Word Power

After selecting your response, put the letter in the space provided.

_____b_____ **1.** The *opposite* of **banal** is
  a. old-fashioned
  b. fresh
  c. common
  d. insensitive

_____b_____ **2.** The *opposite* of **guile** is
  a. cleverness
  b. frankness
  c. exaggeration
  d. anger

_____d_____ **3.** The *opposite* of **affluence** is
  a. anxiety
  b. happiness
  c. abundance
  d. poverty

_____d_____ **4. Lethargy** suggests
  a. snobbery
  b. brilliance
  c. maturity
  d. fatigue

_____c_____ **5. Enigma** is most closely associated with a(n)
  a. location
  b. obligation
  c. riddle
  d. organization

_____a_____ **6.** If people do something in a **clandestine** manner, then they do it
  a. secretly
  b. openly
  c. skillfully
  d. awkwardly

_____c_____ **7. Catharsis** is most closely associated with
   a. illness
   b. travel
   c. purification
   d. caution

_____c_____ **8. dearth : expensive :: a.** plenty : costly
   b. many : priceless
   c. abundant : cheap
   d. saving : free

_____a_____ **9. affinity : fondness :: a.** attraction : devotion
   b. expectation : surprise
   c. bitterness : love
   d. appeal : hate

_____d_____ **10. dichotomy : unity :: a.** abbreviation : shortening
   b. mutiny : revolt
   c. loyalty : praiseworthy
   d. division : wholeness

Completing a Passage

After reading the selection, fill in each space with one of the words listed below.

catharsis	guile	affinity	dichotomy	banal
dearth	lethargy	affluence	enigma	clandestine

ROBERT LINCOLN

Abraham and Mary Lincoln had four children, all sons, but only the eldest, Robert, lived to reach adulthood. Edward (1846–1850) died from diphtheria at age four in Springfield, Illinois; William (1850–1862) died from typhoid fever at eleven in Washington, D.C., during his father's presidency; and Thomas (1853–1871), called Tad, died from tuberculosis at eighteen in Chicago.

Robert Lincoln was born in Springfield, Illinois, in 1843. He graduated from Harvard University in 1864, ranking thirty-second in that class of ninety-nine graduates. He then attended Harvard Law School for a time. During the last year of the Civil War (1861–1865), Robert served as a captain on General Grant's staff.

On the morning of April 14, 1865, the day of his father's assassination by John Wilkes Booth, Robert was back in Washington and had breakfast with his family. He had been present when General Lee had surrendered to General Grant at Appomattox, Virginia, a week earlier, and he told his family the details relating to this momentous event. In the process, he showed his father a photograph of General Lee. After viewing the picture for some time, President Lincoln indicated he thought General Lee's face reflected goodness, not _____guile_____ .

That evening, President and Mrs. Lincoln attended a play, *Our American Cousin*, at Ford's Theater. Robert decided not to accompany his parents, but instead chose to spend a quiet and what might be considered _____banal_____ evening in his room at the White House. He likely was experiencing fatigue and _____lethargy_____ as a result of the climactic events he had recently witnessed that ended the Civil War.

Earlier that day, John Wilkes Booth had held a(n) _____clandestine_____ meeting with his co-conspirators. Booth's motive for assassinating President Lincoln is not considered a(n) _____enigma_____ to historians because it was well known that Booth had a strong _____affinity_____ for the South during the war. In addition, Booth, emotionally unstable throughout his twenty-six-year-old life, had developed a pathological hatred of Lincoln, viewing him as a ruthless dictator. By killing President Lincoln and members of his Cabinet, the latter of which Booth had assigned to his co-conspirators, Booth apparently thought he would put the federal government in such disarray that the South might have a chance to resume and win the war. In any instance, Booth felt that killing Lincoln would avenge the South and serve as a gratifying _____catharsis_____ for his pent-up hatred of the president. He also thought he would be viewed as a hero in the South and eventually in all of the world's history books.

A month after his father's assassination, Robert, his mother, and his brother Tad moved to Chicago. Robert took law courses at the University of Chicago, and he was admitted to the bar in 1867. The following year, Robert married Mary Eunice Harlan. Over the course of the next few years, they had two daughters (Mary and Jessie) and one son (Abraham, but called "Jack").

During the 1870s, Robert Lincoln became a prosperous Chicago lawyer, and he and his family never suffered from a _____dearth_____ of life's necessities but led a life reflecting the _____affluence_____ his successful career had made possible. In 1881 President James Garfield appointed Robert secretary of war (what we now call secretary of defense), and he served in this capacity until 1885. (Ironically, as well as tragically, President Garfield became the second president to be assassinated.) He later served as the United States minister to England and as president of the Pullman Company in Chicago, which made sleeper cars for the railroad. He died at his summer home in Manchester, Vermont, in 1926, just days short of his eighty-third birthday.

There was an undeniable ___*dichotomy*___ between Abraham and Robert Lincoln, both in appearance and in personality; in particular, whereas Abraham Lincoln was tall and slender, his son Robert was short and stocky; in addition, Robert was much more reserved and introverted than his famous father. Nevertheless, Robert's life was one of accomplishments and of honor. (The last person to have direct lineage to Abraham Lincoln was Robert's grandson Robert "Bud" Beckwith, who died in 1985 without leaving any heirs.)

FEATURED WORD: clandestine

Clandestine—something done in secret, often for improper reasons:

- Some of the king's closest advisers held a <u>clandestine</u> meeting to plot his overthrow.

Origin: 1566 <Latin—*clandestinus*—secret, hidden; *clam* (secretly) from base of *celare* (to hide)

Family words: clandestinely (adv), clandestineness (n)

Connotation: *negative*—associated with unlawful acts done in secrecy

Image to remember: thieves meeting in a back room to plot their next crime

Write an original sentence using *clandestine*:

_____

_____

_____

coarse   rough, vulgar, indecent:

Shay had to use <u>coarse</u> sandpaper to remove the coat of paint from the old table.
However, his <u>coarse</u> language almost caused the paint to blister and come off by itself.

course   plan, route, school subject:

The <u>course</u> of action recommended by her lawyer was to file a legal complaint.
The cross-country <u>course</u> is at least five miles long, according to Bruno.
I enjoy my chemistry <u>course</u>, but I find it difficult and time-consuming.

Circle the correct answer:

1. Did you continue with your foreign language coarse / (course) this semester?

2. Occasionally, our coach gets angry, but I've never heard him use (coarse) / course language.

3. The coarse / (course) we took on our car trip followed the beautiful Connecticut River for many miles.

4. The texture of the cloth was (coarse) / course and heavy.

5. The coarse / (course) to follow for good dental health includes brushing and flossing the teeth after every meal if at all possible.

Write original sentences using these words:

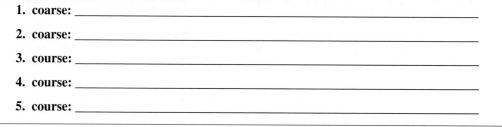

1. **coarse:** _____

2. **coarse:** _____

3. **course:** _____

4. **course:** _____

5. **course:** _____

Learning Challenging Words from Context Clues

1. cogent (KŌ jənt)—adjective

- There are many good reasons for not smoking, but those having to do with health are the most *cogent.*
- The newlyweds bought the insurance policy after Mr. Downey presented them with a number of *cogent* reasons for doing so.

cogent means (a) disturbing (b) persuasive _____ *b* _____ .

2. rationalize (RASH ə nə līz)—verb

- Sometimes we *rationalize* our mistakes rather than taking direct steps to correct them.
- Megan will often *rationalize* her son's misbehavior by saying he's just high-spirited, not deliberately naughty.

rationalize means to (a) make excuses for (b) overreact _____ *a* _____ .

3. sordid (SOR did)—adjective

- The *sordid* details of the mayor's private life may jeopardize his chances for reelection.
- Migrant workers should never have to endure *sordid* working conditions, such as being housed in abandoned railroad boxcars.

sordid means (a) hidden (b) shameful _____ *b* _____ .

4. eclectic (ē KLEK tik)—adjective

- The government adopted an *eclectic* approach rather than a single one in attempting to solve the unemployment problem.
- Ms. Henderson's *eclectic* teaching techniques, ranging from individual instruction to class field trips, result in impressive scholastic achievements by her students.

eclectic means (a) complicated (b) various _____ *b* _____ .

5. usurp (ū SURP)—verb

- My psychology professor said parents should be careful they don't *usurp* their children's rights to make certain decisions.
- When the principal attempted to *usurp* authority rightfully belonging to the superintendent of schools, he was warned and his salary was temporarily decreased.

usurp is related to (a) trespass (b) defend _____ *a* _____ .

6. inundate (IN ən dāt)—verb

- Protests began to *inundate* the TV station when it was announced that the first two rounds of the basketball tournament would not be televised.
- Farmers living near the swollen river feared the raging water would *inundate* their recently planted fields.

inundate is closest in meaning to (a) protest (b) swamp _____ *b* _____ .

7. parochial (pə RŌ kē əl)—adjective

- A counselor needs to have broad rather than *parochial* perspectives.
- An elderly neighbor of mine talks only about his garden and baseball, but despite his *parochial* interests, I enjoy talking with him.

parochial means (a) sophisticated (b) limited _____ *b* _____ .

8. perfunctory (pər FUNK tə rē)—adjective

- Rodney was disappointed with the concert because his favorite band played in a *perfunctory* manner rather than with its usual zest.
- The Caldwells' dog made only a *perfunctory* sniff at the trembling puppy before continuing his jaunt through the neighborhood.

perfunctory is related to (a) superficial (b) thorough _____ *a* _____ .

9. acquiesce (ak wē ES)—verb

- To prevent a strike, the management representative decided to *acquiesce* to the workers' terms.
- Her shocked boyfriend said he would *acquiesce* to breaking up if that's what she really wanted to do.

acquiesce means to (a) agree (b) disagree _____ *a* _____ .

10. **ephemeral** (i FEM ər əl)—adjective

- The popularity of men's leisure suits proved to be *ephemeral* as they are no longer sold or worn.
- Although many children's interest in taking piano lessons proves to be *ephemeral,* Angelina continued to take lessons until she graduated from high school.

ephemeral means (a) unpopular (b) short-lived _____ *b* _____ .

Matching Challenging Words and Definitions

Write each word before its definition.

cogent   sordid   usurp   parochial   acquiesce
rationalize   eclectic   inundate   perfunctory   ephemeral

____*usurp*____ **1.** seize control of, move in on, trespass

____*perfunctory*____ **2.** performed in an uninterested or routine manner

____*sordid*____ **3.** disgraceful, shameful

____*ephemeral*____ **4.** lasting a short time, fleeting

____*parochial*____ **5.** limited or narrow in viewpoint

____*cogent*____ **6.** convincing, persuasive

____*inundate*____ **7.** to overwhelm, to overflow

____*eclectic*____ **8.** from many sources, various

____*acquiesce*____ **9.** to agree to, to submit to

____*rationalize*____ **10.** to explain away, to justify

Fill-Ins with Challenging Words

In each space, write the appropriate word from those listed below.

cogent   sordid   usurp   parochial   acquiesce
rationalize   eclectic   inundate   perfunctory   ephemeral

1. Although he had planned to spend the day working on his car, Andrew reluctantly decided he had better ____*acquiesce*____ to his supervisor's request to work on Saturday.

2. I don't think there is any valid excuse for your discourtesy to Kirsten, so don't try to ____*rationalize*____ your rude behavior to me.

3. After the heavy rain, the overflow from the creek began to ____*inundate*____ the road leading to town.

4. Fatima has ____*eclectic*____ interests, ranging from photography to scuba diving.

5. The couple's pledge to always remain together proved to be _____ ephemeral _____ as they broke up three weeks later.

6. The Pinettes, a retired couple, are anything but _____ parochial _____ in their interests because they enjoy traveling, attending concerts, refinishing furniture, bowling, and canoeing.

7. Every soap opera seems to have at least one major character who leads a(n) _____ sordid _____ life—a life full of deception, infidelity, and crime.

8. The dental hygienist gave me a number of _____ cogent _____ reasons for flossing my teeth after every meal, including the prevention of gum disease.

9. When the student pilot did a casual check of the plane before takeoff, his instructor sternly lectured him for making such a(n) _____ perfunctory _____ inspection.

10. The new custodian was told never to _____ usurp _____ a teacher's authority by disciplining students.

Checking Your Word Power

After selecting your response, put the letter in the space provided.

_____ b _____ **1.** The *opposite* of **acquiesce** is to
   a. agree
   b. refuse
   c. endorse
   d. prove

_____ c _____ **2.** The *opposite* of **cogent** is
   a. smart
   b. forceful
   c. vague
   d. happy

_____ a _____ **3.** The *opposite* of **perfunctory** is
   a. precise
   b. tardy
   c. inconsiderate
   d. calm

_____ d _____ **4.** We are most likely to **rationalize** our
   a. income
   b. dreams
   c. triumphs
   d. mistakes

_b_   **5.** The person most likely to **usurp** authority is a(n)
       a. boss
       b. rebel
       c. police officer
       d. athlete

_b_   **6.** A person with **eclectic** musical interests would probably
       a. like only one type of music
       b. like many types of music
       c. be unable to read music
       d. be an accomplished musician

_a_   **7.** On the other hand, a person with **parochial** musical interests would probably
       a. like only one type of music
       b. like many types of music
       c. be unable to read music
       d. be an accomplished musician

_c_   **8. sordid : honorable :: a.** quiet : silent
       b. sorrow : grief
       c. dirty : clean
       d. funny : dishonorable

_d_   **9. inundate : overwhelm :: a.** overwhelm : challenge
       b. challenge : admit
       c. admit : invent
       d. invent : create

_a_   **10. ephemeral : passing :: a.** temporary : brief
       b. momentary : enduring
       c. impulsive : thoughtful
       d. vanishing : appearing

Completing a Passage

After reading the selection, fill in each space with one of the words listed below.

cogent	sordid	usurped	parochial	acquiesced
rationalizing	eclectic	inundated	perfunctory	ephemeral

ELIZABETH BLACKWELL, M.D.

Elizabeth Blackwell (1821–1910) was the first woman to earn a medical degree in the United States. She was born in England, but she and her family moved to the United States when she was eleven. Her father's occupational pursuits in New York failed, so he moved the family to New Jersey and eventually to Cincinnati in an attempt to establish a successful business. Unfortunately, Mr. Blackwell died before doing so, leaving his family without any financial resources. To support themselves, Elizabeth, her sisters Anna and Marian, and their mother opened a private school.

During the next few years, Elizabeth taught in Cincinnati as well as in communities in Kentucky and North and South Carolina. From childhood on, Elizabeth always had ____eclectic____ interests, ranging from literature to natural science, but during her relatively brief teaching career, she developed a particular interest in medicine, an interest that proved to be enduring rather than ____ephemeral____. She eventually decided to become a doctor, ____rationalizing____ that many women would prefer to consult with a woman physician about their health problems than with a male doctor.

After studying privately with male doctors, who supported her efforts after listening to her ____cogent____ reasons as to why they should help her realize her goal of becoming a physician, Elizabeth ____inundated____ the medical schools in the Northeast with admission applications. However, most of the colleges gave her application only ____perfunctory____ attention because of their ____parochial____ view, the predominant one for that period, that only men possessed the necessary intellectual, emotional, and physical capacities to become doctors, so her admissions requests were quickly rejected.

However, when administration officials at Geneva Medical College in Geneva, New York, received Elizabeth's application, they decided to poll the students on whether she should be admitted. The students, apparently believing the matter was a joke, nonchalantly ____acquiesced____ to her admission request. However, when they discovered that Elizabeth's application was for real, they were at first shocked, then angry.

After Elizabeth arrived at the college and started to attend classes, many students shunned her and some professors openly resented her, even to the extent of prohibiting her from attending certain classroom medical demonstrations, deeming them inappropriate for a woman. Students and professors alike seemed convinced that Elizabeth had ____usurped____ a slot in the medical school that rightfully belonged to a man. Over time, however, students and professors came to admire her for her abilities and persistence. In 1849, Elizabeth graduated first in her class, becoming the first woman to graduate from medical school in the United States.

After further study in France and England, Elizabeth opened a clinic in 1853 in one of the most ____sordid____ slums in New York City. Her sister Emily, who had also become a doctor, and Dr. Marie Zakrzewsha, an immigrant from Poland, joined her medical staff. In addition, a number of the city's leading male physicians supported her clinic by serving as consultants. As the years passed, she helped to establish the New York

Infirmary for Women and Children, as well as the Women's Central Association of Relief during the Civil War; inspired the creation of the U.S. Sanitary Commission; and, with her sister, opened a medical college for women that existed for thirty-one years. She died in 1910 at the age of eighty-nine.

Medical historians agree that Dr. Elizabeth Blackwell deserves much of the credit for the fact that today nearly 30 percent of all doctors in the United States are women and that this percentage will probably grow significantly within the next few years.

FEATURED WORD: parochial

Parochial—(1) refers to a church parish or church school; (2) also means narrowly restricted in scope or outlook:

- Michael attended <u>parochial</u> schools from kindergarten through high school.
- I had <u>parochial</u> views about music in high school, refusing to listen to any type of music except rap and hard rock.

Origin: <French—*parochial* <Latin—*parochialis*—of a parish. *Parochial* to describe a church school dates from the mid-1700s. *Parochial* as a word meaning "limited or narrow in scope or outlook" dates from 1847.

Family words: parochialism (n), parochially (adj)

Connotation: *neutral* or *negative*—neutral when referring to schools with a specific religious affiliation, negative when referring to people who are narrow-minded

Image to remember: a Catholic school

Write original sentences using the two common meanings of *parochial*:

1. _____

2. _____

breath   a noun that refers to the act of inhaling and exhaling:

Bettina took a deep <u>breath</u> before diving into the water.

breathe   a verb that means inhaling and exhaling air:

It was difficult to <u>breathe</u> in the stuffy, hot room.

Circle the correct answer:

1. A respirator was helping the elderly patient to <u>breath</u> / <u>breathe</u>.

2. My sister was holding her breath / <u>breathe</u> to keep from laughing during the minister's long prayer.

Write original sentences using these words:

1. **breath:** _____

2. **breathe:** _____

REVIEW TEST, CHAPTERS 11–17

Word Parts

Matching Word Parts and Definitions

Match each underlined word part with its definition.

A

_c_	**1.** port	**a.** hundred
_e_	**2.** arch	**b.** killing of
_a_	**3.** cent	**c.** carry
_d_	**4.** ven, vent	**d.** come, go
_b_	**5.** cide	**e.** chief, ruler

B

_e_	**1.** circum	**a.** light
_c_	**2.** onym	**b.** condition, quality of
_a_	**3.** photo	**c.** name, word
_d_	**4.** dem	**d.** people
_b_	**5.** age, ance, ship	**e.** around

C

_d_	**1.** claim, clam	**a.** abnormal, faulty
_c_	**2.** greg	**b.** to bring about
_e_	**3.** al	**c.** crowd, group
_a_	**4.** dys	**d.** shout, cry out
_b_	**5.** ize	**e.** having the quality of

D

_c_	**1.** ac	**a.** to blunder, to stray from normal
_a_	**2.** err	**b.** having the quality of
_e_	**3.** medi	**c.** bitterly sharp, insightful
_d_	**4.** be	**d.** to be
_b_	**5.** ic	**e.** middle

E

_b_	**1.** sol	**a.** done in the manner of
_e_	**2.** polis, urb	**b.** alone
_d_	**3.** ish	**c.** draw, pull
_a_	**4.** ly	**d.** descriptive of
_c_	**5.** tract	**e.** city

Fill-Ins with Word Parts

Select the appropriate word part so the proper word is formed in each sentence.

ped   micro   scrib   poten   leg

1. Their young daughter was enjoying _____*scrib*_____ bling in her coloring book with her new crayons.

2. Is it _____*leg*_____ al to park on this side of the street?

3. Though the _____*micro*_____ scopes we used in the laboratory were obviously old, they were powerful and easy to focus.

4. I have heard of manicures, but what are _____*ped*_____ icures?

5. Wow! That's the most _____*poten*_____ t cup of coffee I've ever drunk. I'll be awake all night!

Challenging Words

Matching Challenging Words and Definitions

Write each word before its definition.

A

cogent   sordid   usurp   eclectic   rationalize   acquiesce

___*rationalize*___ **1.** to explain away, to justify

___*sordid*___ **2.** shameful, disgraceful

___*eclectic*___ **3.** various, from many sources

___*acquiesce*___ **4.** to agree to, to submit to

___*cogent*___ **5.** persuasive, convincing

___*usurp*___ **6.** to overthrow, to seize control of

B

podiatry   proscribe   archetype   convene   potency   microbiology

___*proscribe*___ **1.** to prohibit, to ban, to outlaw

___*potency*___ **2.** strength, powerfulness

___*archetype*___ **3.** original model after which other things are patterned

___*microbiology*___ **4.** the study of extremely small organisms

___*podiatry*___ **5.** study and treatment of foot ailments

___*convene*___ **6.** to meet, to assemble, to come together

C

inundate   perfunctory   ephemeral   catharsis   guile   affinity

__guile__   **1.** deceit

__ephemeral__   **2.** temporary, fleeting, lasting for just a short time

__affinity__   **3.** natural liking for or ability to do, a strong attraction to

__inundate__   **4.** to overflow, to flood, to overwhelm

__catharsis__   **5.** a cleansing, a release of pent-up emotions

__perfunctory__   **6.** done in an unenthusiastic, superficial, or routine manner

D

dichotomy   banal   dearth   lethargy   affluence   enigma

__affluence__   **1.** wealth, prosperity, riches

__dearth__   **2.** scarcity, insufficiency

__enigma__   **3.** mystery, puzzle

__banal__   **4.** run of the mill, lacking originality, boring, stale

__lethargy__   **5.** sluggishness, lack of energy

__dichotomy__   **6.** division into two parts, split

E

debacle   deprivation   garrulous   meticulous   nebulous   specious

__meticulous__   **1.** precise, extremely particular, thorough

__debacle__   **2.** complete failure

__nebulous__   **3.** hazy, vague, murky

__garrulous__   **4.** talkative, gabby

__specious__   **5.** misleading, deceitful, false

__deprivation__   **6.** hardship, lack of the necessities of life

F

dystrophy   ostracize   hypothetical   immutable   impeccable   gregarious

__immutable__   **1.** changeless, constant

__dystrophy__   **2.** wasting away of muscles

__impeccable__   **3.** spotless, flawless

__hypothetical__   **4.** assumed, inferred, supposed

__gregarious__   **5.** sociable, friendly, companionable

__ostracize__   **6.** to exclude, to shut out

Completing a Passage

After reading the selection, fill in each space with one of the words listed below.

bereft	alienation	aberration	exacerbate
repudiates	deleterious	sophomoric	clamorous

A BLIP ON PRO FOOTBALL'S RADAR SCREEN

Professional football fans, from the mildly interested to the most loyal, enthusiastic, and _____clamorous_____ ones, are justifiably awed by the extraordinary abilities of today's players. Unfortunately, though, it's no longer an _____aberration_____ to read in the sports pages about some pro player being arrested for a serious offense, such as a DUI, possession of drugs, or a physical assault. Such criminal behavior has resulted in the _____alienation_____ of many once-devoted pro football fans. Other fans have become disenchanted when a multimillionaire player on their favorite team _____repudiates_____ a generous three-year contract offer, insisting instead that the contract be for six years, contain a no-cut clause, and be for gazillions of dollars. If the resentful team owners eventually cave in to such outrageous demands, the player will often _____exacerbate_____ the smoldering situation by demanding he also be given a huge signing bonus.

There are also too many professional football players who are _____bereft_____ of good old-fashioned sportsmanship and humility. Some players dance and sashay in the end zone after scoring a touchdown, while others jump wildly up and down while pounding their chest after making a tackle. _____Deleterious_____ behaviors like the preceding demonstrate a lack of respect for both their opponents and the game itself. These classless players act as if they had just won World War II all by themselves. Their attention-seeking and childish behavior is a major turn-off to many longtime fans of the game.

Yes, every season professional football teams draw thousands of fans to their stadiums, and millions more watch the games on television. Yet for some fans, the integrity of pro football is undermined by the sometimes criminal and often _____sophomoric_____ behavior of too many of its players.

Unscrambling Words

Unscramble each "word" to discover one you have studied, using the sentence as a clue to the word's identity.

CLUE	SCRAMBLED	UNSCRAMBLED
Example: Over the years, the three cities grew to form one big metropolitan area.	pelosigam	megapolis
1. Good old Chris will believe anything.	buielllg	gullible
2. That's the common way most folks speak in this part of the country.	qlolalociu	colloquial
3. She thinks she can get away with anything.	tinyipun	impunity
4. I use this adjective to describe the Middle Ages.	veedialm	medieval
5. I'm confident this plan is a good one.	abeilv	viable
6. Aren't you being this way when you say he is a "tall giant"?	ddnuanter	redundant
7. Is your aunt actually one hundred years old?	nacanenteri	centenarian

Analogies

After selecting your response, put the letter in the space provided.

_____a_____ **1. felicitous: fortunate :: a.** energetic : lively
   b. intense : dull
   c. lucky : unlucky
   d. clumsy : graceful

_____d_____ **2. trepidation: trembling :: a.** foolishness : giggling
   b. courage : crying
   c. curious : nosy
   d. fear : quaking

_____b_____ **3. collateral: guarantee :: a.** pledge : election
   b. pledge : promise
   c. pledge : abandon
   d. pledge : collect

_____c_____ **4. ostensibly : insincerity ::** **a.** honesty : insensitivity
b. importantly : surprisingly
c. supposedly : phoniness
d. impressively : insecurity

_____a_____ **5. fetish: fixation ::** **a.** fixation : compulsion
b. compulsion : talent
c. talent : justice
d. justice : dishonorable

_____c_____ **6. portage: transport ::** **a.** establish : estimate
b. formal : irregular
c. essential : necessary
d. defend : carry

Mastering Confusing Words

Circle the correct answer.

1. I wasn't (conscience /(conscious)) of the fact that Amanda had finished her degree requirements last semester.

2. Do you think a green sofa would ((complement)/ compliment) or clash with the room's other colors?

3. We've had so much dreary (weather /(weather)) this month that I can't remember the last time the sun ((shone)/ shown).

4. It was wonderful to (breath /(breathe)) fresh air again after being cooped up in the lab all afternoon.

5. I would like to (complement /(compliment)) Jaden for the (coarse /(course)) of action he recommended because I think it will settle our problem once and for all.

6. We were both out of ((breath)/ breathe) after running to catch the bus before it left, but we made it in time.

7. There was a large ((hole)/ whole) in the heel of one of the socks, so I threw the (hole /(whole)) pair away.

8. Do you know (weather /(whether)) Aleah has to work this evening?

Crossword Puzzle

Solve the crossword by using the following words.

genocide felicitous abeyance photosynthesis clandestine
acronym collateral circumspect parochial retraction legacy
sagacious fetish trepidation soliloquy demagogue proscribe

¹a	c	r	o	n	y	m	²p	a	r	o	c	h	i	a	l
b															
³f	e	t	i	s	h										
y															
a			⁴c								⁵s				
n			i		⁶s	a	⁷g	a	c	i	o	u	s		
c			r				e				l			⁸t	
⁹r	e	t	r	a	c	t	i	o	n		i			r	
			u				o				l			e	
			m				c				o			p	
¹⁰p	h	o	t	o	s	y	n	t	h	e	s	i	s	i	
			p				d				u			d	
		¹¹d	e	m	a	g	o	g	u	e		y		a	
		c												t	
¹²c	o	l	l	a	t	e	r	a	l	¹³l	e	g	a	c	y	i
														o	
¹⁴c	l	a	n	d	e	s	t	i	n	e				n	
¹⁵f	e	l	i	c	i	t	o	u	s						
					¹⁶p	r	o	s	c	r	i	b	e		

ACROSS

1. formed from the first letters in a series of words
2. limited or narrow in viewpoint
3. extreme attraction, obsessive fixation
6. wise
9. a taking back
10. process by which plants make food for themselves
11. person who seeks power by appealing to people's fears
12. security pledged in return for a loan
13. inheritance
14. done in secret
15. fortunate, timely, appropriate
16. to prohibit

DOWN

1. temporary suspension
4. cautious
5. speech to oneself
7. extermination of a whole group of people
8. fear, dread

Part **TWO** Academic Terms

Part Two of *Building Vocabulary for College* enables you to become familiar with many of the academic terms associated with subjects you probably will be required to study in college, such as history, as well as those you may elect to take, such as computer science. Learning the definitions of these terms is unquestionably an asset as they often hold the key to understanding the fundamental concepts presented in college courses.

The academic terms and definitions featured in the twelve chapters of Part Two are similar to those you would find in the glossaries of textbooks. The prefixes, suffixes, and roots you studied in Part One have been underlined so you can use your knowledge about them to deepen your understanding of the academic terms.

STUDYING THE ACADEMIC TERMS

- Take advantage of pictures and other visual aids that may be available to acquaint you with some of the academic terms.

- As you were directed to do with the challenging words in Part One, familiarize yourself with each academic term's pronunciation, part of speech, and definition, noting (1) the word is spelled phonetically so you will know how it is pronounced; (2) a space separates each syllable, with the accented syllable printed in capital letters; (3) whether the term contains an underlined word part you have studied; (4) vowels with long sounds have a line over them; (5) the schwa sound—*uh*—is represented by ə, which resembles a reversed, upside-down *e*; and (6) the term's part of speech.

  Examples: connotation (kon ə TĀ shən)—noun
  mutation (mū TĀ shən)—noun

  Note: The pronunciation given for each term in Part Two is a common one, but there may be other acceptable pronunciations.

- Read the sample sentence that follows the term's definition to deepen your understanding of the term.

DOING THE EXERCISES

- Follow the directions for completing the chapter's four sets of exercises.
- Complete the **Featured Word** and **Mastering Confusing Words** lessons.
- Be prepared for review tests after completing chapters 18–23 and chapters 24–29.

Learning Literature and Composition Terms from Context Clues: Set 1

Literature and composition embrace all human experiences—common, unique, sad, joyful, expected, unexpected, disenchanting, and inspirational. These subjects can provide excellent opportunities to gain valuable insights into life. The following terms are commonly used in both literature and composition, so knowledge of them will be beneficial to you.

1. **bibliography** (bib lē OG rə fē)—noun

   A list of books and other readings on a particular subject.

   A research paper's *bibliography* must list all the sources used for information.

2. **connotation** (kon ə TĀ shən)—noun

   A word's suggested meanings or emotional associations, as contrasted to its strict, exact meaning.

   The denotation of *home* is "residence," but the *connotation* of *home* suggests feelings of love and security.

3. **denotation** (dē nō TĀ shən)—noun

   The strict, exact meaning of a word.

   The *denotation* of *father* is "male parent."

4. **figures of speech** (FIG yərs uv SPĒCH)—noun

   Expressions in which the words are not meant in their literal sense but are intended to be interpreted in an imaginative way.

   To present information in an original and colorful manner, writers often use *figures of speech,* such as metaphors, personification, and similes (see below).

5. **genre** (ZHAN rə)—noun

   A category or type of literature, such as novel, autobiography, or short story.

   Biography, an account of a person's life, is the most popular *genre* of literature for many readers.

6. literal (LIT ər əl)—adjective

Refers to the strict meaning of a word or phrase.

The *literal* meaning of *mother* is "female parent."

7. metaphor (MET ə for)—noun

A figure of speech in which two unlike things are compared or one thing is said to be another thing; the word *like* or *as* is not used in the comparison. (See *simile* below.)

"On Saturday evenings, Whitney's car was a panther that slinked down Main Street, daring anyone or anything to challenge it" is an example of a *metaphor.*

8. personification (pər son ə fa KĀ shən)—noun

A figure of speech in which a thing is given human qualities or performs human actions.

"The tulips danced and smiled when the old gardener came their way" is an example of *personification.*

9. prose (PRŌZ)—noun

The ordinary form of language; that is, writing or speech that is not poetry.

Novels and short stories are almost always written in *prose.*

10. simile (SIM ə lē)—noun

A figure of speech in which two unlike things are compared by using the word *like* or *as.*

"The frisky puppy is like an unguided missile" is an example of a *simile.*

Matching Academic Terms and Definitions: Set 1

Match each definition with the term it defines.

_e_	**1.** prose	**a.** imaginative expressions
_i_	**2.** genre	**b.** adjective referring to the exact meaning of a word or phrase
_g_	**3.** bibliography	
_c_	**4.** denotation	**c.** noun referring to the actual meaning
_f_	**5.** connotation	**d.** giving a thing human qualities
_b_	**6.** literal	**e.** writing that is not poetry
_a_	**7.** figures of speech	**f.** suggested meaning of a word
_h_	**8.** simile	**g.** list of readings or references
_j_	**9.** metaphor	**h.** comparison using *like* or *as*
_d_	**10.** personification	**i.** form of literature
		j. comparison not using *like* or *as*

Fill-Ins with Academic Terms: Set 1

In each space, write the appropriate term from those listed below.

bibliography	figures of speech	metaphor	simile
connotation	genre	personification	
denotation	literal	prose	

1. "Grover's motorboat is like a rocket" is a _____ *simile* _____.

2. "Diego was a perfectly tuned machine; he ran relentlessly mile after mile" is a _____ *metaphor* _____.

3. Personification, metaphors, and similes are _____ *figures of speech* _____.

4. Most magazines are written in _____ *prose* _____.

5. At the end of your term paper, include a _____ *bibliography* _____ containing all the references you have used.

6. The _____ *connotation* _____ of the word *football* includes fall afternoons, marching bands, and roaring crowds.

7. The _____ *denotation* _____ of the word *football* includes a game with eleven players on each team.

8. Poetry is another _____ *genre* _____ of literature.

9. "The tree stuck out its leg and tripped me" is _____ *personification* _____.

10. The _____ *literal* _____ meaning of *morning* is the time between 12:00 A.M. and 12:00 P.M.

Related Meanings: Set 1

If the words opposite each other are similar in meaning, write Yes *in the space; if they are unrelated, write* No.

1. prose — *No* rhyming words
2. genre — *No* family history
3. bibliography — *Yes* list of readings
4. denotation — *Yes* word's actual meaning
5. connotation — *No* word's opposite meaning
6. literal — *No* reading ability
7. figures of speech — *Yes* fanciful expressions
8. simile — *No* comparison without *like* or *as*
9. metaphor — *No* comparison with *like* or *as*
10. personification — *No* sociable

Writing Your Own Definitions: Set 1

Write either an original sentence or a definition for each term that clearly demonstrates your mastery of its meaning as used in literature and composition.   Answers will vary.

1. bibliography _____

_____

2. connotation _____

_____

3. denotation _____

_____

4. figures of speech _____

_____

5. genre _____

_____

6. literal _____

_____

7. metaphor _____

_____

8. personification _____

_____

9. prose _____

_____

10. simile _____

_____

Learning Literature and Composition Terms from Context Clues: Set 2

1. **alliteration** (ə lit ə RĀ shən)—noun

   The repetition of the first sound, usually a consonant, in a series of words. "Francis is fair, frank, friendly, and famous" is an example of *alliteration.*

2. **hyperbole** (hī PUR bə lē)—noun

   A figure of speech in which exaggerated words are used for emphasis.

   "The closet in my room is so small that an ant wouldn't have enough room to turn around" is an example of *hyperbole.*

3. **plagiarism** (PLĀ jə riz əm)—noun

   The copying of words or ideas of another writer and then presenting them as one's original work.

   You must give credit to the author of the words you are using; otherwise, you will be guilty of *plagiarism.*

4. **satire** (SAT īr)—noun

   The use of sarcastic humor to expose injustice or stupidity.

   The sports columnist's *satire* was obvious when she wrote that the owner of the basketball team should feel guilty for not buying his star player a luxurious house because the player was making "only" 27 million dollars a year.

5. **analogy** (ə NAL ə jē)—noun

   A comparison in which similarities are found between two unlike things.

   An *analogy* is often expressed as a simile, as in "The football game was like a battle between gladiators."

6. **antagonist** (an TAG ə nist)—noun; **protagonist** (prō TAG ə nist)—noun

   The antagonist is the character in a story who opposes the hero or heroine, known as the protagonist.

   In John Updike's "The Christian Roommates," Lester Spotted Elk was the *antagonist* of Orson, the *protagonist,* when Orson was in high school.

7. **canon** (KAN ən)—noun

   The works of an author that are considered authentic.

   Romeo and Juliet is just one of over thirty plays included in William Shakespeare's *canon.*

8. flashback (FLASH bak)—noun

An interruption in the flow of a story, play, or film to present action that occurred earlier.

A *flashback* in the movie showed the old man as a college student.

9. foreshadowing (fŏr SHAD ō ing)—noun

A hint in the story or drama of some coming event, often a tragic one.

The king's nightmare was a *foreshadowing* of the tragic battle that would result in his death the next day.

10. synopsis (si NOP sis)—noun

A summary of the main points of a story or other literary work.

Our assignment was to write a *synopsis* of Katherine Mansfield's short story "The Garden Party."

11. anthology (an THOL ə jē)—noun

A book or collection of selected writings.

Our literature class is using an *anthology* containing short stories, poems, and plays.

Matching Academic Terms and Definitions: Set 2

Match each definition with the term it defines.

h	**1.** hyperbole	**a.** hero or leading character in a story
e	**2.** alliteration	**b.** authentic works of an author
i	**3.** antagonist	**c.** hint in the story of a coming event
k	**4.** flashback	**d.** representing the words or ideas of
g	**5.** synopsis	another author as one's own
a	**6.** protagonist	**e.** a string of words with the same initial
c	**7.** foreshadowing	sound
l	**8.** anthology	**f.** sarcastic humor
j	**9.** analogy	**g.** summary
b	**10.** canon	**h.** exaggeration for the sake of effect
f	**11.** satire	**i.** person who opposes the hero
d	**12.** plagiarism	**j.** comparison of unlike things
		k. interruption in a story to present a previous scene
		l. collection of selected writings

Fill-Ins with Academic Terms: Set 2

In each space, write the appropriate term from those listed below.

alliteration	satire	protagonist	foreshadowing
hyperbole	analogy	canon	synopsis
plagiarism	antagonist	flashback	anthology

1. The ___protagonist___ in this story is a young woman who eventually triumphs over her chief ___antagonist___, an evil man who seeks revenge against her and her family.

2. I'm writing a(n) ___synopsis___ of Robert Frost's poem "The Death of the Hired Man," which is contained in the ___anthology___ of poems, essays, plays, and short stories we're using in our American literature class.

3. As the ship slowly sinks to the bottom of the ocean, there is a(n) ___flashback___ of the captain as a young man eagerly enlisting in the Navy.

4. The author uses a comical ___analogy___, comparing the young girl's mind to a glass of fizzy root beer.

5. There is no question Shakespeare wrote *King Lear,* so that is why it is included in the Shakespearean ___canon___.

6. "Bruce brutally batted ball after ball" is an example of ___alliteration___.

7. "I drove a million miles during my week's vacation" is obviously ___hyperbole___.

8. Max didn't want to be guilty of ___plagiarism___, so he put quotation marks around the words and cited the author's name in his bibliography.

9. In his letter to the editor, Rex used bitter humor, or ___satire___, to voice his criticisms about the school's new parking regulations.

10. The wilted rose in the bride's wedding bouquet provided a(n) ___foreshadowing___ that the couple's love would not endure.

Related Meanings: Set 2

If the words opposite each other are similar in meaning, write Yes *in the space; if they are unrelated, write* No.

1. plagiarism   _No_   summarizing a play
2. alliteration   _Yes_   series of words with the same first sound
3. satire   _No_   concluding remarks
4. hyperbole   _Yes_   overstatement
5. flashback   _Yes_   return to a previous time
6. synopsis   _No_   comparison of unlike things
7. antagonist   _Yes_   opponent
8. analogy   _No_   a summary

9.	anthology	_No_	study of myths and primitive religions
10.	canon	_Yes_	genuine books of an author
11.	protagonist	_Yes_	hero
12.	foreshadowing	_Yes_	indication of a coming event

Writing Your Own Definitions: Set 2

Write either an original sentence or a definition for each term that clearly demonstrates your mastery of its meaning as used in literature and composition.   Answers will vary.

1. alliteration _____

_____

2. hyperbole _____

_____

3. plagiarism _____

_____

4. satire _____

_____

5. analogy _____

_____

6. antagonist _____

_____

7. protagonist _____

_____

8. canon _____

_____

9. flashback _____

_____

10. foreshadowing _____

_____

11. synopsis _____

_____

12. anthology _____

_____

A

After reading the selection, fill in each space with one of the terms listed below.

denotation	simile	genres	personification	bibliography
metaphor	prose	literal	connotation	figures of speech

LITERARY TERMS

Figures of speech play a prominent role in both _____*prose*_____ and poetry. For example, the _____*simile*_____ "Tyrone was like a tornado on the basketball floor," the _____*metaphor*_____ "Tyrone was a tornado on the basketball floor," and the _____*personification*_____ "The tornado spread its arms to embrace three entire counties before it breathed its last" could appear not only in poetry but also in such varied _____*genres*_____ as biography and science fiction.

To test the validity of the preceding assertion, make a random _____*bibliography*_____ of a variety of books and poems, and then scan through them to see if you can identify examples of how *figures of speech* enrich and empower the writing. Chances are that you will find many examples.

Denotation and connotation are also important contributors to writing. _____*Denotation*_____ refers to the _____*literal*_____ or dictionary meaning of a word (*bomb*—an explosive weapon), whereas _____*connotation*_____ refers to the associated or suggested meaning of a word (*bomb*—a miserable failure).

To illustrate to yourself how words have both denotative and connotative meanings, write down the dictionary meaning of *rat*, and then list what meanings you associate with this word.

B

After reading the selection, fill in each space with one of the terms listed below.

protagonist	alliteration	antagonist	canon	synopsis	analogy
anthology	flashbacks	foreshadowing	hyperbole	satire	plagiarism

SUE GRAFTON'S MYSTERY NOVELS

For thousands of mystery fans, the _____*canon*_____ of "must read" mystery novels is incomplete unless it includes the extensive _____*anthology*_____ of Sue Grafton's books. The titles of her numerous novels are almost in _____*alliteration*_____, as the first is entitled *A Is for Alibi,* the second *B Is for Burglary,* the third *C Is for Corpse,* and so on through over half of the alphabet—and she's still writing. The _____*protagonist*_____ in all of Grafton's

novels is a young woman private investigator, Kinsey Millhone; however, the
__antagonist__ in each book can vary from a vicious young man to a sweet old lady.

Grafton's novels are unquestionably unique, so she certainly can't be accused of
__plagiarism__ . Her books feature passion, humor, suspense, danger, and sarcastic
__satire__ to describe the people and situations with which Kinsey becomes
entangled. Grafton also uses __flashbacks__ to give readers a glimpse into a character's past as well as __foreshadowing__ to drop hints of what may happen in the future. It
is certainly __hyperbole__ to say that writing a __synopsis__ of a Grafton
mystery novel is as easy as writing one about the performance of a well-crafted car,
because such an __analogy__ does not take into account the unpredictable twists,
turns, and surprises a Grafton book always contains.

FEATURED WORD: hyperbole

Hyperbole—a figure of speech in which exaggeration is used for emphasis or effect:

- In the first fifteen minutes after she bought her first cell phone, my daughter called everyone she knew and 300 people she didn't.

Origin: 1529 <Latin—*hyperbole* <Greek—*hyperballein* (to throw over or beyond), from *hyper*
(beyond) and *bol* (stem of *ballein*, meaning to throw)

Family words: hyperbolic (adj), hyperbolical (adj), hyperbolically (adv), hyperbolize (v)

Image to remember: Someone telling a story in an exaggerated and dramatic way

Write an original sentence using *hyperbole*:

_____

_____

_____

loose   not tight, unfastened:

My seven-year-old brother has some <u>loose</u> teeth.

One of the bolts on the swing set was <u>loose,</u> so I tightened it.

lose   to suffer defeat or to misplace:

After leading the entire game, I didn't think the Bulldogs would <u>lose</u>, but they did.

Valerie, did you <u>lose</u> your Spanish book?

Circle the correct answer:

1. I thought the Mustangs would <u>loose</u> /(<u>lose</u>) the game after their star player fouled out, but they hung on and won by three points.

2. One of the hinges on the back door is (<u>loose</u>)/ <u>lose</u>.

3. Don't <u>loose</u> /(<u>lose</u>) the car keys again, young man.

Write original sentences using these words:

1. **loose:** _____

2. **lose:** _____

Learning Oral Communication Terms from Context Clues: Set 1

Because communicating with family, friends, associates, and countless others plays such a key role in our lives, college students, regardless of their majors, are usually required to take at least one course in oral communications (speech) to enhance their ability to interact formally and informally with others, whether in a one-to-one, small-group, or large-group situation. The terms presented in this and the following lesson are among those frequently used in introductory oral communication courses. In addition, a review of the **literature** and **composition** terms preceding these lessons is advisable as many of these words are also used in oral communication courses.

1. <u>**venue**</u> (VEN yoo)—noun

   The place where communication, such as a speech, takes place.

   Often, *venue* refers not only to the place where communication takes place, but also to the specific occasion and purpose of the communication.

2. <u>**context**</u> (KON tekst)—noun

   The environment in which communication takes place.

   Context includes the physical, social, and psychological conditions existing when communication takes place.

3. <u>**encoding**</u> (en KŌHD ing)—noun

   The transformation of a thought into a message.

   Encoding includes all the mental processes involved in converting ideas, feelings, opinions, and so forth into messages.

4. <u>**decoding**</u> (dē KŌHD ing)—noun

   The transformation of a message into meaning.

   Decoding includes all the mental processes involved in converting messages into meaning.

5. <u>**catalyst**</u> (KAT ə list)—noun

   Anything that improves communication.

   Humor can often serve as a *catalyst* for enriching communication.

6. **noise** (noiz)—noun

Anything that hinders communication.

Preoccupation with factors unrelated to the speaker's remarks is an example of communication *noise*.

7. **speaking** (SPEEK ing) **voice** (vois)—adjective + noun

Refers to the basic factors relating to speech.

The basic factors relating to *speaking voice* include **volume** (loudness, softness), **pitch** (highness, lowness), **inflections** (variations of pitch), **tempo** (speaking rate), **tone** (attitude toward a subject, such as humorous or serious), **diction** (choice and use of words), and **pronunciation.**

8. **active** (AK tiv) and **passive** (PAS iv) **voice** (vois)—adjectives + noun

A verb is in the active voice when the subject of the sentence does the action the verb describes:

> Karen <u>washed</u> the car.

A verb is in the passive voice when it acts upon the subject:

> The car <u>was</u> <u>washed</u> by Karen.

Generally, it is best to use the *active voice* for both writing and speaking because it produces more direct, powerful, and interesting communication than the *passive voice* does.

9. **enunciation** (i NUN sē Ā shən)—noun

Refers to the correct and precise pronunciation of words.

In casual conversations, it's usually okay for us to mispronounce or slur certain words, such as saying "accidently" instead of "accidentally" and "wif" instead of "with," but in more formal speaking situations, we should make sure our *enunciation* of all words is appropriate.

10. **impromptu speaking** (im PROMP too SPEEK ing)—adjective + noun

Speaking done with little or no advance preparation.

Though always a challenge, *impromptu speaking* can be effective and rewarding if the speaker focuses upon one or two main ideas and then provides specific examples for clarification or support.

Matching Academic Terms and Definitions: Set 1

Match each definition with the term it defines.

_f_	**1.** venue	**a.** transformation of a message into meaning
_c_	**2.** context	**b.** when the subject of the sentence does
_i_	**3.** encoding	the action the verb describes
_a_	**4.** decoding	**c.** the environment in which communication
_h_	**5.** catalyst	takes place
_d_	**6.** noise	**d.** anything that hinders communication
_j_	**7.** speaking voice	**e.** speaking done with little or no advance
_b_	**8.** active voice	preparation
_k_	**9.** passive voice	**f.** the place where communication takes place
_g_	**10.** enunciation	**g.** the correct and precise pronunciation
_e_	**11.** impromptu speaking	of words

h. anything that improves communication

i. transformation of a thought into a message

j. refers to the basic factors relating to speech

k. when the verb acts upon the subject

Fill-Ins with Academic Terms: Set 1

In each space, write the appropriate term from those listed below.

venue	encoding	catalyst	speaking voice	passive	impromptu
context	decoding	noise	active	enunciation	

1. "The meal was cooked by Jeff" is in the _____passive_____ voice, whereas "Jeff cooked the meal" is in the _____active_____ voice.

2. My instructor gave me three minutes to prepare for a(n) _____impromptu_____ speech on my favorite movie.

3. My emotions and thoughts whirled around before _____encoding_____ took place; then I was able to explain why *Sleepless in Seattle* was my favorite movie.

4. The _____venue_____ for Dr. Wallace's speech will be the convention room on the first floor of the Dickson Inn on Essex Street.

5. Good acoustics is a(n) _____catalyst_____ contributing to effective communication.

6. His _____enunciation_____ of some words was faulty as he said "incidently" instead of "incidentally" and "choclate" instead of "chocolate."

7. Today's class was devoted to _____speaking voice_____, so we discussed such matters as volume, tone, and tempo when we gave a speech.

8. The _____decoding_____ of a complex message can be aided by listing the main ideas it contains and then writing a summary of the ideas in your own words.

9. The **context**, or environment, in which a speech takes place includes a number of physical, social, and psychological factors, such as the size of the room, the room's temperature, and the ages, backgrounds, and attitudes of the listeners.

10. In oral communications, the term **noise** doesn't refer only to loud, disturbing sounds; it refers to anything hampering the effective interchange of information.

Related Meanings: Set 1

If the words opposite each other are similar in meaning, write Yes *in the space; if they are unrelated, write* No.

1. catalyst	Yes	something that aids communication
2. context	No	interpretation of a message
3. speaking voice	No	oral commands
4. impromptu speaking	Yes	talking on the spur of the moment
5. active and passive voices	No	the loudness and softness of sound
6. decoding	Yes	conversion of messages into meaning
7. venue	Yes	location where a speech is given
8. noise	No	sound effects used to aid communication
9. enunciation	No	feedback provided by an audience
10. encoding	Yes	conversion of thoughts into messages

Writing Your Own Definitions: Set 1

Write either an original sentence or a definition for each term that clearly demonstrates your mastery of its meaning as used in oral communications.   Answers will vary.

1. **venue** _____

   _____

2. **context** _____

   _____

3. **encoding** _____

   _____

4. **decoding** _____

   _____

5. **catalyst** _____

   _____

6. noise _____

_____

7. speaking voice _____

_____

8. active voice _____

_____

9. passive voice _____

_____

10. enunciation _____

_____

11. impromptu speaking _____

_____

Learning Oral Communication Terms from Context Clues: Set 2

1. <u>transitions</u> (tran ZISH əns)—noun

   Words and phrases a speaker uses to move from one major point to another.
   Examples of *transitions* often used by speakers include these: **to add
   information**—and, also, in addition, furthermore, moreover, besides; **to
   compare**—similarly, likewise, by the same token, in the same vein; **to
   contrast**—but, on the other hand, yet, however, although, in contrast, on the
   contrary, nevertheless; **to relate time**—then, when, afterward, meanwhile,
   during, thereafter; **to clarify**—for example, for instance, specifically; **to
   emphasize**—more important, to be sure, indeed, as long as, provided that,
   unless; **to show cause and effect**—as a result, because, therefore, thus, then,
   since, hence; **to summarize**—therefore, in summary, consequently, as a result.

2. **kinesics** (kə NĒS iks)—noun

   Refers to body movements or body language.
   Communication is influenced by *kinesics,* or body movements, which include
   gestures, posture, facial expressions, and eye behavior.

3. **rapport** (ra POR)—noun

A harmonious or sympathetic connection between a speaker and his or her audience.

To communicate effectively, speakers must establish *rapport* with their audience; humor is often used for this purpose.

4. **prem**ise (PREM is)—noun

An assertion made by a speaker that serves as a basis for an argument or for a conclusion.

The speaker's *premise* was that students should not have to pay to attend any athletic or musical events on campus because they already pay an activity fee each semester.

5. **fallacies** (FAL ə sēs)—noun

Mistakes in reasoning.

Among the common *fallacies* speakers sometimes commit are these: **Hasty Generalization**—basing a conclusion on too little evidence; for example, saying "Connecticut drivers are reckless" based on seeing only two Connecticut motorists driving in this manner. **Either–Or**—stating there are only two alternatives when there are more than that; for example, saying "To avoid a vitamin C deficiency, a person must drink either orange or grape juice every day" when in truth there are numerous other sources of vitamin C. **Ad Hominem**—attacking the person personally rather than the person's argument; for example, saying "Lawrence argues he's the best candidate for the school board, but I know for a fact he wasn't popular in high school, and besides, he's divorced." **Prestige Jargon**—using impressive language in an attempt to gain importance or acceptance of an argument; for example, saying "A student should faithfully attend his or her classes as there is a plethora of research connoting a positive correlation between a student's class attendance and his or her overall scholastic performance," instead of simply saying, "Students should attend their classes because good attendance is related to good grades."

6. **nonsex**ist **language** (NON SEKS ist LANG gwij)—adjective + noun

Communication reflecting gender fairness.

To avoid stereotyping, insensitivity, and unfairness, speakers should use *nonsexist language.* For example, speakers should say police officers, **not** policemen or policewomen; mail carriers, **not** mailmen or mailwomen; sales representatives, **not** salesmen or salesladies; humankind, **not** mankind.

7. **objective** (əb JEK tiv)—adjective
   subjective (səb JEK tiv)—adjective

   When speakers are objective, personal feelings or biases do not influence their remarks; however, when speakers are subjective, their personal feelings or biases do influence their remarks.

   It is appropriate for speakers to be *objective* when they state the facts involved in an experience, event, or outcome; on the other hand, it is appropriate for speakers to be *subjective* when they remark about their reactions regarding the experience, event, or outcome.

8. **critique** (kri TEEK)—noun

   A careful, in-depth review of something, such as a movie, book, piece of artwork, organization, or product.

   The speaker gave a *critique* of the student support programs currently existing on campus. For the most part, she was complimentary of the programs and the people responsible for them; however, she felt the financial aid office was significantly understaffed.

9. **deduction** (dē DUK shən)—noun
   induction (in DUK shən)—noun

   Deduction is reasoning that starts with an accepted principle and leads to specific instances that support the accepted principle.

   Induction is the drawing of a conclusion after gathering appropriate information.

   A speaker can often use *deduction* and/or *induction* to justify his or her opinions, assumptions, conclusions, and suggestions, as in these examples: **Deduction**— At the study skills seminar, the speaker urged us to devote the majority of our studying time on the information our instructors emphasize in class; he said numerous studies conducted over the years indicate that most college students who follow this principle achieve high grades. **Induction**—The speaker also said the data he has collected during the past eight semesters reveal that students who study at the same time and at the same place usually achieve higher grades than students who study at various times and at various places; therefore, he has concluded that studying at a specific time and at a specific place is another principle college students would be wise to follow.

10. **multimedia presentation** (MUL ti MĒ dē ə PREZ ən TĀY shən)—adjective + noun

    A talk or similar event that uses several forms of communication, such as slides, videos, and films.

    The speaker's *multimedia presentation* was impressive as she used a computer to display various charts, photographs, and video clips on a large screen.

Matching Academic Terms and Definitions: Set 2

Match each definition with the term it defines.

_h___ **1.** transitions

_j___ **2.** kinesics

_g___ **3.** rapport

_i___ **4.** premise

_a___ **5.** fallacies

_c___ **6.** nonsexist language

_k___ **7.** objective

_e___ **8.** subjective

_l___ **9.** critique

_f___ **10.** deduction

_d___ **11.** induction

_b___ **12.** multimedia presentation

a. mistakes in reasoning

b. a talk that uses a variety of sources, such as graphs and slides

c. communication reflecting gender fairness

d. reasoning that draws a conclusion after making observations

e. reflecting personal feelings or biases

f. reasoning that begins with an accepted principle

g. harmonious connection between speaker and audience

h. connections between words and phrases

i. assertion that serves as a basis for an argument

j. body movements

k. lacking personal feelings or biases

l. in-depth review of a product, organization, or event

Fill-Ins with Academic Terms: Set 2

In each space, write the appropriate term from those listed below.

| transitions | kinesics | rapport | premise | fallacies | nonsexist language |
| objective | subjective | critique | deduction | induction | multimedia |

1. Our instructor's use of _____kinesics_____, especially his gestures and facial expressions, effectively convey his sense of humor as well as the main points he wishes to stress during class discussions.

2. The speaker's basic assumption was that all college students enjoy team sports, and since we were college students, we all enjoyed team sports; however, his _____premise_____ was faulty from the beginning because a number of my friends and I don't care about team sports at all.

3. The speaker also used _____induction_____ as he said he had observed over the years that students gain an average of ten pounds during their first year of college, so he has concluded that we will too; but I sure hope he's wrong, at least in my case.

4. I appreciate Professor Libby's use of _____transitions_____, such as "for example" or "for instance," when she explains difficult concepts.

5. She has excellent _____ *rapport* _____ with us as she calls on us by name and obviously appreciates what we have to say.

6. Although jury members may not like the looks of the defendant, they should remain _____ *objective* _____ and base their verdict on the evidence presented during the trial.

7. Today's history class was particularly interesting because of Dr. Hewitt's _____ *multimedia* _____ presentation, which included newspaper articles, photos, and film clips about World War II.

8. "Flight attendant" instead of "stewardess" is an example of _____ *nonsexist language* _____.

9. Attacking a person personally instead of his or her argument and making a hasty generalization are examples of _____ *fallacies* _____.

10. Although Todd and Bridget's love for that part of the city obviously influenced their decision about which apartment to rent, I think it was okay for them to be _____ *subjective* _____ in this instance, don't you agree?

11. My _____ *deduction* _____ is that it's important to feel "at home" where you live, even if where you live causes some minor inconveniences.

12. In communications class today, Jarrett gave an impressive _____ *critique* _____ of last weekend's rock concert. Although he praised the band's musicianship and choice of numbers, he said the lead singer overpowered the other singers and that the band's sound system was inadequate, at least for Hudson Hall, the place where the concert was held.

Related Meanings: Set 2

If the words opposite each other are similar in meaning, write Yes *in the space; if they are unrelated, write* No.

1. subjective	No	insulting
2. rapport	Yes	harmony
3. fallacies	No	jokes
4. transitions	Yes	connecting words
5. objective	No	agreeable
6. multimedia presentation	Yes	talk using various audio and visual aids
7. induction	Yes	drawing a conclusion after gathering evidence
8. premise	No	obligation
9. nonsexist language	No	stereotyping talk
10. critique	Yes	careful evaluation
11. deduction	No	brief speech
12. kinesics	Yes	body language

Writing Your Own Definitions: Set 2

Write either an original sentence or a definition for each term that clearly demonstrates your mastery of its meaning as used in oral communications.   Answers will vary.

1. **transitions** _____

   _____

2. **kinesics** _____

   _____

3. **rapport** _____

   _____

4. **premise** _____

   _____

5. **fallacies** _____

   _____

6. **nonsexist language** _____

   _____

7. **objective** _____

   _____

8. **subjective** _____

   _____

9. **critique** _____

   _____

10. **deduction** _____

    _____

11. **induction** _____

    _____

12. **multimedia presentation** _____

    _____

Completing a Passage: Oral Communications

After reading the selection, fill in each space with one of the terms listed below.

enunciation	rapport	active	venue	multimedia
impromptu	catalyst	passive	premise	

SPEECH GUIDELINES

If you are scheduled to speak formally rather than in a(n) ___impromptu___ manner, one of the first things you need to consider, after deciding on a topic appropriate for your audience, is the ___venue___ . If, for example, you will be speaking in a fairly small room before twenty to thirty people, then you might decide that a(n) ___multimedia___ presentation, such as PowerPoint and video clips, would enrich your speech.

Another initial consideration is whether the purpose of your speech is to inform, entertain, persuade, inspire, or motivate. When your purpose is to persuade, it is particularly important that your major assertion or ___premise___ is clear and supported as specifically as possible, such as with facts and examples.

Keep in mind your audience: Will they be people who are familiar or unfamiliar with your topic? What will be the age range of most of them? Would humor serve as an effective ___catalyst___ to establish ___rapport___ with them, or should you adopt some other approach?

Research the topic of your speech to make sure your information is up-to-date, although you certainly can use a personal story or two, especially if it helps to make abstract or confusing information clearer. Whenever possible, speak in the ___active___ rather than in the ___passive___ voice, as it is more direct, powerful, and interesting. And be sure your ___enunciation___ is precise and your voice loud enough so everyone can hear; you may want to consider using a microphone.

Finally, it's generally best to make sure your speech doesn't exceed twenty minutes, as even the best audiences can become restless or overloaded with information in that amount of time.

Rapport—a relationship exhibiting mutual trust and emotional connection:

- Excellent <u>rapport</u> between the conductor and orchestra was evident throughout the concert.

Origin: <French—*rapporter*—bring back; *re* (again) and *apporter* (to bring) (the "harmonious connection" meaning dates from the mid-1800s)

Image to remember: people enjoying each other's company

Write an original sentence using *rapport*:

_____

_____

_____

MASTERING CONFUSING WORDS | **threw / through**

threw   pas tense of *throw*:

Stan <u>threw</u> his tools in the back of his pickup and left for work.

through   from one side to the other; also means completed:

Dora looked <u>through</u> her clothes to find something she thought would be appropriate to wear to the party.

When Ramon got <u>through</u> painting the porch, it was six o'clock, so he decided to call it a day.

Circle the correct answer:

1. Lance walked <u>threw /(through)</u> the computer lab looking for someone to help him.

2. I (threw)/ <u>through</u> the trash into the waste basket.

3. Ashley wondered if she'd ever get <u>threw /(through)</u> writing her paper.

Write original sentences using these words:

1. **threw:** _____

2. **through:** _____

Learning Psychology Terms from Context Clues: Set 1

Psychology is devoted to the systematic study of behavior as well as to the motives for that behavior. Psychology has been found to be an appropriate college major for not only students planning a career in this field, but also for students planning careers in law, business, social work, teaching, and other professions as well. Mastery of the psychological terms included in this chapter can contribute to your basic understanding of this intriguing subject.

1. **control group** (kən TRŌL GROOP)—adjective + noun

   A group of subjects (people or other organisms) exposed to all the features of a particular experiment <u>except</u> for the variable being studied (see 3). The characteristics of the control group are always matched as closely as possible to those of the experimental group, and the control group is often "treated" with a *placebo* (see 4) instead of the actual variable.

2. **experimental group** (ik SPER ə MEN təl GROOP)—adjective + noun

   A group of subjects exposed to the variable being investigated in an experiment. The researcher is attempting to discover the effects of the variable on the subjects. The people in the experimental and control groups are of the same age and state of health and follow the same diet and physical routine. However, those in the *experimental group* are receiving a daily vitamin D pill to see if this vitamin can help to reduce their bone loss as they age. Those in the *control group,* rather than receiving a vitamin D pill, are being given a *placebo* (see 4). The experimental and the control groups are unaware which of them is receiving the real variable and which one is receiving the fake one, that is, the placebo.

3. **variable** (VAR ē ə bəl)—noun

   In an experiment, the condition or factor that can be changed or manipulated. (In 2, vitamin D was the *variable.*)

4. **placebo** (plə SĒ bō)—noun

   An inactive substance used as a control in an experiment to determine the effectiveness of a medicinal drug or treatment; because a *placebo* has no medicinal value, it can serve as a valid comparison to the drug or treatment being tested. However, it can also produce psychological benefits because people sometimes feel better simply because they are taking what they believe is "medicine."

   The experimental group was given a daily vitamin D pill, whereas the control group was given a pill that looked like a vitamin D pill but was actually a *placebo* containing sugar.

5. **empirical** (em PIR ə kəl)—adjective

   Relating to what has been precisely experienced or observed in experiments.
   The *empirical* facts were recorded so that the experiment could be evaluated.

6. **hypothesis** (hī POTH ə sis)—noun

   A logical explanation that needs further investigation before it can be said to be true.
   The *hypothesis* that poliomyelitis was caused by a virus proved to be true when the virus was identified in the 1950s.

7. **cognitive** (KOG nə tiv)—adjective

   Relating to knowing, understanding, and thinking.
   A major stage in a child's *cognitive* development is reached when he or she becomes capable of abstract reasoning.

8. **intrinsic motivation** (in TRIN sik mō tə VĀ shən)—adjective + noun

   A reason or desire for action that comes from within the individual.
   Carolyn wants to prove to herself that she can improve her grades, so her commitment to additional study time for every subject she's taking is the result of *intrinsic motivation.*

9. **extrinsic motivation** (eks TRIN sik mō tə VĀ shən)—adjective + noun

   A reason or desire for action that comes from outside the individual.
   Maddox's increased studying this semester results from *extrinsic motivation,* as his parents promised to give him $1,000 if he improves all his grades.

10. **introvert** (IN trə VURT)—noun

    A person concerned mainly with his or her own thoughts and feelings.
    An *introvert* can become so obsessed with himself or herself that he or she has little social interaction with others.

11. extrovert (EK strə VURT)—noun

A person who has an outgoing, friendly personality.

Latoya is an *extrovert,* so she felt right at home mingling with all the guests.

Matching Academic Terms and Definitions: Set 1

Match each definition with the term it defines.

_e_	1. variable	**a.** an inactive substance often used in experiments
_i_	2. introvert	**b.** logical explanation that will be tested for its validity
_j_	3. experimental	
_d_	4. extrinsic	**c.** person with a friendly, outgoing personality
_f_	5. empirical	**d.** motivation coming from outside an individual
_c_	6. extrovert	**e.** factor manipulated in an experiment
_b_	7. hypothesis	**f.** evidence directly experienced or observed
_g_	8. intrinsic	**g.** motivation coming from within an individual
_k_	9. cognitive	**h.** group exposed to all features of the experiment except for the variable
_h_	10. control	
_a_	11. placebo	**i.** person concerned mainly with his or her own feelings
		j. group exposed to all features of the experiment, including the variable
		k. term associated with intellectual abilities

Fill-Ins with Academic Terms: Set 1

In each space, write the appropriate term from those listed below.

introvert	experimental	extrovert	empirical	intrinsic	control
placebo	cognitive	hypothesis	extrinsic	variable	

1. As people mature, their _____*cognitive*_____ skills become more developed, so they are capable of solving more complex problems.

2. Niacin was the _____*variable*_____ used in the experiment to see if it would help to reduce high cholesterol readings. My folks were in the _____*experimental*_____ group, so they received a daily niacin capsule; another couple I know were in the _____*control*_____ group, so they were given a(n) _____*placebo*_____, which was simply a capsule with nothing in it.

3. The _____*empirical*_____ evidence gathered from the experiment indicated that niacin could help reduce cholesterol to some extent.

4. Roger is a(n) _____*extrovert*_____, as he loves to be around people and talk about every subject imaginable.

5. _____*Intrinsic*_____ motivation is apparently responsible for Rory working out every other day in the weight room, as he said he hopes to make the varsity football team next season.

6. I'm surprised Rory is so motivated to be on the debate team; because I seldom see him around other people, I assumed he was a(n) _____introvert_____ .

7. My _____hypothesis_____ is that he has probably overcome much of his former shyness and lack of sociability because he's older and has made some friends.

8. Olivia is practicing the flute a couple of hours every day because of _____extrinsic_____ motivation, as her grandparents promised her a Florida vacation in the spring if she did so.

Related Meanings: Set 1

If the words opposite each other are similar in meaning, write Yes *in the space; if they are unrelated, write* No.

1. extrinsic motivation   _No_   comes from within a person
2. extrovert   _Yes_   life of the party
3. variable   _No_   unrealistic expectations
4. empirical   _Yes_   observed evidence in an experiment
5. intrinsic motivation   _No_   due to threats of punishment
6. experimental group   _Yes_   those in an experiment subjected to the variable
7. introvert   _Yes_   one who is self-obsessed
8. cognitive   _Yes_   intellectual capacities
9. hypothesis   _No_   insightful, accurate
10. control group   _Yes_   those in an experiment not subjected to the variable
11. placebo   _No_   an experimental drug

Writing Your Own Definitions: Set 1

Write either an original sentence or a definition for each term that clearly demonstrates your mastery of its meaning as used in psychology.   Answers will vary.

1. **empirical** _____

_____

2. **control group** _____

_____

3. **extrinsic motivation** _____

_____

4. **cognitive** _____

_____

5. **extrovert** _____

_____

6. intrinsic motivation _____

_____

7. experimental group _____

_____

8. hypothesis _____

_____

9. variable _____

_____

10. introvert _____

_____

11. placebo _____

_____

Learning Psychology Terms from Context Clues: Set 2

1. ego (Ē gō)—noun

2. id (ID)—noun

3. superego (SOO pər Ē gō)—noun

Ego, id, and superego are terms associated with Sigmund Freud (1856–1939), the founder of psychoanalysis. The ego is the conscious part of the personality and is responsible for logical thinking.

The id is the instinctive part of the personality, including the sexual and aggressive instincts, that seeks immediate gratification. Freud maintained that the id is the first system to develop within a person because it is most closely related to the biological realm. The id is the "home" of all psychological energy, or libido (Latin for "lust").

The superego is the moralistic part of the personality, including beliefs about what conduct is right or wrong.

The *ego* has to resolve the conflicting demands of the *id, superego,* and external reality. The *id* is the pleasure-loving, selfish side of a person's personality that seeks immediate gratification regardless of consequences. The *superego,* or conscience, is largely a product of parental and societal influences.

4. **psychoanalysis** (SĪ kō ə NAL ə sis)—noun

Method of treating emotional disorders through free association: having the patient talk freely about personal experiences, particularly those relating to childhood and dreams.

Sigmund Freud developed *psychoanalysis,* a method that encourages the patient to use free association, that is, to discuss anything that comes to mind, in the hope that hidden emotional conflicts will be uncovered.

5. **defense mechanisms** (də FENS MEK ə NIZ əms)—adjective + noun

Unconscious strategies used to protect ourselves against unpleasant emotions or to maintain our self-images.

Repression (selective forgetting) and rationalization (excuse making) are common *defense mechanisms.*

Sigmund Freud introduced the practice of *psychoanalysis* to help patients understand their hidden desires and emotions. *(AP Photo/Sigmund Freud Museum)*

6. therapeutic (ther ə PŪ tik)—adjective

Relating to the treatment of disease, especially something intended to bring about healing.

Kara says that playing her clarinet has a *therapeutic* effect on her when she is emotionally upset.

7. neurosis (nyoo RŌ sis)—noun

An emotional disorder characterized by anxiety or other symptoms. A neurosis is not due to a physical or mental disease, and the sufferer does not lose contact with reality. A neurosis is not as severe a disorder as a *psychosis* (see below).

Claustrophobia is a common *neurosis* in which a person becomes extremely anxious in enclosed places, such as in an elevator or in a small room without windows.

8. psychosis (sī KŌ sis)—noun

A severe mental disorder involving personality disorganization and a lack of contact with reality.

A person suffering from a *psychosis* is considered insane.

9. psychosomatic (SĪ kō sō MAT ik)—adjective

Relates to the presence of physical symptoms that are due to emotional causes.

Psychosomatic is the term often used to reflect the influence the mind can have on the body. For example, a patient may have severe headaches because of stress (psychosomatic related), not because of some physical problem.

10. Oedipus complex (ED ə pəs kəm PLEKS)—adjective + noun

A psychoanalytic theory that children commonly have a subconscious sexual attraction to the parent of the opposite sex and hostility for the parent of the same sex. *Oedipus* comes from Greek mythology in which a son unwittingly kills his father and marries his mother.

The *Oedipus complex,* a theory developed by Freud to explain conflicts between a child and his or her parent of the opposite sex, is not subscribed to by all psychologists.

11. behavior therapy (bē HĀV yər THER ə pē)—adjective + noun

A psychological approach for treating emotional disturbances that emphasizes taking direct physical action to restore good mental and emotional health. The goal of behavior therapy is to help the patient modify and gain control over unwanted behavior. Gradually exposing the individual to situations he or she finds difficult to experience is a technique often used in this therapy.

Dr. Lown used *behavior therapy* to help her patient overcome his fear of elevators. The first week, she had her patient travel to the second floor and then back on an elevator; she gradually increased the number of floors the patient traveled until his anxiety regarding elevators was overcome.

12. cognitive therapy (KOG nə tiv THER ə pē)—adjective + noun

The goal of this type of therapy is to help individuals change unproductive thought patterns to those that are more realistic and beneficial. Many therapists use a combination of cognitive-behavior therapies in working with their patients.

After being counseled for several months in *cognitive therapy* techniques, my friend is confident he can now cope with his public speaking fears.

Matching Academic Terms and Definitions: Set 2

Match each definition with the term it defines.

_c_	**1.** therapeutic	**a.** refers to physical complaints related to emotional disorders
_l_	**2.** psychoanalysis	
_i_	**3.** defense mechanisms	**b.** the part of the personality concerned with right and wrong
_k_	**4.** behavior therapy	
_h_	**5.** ego	**c.** a term used for the positive treatment of illnesses
_j_	**6.** psychosis	
_b_	**7.** superego	**d.** a psychological approach designed to help the individual change harmful thought patterns to more constructive ones
_f_	**8.** id	
_g_	**9.** neurosis	
_d_	**10.** cognitive therapy	**e.** the theory that children often have an unconscious sexual attraction to the parent of the opposite sex
_e_	**11.** Oedipus complex	
_a_	**12.** psychosomatic	**f.** the instinctive part of the personality that seeks immediate gratification

g. an emotional disorder in which the individual retains contact with reality

h. the part of the personality responsible for logical thinking

i. attitudes or strategies used to protect one's emotions or self-image

j. a severe mental disorder in which the person has lost contact with reality

k. a psychological approach that emphasizes gaining control over unwanted behavior rather than spending significant time exploring the individual's past mental and emotional histories

l. a psychological approach that uses talk (free association) to explore an individual's childhood as well as his or her dreams in an effort to uncover the root causes of emotional distress

Fill-Ins with Academic Terms: Set 2

In each space, write the appropriate term from those listed below.

cognitive	ego	psychosis	psychoanalysis	id
therapeutic	Oedipus complex	intrinsic	psychosomatic	
defense mechanisms	behavior	superego	neurosis	

1. An individual who lacks contact with reality and has major personality disorganization is suffering from a(n) _____ psychosis _____ .

2. The _____ id _____ seeks immediate gratification regardless of the consequences, while the _____ superego _____ strives to maintain moral standards; the _____ ego _____ , responsible for logical thinking, attempts to reconcile the two.

3. Although my business partner is often plagued by anxiety, he is able to meet his responsibilities; nevertheless, he's seeing a psychologist for help in overcoming his _____ neurosis _____ .

4. Exercise has been found to be _____ therapeutic _____ for the relief of stress.

5. After someone else was given the promotion he had also requested, Ted said that was okay with him because the salary raise wasn't much, and besides, he didn't think he would like the people he would have had to work with anyway. Ted's statements represent the possible use of _____ defense mechanisms _____ .

6. During _____ psychoanalysis _____ , in which Martin talked a lot about his childhood, the psychiatrist suggested that Martin had possessed a(n) _____ Oedipus complex _____ when he was a youngster, and that was the reason he had never been able to get along well with his father.

7. Valerie was flabbergasted when the doctor stated his belief that her back pain was due to _____ psychosomatic _____ problems, not physical ones.

8. When treating certain patients, numerous psychologists often combine _____ cognitive _____ therapy, which stresses the development of healthy thought patterns, and _____ behavior _____ therapy, which stresses direct physical action to overcome emotional problems.

9. _____ Intrinsic _____ motivation comes from within a person.

Related Meanings: Set 2

If the words opposite each other are similar in meaning, write Yes *in the space; if they are unrelated, write* No.

1. cognitive therapy   _Yes_   psychological treatment stressing logical thought patterns

2. ego   _Yes_   logical, conscious side of one's personality

3. defense mechanisms   _No_   motivational strategies

4. neurosis   _No_   lack of a sense of reality

5. Oedipus complex   <u>No</u>   abnormal fear of strangers

6. therapeutic   <u>Yes</u>   helpful to healing

7. superego   <u>Yes</u>   honest and moral side of one's personality

8. behavior therapy   <u>Yes</u>   psychological treatment emphasizing action

9. psychosomatic   <u>Yes</u>   root of physical problem lies in an emotional disorder

10. psychosis   <u>No</u>   healthy cleansing of emotions

11. id   <u>Yes</u>   instinctive, selfish side of one's personality

12. psychoanalysis   <u>Yes</u>   psychological treatment with emphasis on rambling talk, or free association, to uncover hidden causes of emotional problems

Writing Your Own Definitions: Set 2

Write either an original sentence or a definition for each term that clearly demonstrates your mastery of its meaning as used in psychology.   Answers will vary.

1. **superego** _____

   _____

2. **therapeutic** _____

   _____

3. **behavior therapy** _____

   _____

4. **psychosomatic** _____

   _____

5. **id** _____

   _____

6. **Oedipus complex** _____

   _____

7. **defense mechanisms** _____

   _____

8. **psychoanalysis** _____

   _____

9. **psychosis** _____

   _____

10. cognitive therapy _____

_____

11. ego _____

_____

12. neurosis _____

_____

Completing a Passage: Psychology

After reading the selection, fill in each space with one of the terms listed below.

intrinsic motivation	psychosis	therapeutic	ego
defense mechanisms	psychoanalysis	cognitive therapy	
neurosis	psychosomatic	behavior therapy	

PANIC ATTACKS

Panic attacks are sudden onsets of intense fear, anxiety, and a feeling of unreality; they are often accompanied by sweating, dizziness, and a pounding heartbeat. People from all walks of life, including athletes, singers, actors, broadcasters, ministers, teachers, doctors, and many others, have been the victims of panic attacks.

All of the causes of panic attacks have not been identified, but stress and emotional problems are generally thought to be major ones. People experiencing a panic attack for the first time often think they are having a heart attack, stroke, or some other medical catastrophe, including "going crazy." Understandably, they will frequently rush to the nearest emergency room. After undergoing a medical exam, they may be told that there is nothing wrong with them physically, which suggests that their problem may be _____psychosomatic_____ in nature. Although grateful to be told they are okay physically, it is often a blow to a panic attack sufferer's _____ego_____ to be told that an emotional disorder may have triggered their terrible discomfort.

Panic attacks are one of the most common psychological problems in our society, as figures indicate that one out of every twenty people experiences a panic attack some-time in his or her life. People with a chronic panic disorder suffer from a _____neurosis_____, not a _____psychosis_____, as they do not lose touch with reality despite the anxiety that so often overwhelms them. Such people frequently rearrange major parts of their lives in an effort to avoid having a panic attack. For example, if they had their first attack while shopping at a mall, attending a movie, or driving a car, they will completely avoid these activities, sometimes becoming so fearful they seldom leave home, using all sorts of _defense mechanisms_ to explain their puzzling behavior to friends and family members.

Fortunately, people who suffer from panic attacks can be helped by ___therapeutic___ medicines and effective counseling techniques. Regarding the latter, both ___behavior therapy___ and ___cognitive therapy___, with their emphasis on action and correct thought patterns, have a history of success in helping people to overcome their panic attacks. ___Psychoanalysis___, though requiring more time because of the free association talk involved, can also be helpful; however, many psychologists prefer a combination of the other two methods.

For many sufferers, ___intrinsic motivation___ leads them to seek help, but whatever motivates a person to get help, he or she is wise to do so, as from 70 to 90 percent of those who receive treatment are eventually freed from their terrifying panic attacks.

FEATURED WORD: psychosomatic

Psychosomatic—pertaining to the relationship between body and mind:

- In the interview, the doctor was quoted as saying he believed that over half of all illnesses are triggered by <u>psychosomatic</u> factors, so he urged his colleagues to be aware of patients' emotional backgrounds when exploring the causes of their physical complaints.

Origin: late 1930s <Greek—*psyche* (mind) and *soma* (body)

Family words: psychotherapy (n), psychotherapeutics (n)

Image to remember: person being counseled to improve his or her emotional situation in order to overcome his or her physical problems

Write an original sentence using *psychosomatic*:

_____

_____

_____

MASTERING CONFUSING WORDS	farther / further

farther   refers to physical distance:

> We decided not to hike any <u>farther</u> because it was getting dark.

further   indicates to a greater extent or degree:

> The happy couple said they would announce their plans in <u>further</u> detail in a couple of weeks.

> The governor said the budget would take <u>further</u> study before a final decision could be reached.

Circle the correct answer:

1. After moving to the Southwest, Hakeem had no farther / further problems with asthma.

2. How much farther / further is it to the coast?

3. Until farther / further notice, Essex Street will be closed for repairs.

Write original sentences using these words:

1. farther: _____

2. further: _____

Learning Sociology Terms from Context Clues: Set 1

Sociology is concerned with the systematic study of human society, including the social interactions among nations, communities, and families. Sociology includes many subfields, such as gerontology, social psychology, and religious and educational sociology, among many others. Mastery of the terms in this lesson and the following lesson can give you insight into this interesting and valuable social science.

1. **acculturation** (ə kul chə RĀ shən)—noun

   Modification of a culture as a result of contact with another culture.
   The *acculturation* of the Japanese to many aspects of Western culture began after World War II.

2. **agrarian** (ə GRAR ē ən)—adjective

   Relates to rural life, agricultural groups, and farm ownership.
   The United States has moved from a predominantly *agrarian* to an urban society.

3. **culture** (KUL chər)—noun

   The patterns of life shared by the members of a society and transmitted from one generation to another.
   Eating three meals a day is part of our *culture*.

4. **demography** (di MOG rə fē)—noun

   The statistical study of human populations, such as information about the number of births, deaths, and marriages.
   A study of *demography* reveals that one of the highest birthrates in the United States occurred in the late 1940s.

5. **mores** (MŌR āz)—noun

   Social norms that reflect the moral standards of a society.
   Marrying a close relative is opposed by the *mores* of most societies.

6. **peer group** (PĒR GROOP)—noun + noun

   A grouping of individuals of the same general age and social position.
   As a child becomes older, his or her *peer group* has more influence.

7. **sibling** (SIB ling)—noun

One of two or more individuals having one common parent; a brother or sister.
Jack, my oldest *sibling,* is studying law at a university in New Jersey.

8. **social norms** (SŌ shəl NORMZ)—adjective + noun

Standards that guide people in what they should or should not do in any
particular social situation.
Laws are serious and formal *social norms.*

9. **stereotype** (STER ē ə tīp)—noun; verb

A standardized image applied to individuals who are identified with a particular
group (noun); to make a stereotype of (verb).
The *stereotype* of the cowboy of the Old West is that of a fearless, rugged,
independent man.

10. **urbanism** (UR bə niz əm)—noun

Patterns of life characteristic of cities.
Some of the benefits of *urbanism* include access to outstanding museums,
theaters, and restaurants.

11. **values** (VAL yo͞oz)—noun

Ideas about what is good, proper, wise, and worthwhile.
Achieving success in work is one of society's *values.*

Matching Academic Terms and Definitions: Set 1

Match each definition with the term it defines.

_e_	**1.** social norms	**a.**	adopting new patterns of life
_g_	**2.** mores	**b.**	a fixed view of individuals
_i_	**3.** values	**c.**	customs and values shared by a society
_c_	**4.** culture	**d.**	a brother or sister
_k_	**5.** peer group	**e.**	standards for social behavior
_b_	**6.** stereotype	**f.**	refers to country life and farming
_h_	**7.** demography	**g.**	guides that provide moral standards
_a_	**8.** acculturation	**h.**	study of population figures
_j_	**9.** urbanism	**i.**	ideas about what is beneficial
_f_	**10.** agrarian	**j.**	refers to cities
_d_	**11.** sibling	**k.**	individuals of similar backgrounds

Fill-Ins with Academic Terms: Set 1

In each space, write the appropriate term from those listed below.

acculturation	demography	social norms	values
sibling	mores	stereotype	agrarian
culture	peer group	urbanism	

1. A word referring to city life is _____ urbanism _____ .

2. Guides that help us to decide how we should behave when in public are _____ social norms _____ .

3. Because friends are important to all of us, we wish to be accepted by our _____ peer group _____ .

4. Human population figures have to do with the subject of _____ demography _____ .

5. Do you know whether Todd's _____ sibling _____ is a brother or a sister?

6. Strict guides concerned with society's important moral standards are called _____ mores _____ .

7. Getting a good education is one of the _____ values _____ of our society because of education's personal and vocational benefits.

8. A person who is overly aggressive, loud, and deceptive is the _____ stereotype _____ many people have of a used-car salesman.

9. Iowa and Nebraska are considered _____ agrarian _____ states because of the importance of agriculture to their economy.

10. Laws, religion, and manners are part of our _____ culture _____ .

11. A United States citizen who moves to the Philippines undergoes a(n) _____ acculturation _____ process because of the necessity to acquire new ways of functioning in a different society.

Related Meanings: Set 1

If the words opposite each other are similar in meaning, write Yes *in the space; if they are unrelated, write* No.

1. social norms   Yes   behavior guides
2. mores   Yes   moral guidelines
3. values   Yes   ideals
4. culture   No   advanced civilization
5. peer group   No   those of the upper class
6. stereotype   Yes   common image
7. demography   No   study of land
8. acculturation   No   universal praise

9. urbanism   _Yes_ relates to cities
10. agrarian   _Yes_ rural
11. sibling   _No_ cousin

Writing Your Own Definitions: Set 1

Write either an original sentence or a definition for each term that clearly demonstrates your mastery of its meaning as used in sociology.   Answers will vary.

1. acculturation _____

_____

2. agrarian _____

_____

3. culture _____

_____

4. demography _____

_____

5. mores _____

_____

6. sibling _____

_____

7. peer group _____

_____

8. social norms _____

_____

9. stereotype _____

_____

10. urbanism _____

_____

11. values _____

_____

Learning Sociology Terms from Context Clues: Set 2

1. **bureaucracy** (bū ROK rə sē)—noun

   Government structure operated by numerous offices and officials, with clearly defined responsibilities; often characterized by the following of inflexible rules and the creation of endless red tape.

   The Duncans did not let the irritating *bureaucracy* discourage them from attempting to adopt a child.

2. **ethnic group** (ETH nik GROOP)—adjective + noun

   A group within a society that shares the same traits, such as race, nationality, religion, language, and customs.

   Immigrants from Germany were an *ethnic group* that helped to settle Cincinnati, Ohio.

3. **ethnocentrism** (eth nō SEN triz əm)—noun

   The attitude that one's own race, nation, or culture is superior to all others.

   When people are initially exposed to a different culture, they may fall victim to *ethnocentrism,* a feeling that the new culture is inferior to the one to which they are accustomed.

4. **folkways** (FŌK wāz)—noun

   Social customs approved by society; unlike mores, folkways are not considered morally significant, so they are not strictly enforced.

   One of the *folkways* in our society is that a person should dress at least fairly formally when attending church, but it is not considered a serious offense if someone shows up wearing jeans.

5. **Malthusian theory** (mal THOO zē ən THE ə rē)—adjective + noun

   Thomas R. Malthus's (1766–1834) theory that if population is not controlled, the result will be famine, war, and other tragedies.

   The *Malthusian theory* was one of the first theories to predict that world hunger would result if population growth got out of control.

6. **matriarchal family** (mā trē AR kəl FAM ə lē)—adjective + noun

   A family headed by the mother.

   Because my father was frequently absent on business trips, ours was a *matriarchal family;* mother was dominant and made the major family decisions.

7. **patriarchal family** (pā trē AR kəl FAM ə lē)—adjective + noun

A family headed by the father.

A *patriarchal family* is most often portrayed in American literature, that is, a family dominated by the father's influence.

8. **sanction** (SANK shən)—noun

A mechanism of social control for enforcing a society's standards.

Because of the recent disturbances involving young people, the city council has enacted a 10:00 P.M. curfew for all teenagers; this *sanction* will be in effect for the remainder of the summer.

9. **status** (STĀ təs)—noun

A person's social standing in society.

Doctors enjoy a high social *status* in most communities.

10. **utopia** (ū TŌ pē ə)—noun

An imaginary place where everything is perfect.

Some young people yearn to go to Hollywood because they think this city must be *utopia*.

11. **gerontology** (JER ən TOL ə jē)—noun

The scientific study of aging.

As the population continues to grow and life expectancy increases, more sociologists are specializing in *gerontology* than ever before.

12. **geriatrics** (JER ē AT riks)—noun

The branch of medicine dealing with the diseases and care of the elderly.

My grandparents' doctor is Dr. Rostelli, a specialist in *geriatrics*.

Matching Academic Terms and Definition: Set 2

Match each definition with the term it defines.

i	1. matriarchal family	**a.**	perfect community
g	2. patriarchal family	**b.**	scientific study of aging
e	3. geriatrics	**c.**	organization with rigid rules
a	4. utopia	**d.**	punishment or approval
h	5. ethnocentrism	**e.**	medicine specializing in the treatment
j	6. Malthusian theory		of the elderly
b	7. gerontology	**f.**	people sharing certain characteristics
d	8. sanction	**g.**	father dominant
k	9. status	**h.**	belief that one's own culture is the best
f	10. ethnic group	**i.**	customs not strictly enforced

_____c_____ **11.** bureaucracy
_____i_____ **12.** folkways

j. the idea that uncontrolled population leads to serious problems

k. one's position in society

l. mother dominant

Fill-Ins with Academic Terms: Set 2

In each space, write the appropriate term from those listed below.

bureaucracy	folkways	patriarchal family	utopia
ethnic group	Malthusian theory	sanction	geriatrics
ethnocentrism	matriarchal family	status	gerontology

1. Marybeth was accused of ____ethnocentrism____ after stating that England's culture is superior to the culture of any other country.

2. People who are of French descent have been a significant ____ethnic group____ in Maine's history.

3. The newspaper's editor blamed the state ____bureaucracy____ for the endless paperwork involved in the proposed construction of a new city bridge.

4. According to ____Malthusian theory____ , controlled population growth is essential to avoid serious societal problems.

5. Because his father died when Wallis was only two years old, he was raised in a(n) ____matriarchal family____ .

6. My Aunt Dolores was a part of a(n) ____patriarchal family____ ; her father dominated all family matters.

7. Because of the growth in our aging population, there is a need for more doctors specializing in ____geriatrics____ .

8. Among the ____folkways____ in our society is the expectation that store clerks will be courteous to customers.

9. An example of a(n) ____sanction____ in the military is demotion to a lower rank.

10. Mr. Porter, a popular coach and biology teacher, enjoys a respected ____status____ in the community.

11. Maura's idea of ____utopia____ is Arizona because of its warm, dry climate and its opportunities for geological exploration.

12. After Peyton received her B.A. in sociology, she decided to pursue a master's degree in ____gerontology____ as she is interested in learning more about the aging process.

Related Meanings: Set 2

If the words opposite each other are similar in meaning, write Yes *in the space; if they are unrelated, write* No.

1. gerontology   <u>No</u>   medical specialty concerned with the diseases of children

2. matriarchal family   <u>Yes</u>   family headed by mother
3. patriarchal family   <u>Yes</u>   family headed by father
4. bureaucracy   <u>Yes</u>   structure with numerous regulations
5. utopia   <u>Yes</u>   heaven on earth
6. ethnocentrism   <u>No</u>   dictator in power
7. Malthusian theory   <u>No</u>   belief that earth formed 10 thousand years ago
8. folkways   <u>Yes</u>   traditions expected to be observed
9. sanction   <u>Yes</u>   something that tends to reinforce or discourage certain actions

10. status   <u>No</u>   penalty for misbehavior
11. ethnic group   <u>No</u>   individuals in local power
12. geriatrics   <u>Yes</u>   medical specialty concerned with the aged

Writing Your Own Definitions: Set 2

Write either an original sentence or a definition for each term that clearly demonstrates your mastery of its meaning as used in sociology.   Answers will vary.

1. **bureaucracy** _____

_____

2. **ethnic group** _____

_____

3. **ethnocentrism** _____

_____

4. **folkways** _____

_____

5. **gerontology** _____

_____

6. **Malthusian theory** _____

_____

7. matriarchal family _____

_____

8. patriarchal family _____

_____

9. geriatrics _____

_____

10. status _____

_____

11. utopia _____

_____

12. sanction _____

_____

Completing a Passage: Sociology

After reading the selection, fill in each space with one of the terms listed below.

urbanism	stereotype	bureaucracy	ethnocentrism	ethnic group
status	social norms	peer groups	demography	agrarian

OPINION POLLS

The growth of creditable opinion polls dates back to the 1930s, when government, business, and educational organizations began to need more systematic methods for gathering information. Sociologists played a major part in the growth of opinion polls and other data-gathering techniques as the heart of their work involves ___*demography*___ , that is, the statistical study of birth, deaths, marriages, and other such information.

By having available the data provided by opinion polls, sociologists are able to identify shifts, if any, in the nation's ___*social norms*___ , such as whether something once considered socially unacceptable has now become socially acceptable. Opinion polls also help sociologists determine whether the ___*status*___ of people engaged in various occupations has undergone a change; for example, a recent poll revealed that the social ranking of cosmetologists (cosmetics specialists) has risen significantly in the last decade while the ranking of car salesmen has remained the same, an indication that people continue to ___*stereotype*___ them as slick and dishonest people.

Government officials are also interested in the information yielded by polls because they must stay current regarding all matters affecting the people, whether those are related to ___urbanism___ (cities) or ___agrarian___ (rural) life. However, after studying this information, they often add even more rules and regulations to an already complex ___bureaucracy___. Politicians and businesspeople also rely on opinion polls to identify voters' attitudes and consumers' views on existing or new products.

To have validity, an opinion poll must be a representative sample that accurately mirrors the population under study. For example, if a poll's purpose it to gather information about the religious views of students attending U.S. colleges, then steps must be taken to ensure that the polling sample is sufficiently large and varied so that it truly represents these students. In such a poll, the opinions of ___peer groups___ are essential, but efforts must be made to rule out the domination of any one ___ethnic group___ because students who share the same race, language, customs, and nationality would not be representative of all students attending U.S. colleges. And because most people express at least a degree of ___ethnocentrism___ when it comes to cultural matters (which includes religious views), efforts must also be made to poll college students from foreign countries as well as those from the United States.

Though many people are skeptical of the accuracy of opinion polls, sociologists and others have faith in them if they are based on a representative sample of the group under study, if the polling questions (and interviews, if conducted) are free of bias and well written, and if the data gathered are analyzed correctly.

Gerontology—the scientific study of the biological, psychological, and sociological factors involved in the aging process:

- <u>Gerontology</u>, the scientific study of aging, is a subfield of sociology.

Origin: 1903, coined in England <Greek—*geron* (old man) and <French—*logie* (study of)

Family words: gerontological (adj), gerontologist (n)

Image to remember: elderly people, retirees

Write an original sentence using *gerontology*:

_____

_____

_____

desert   (1) dry, barren land; (2) forsaking one's duty:

This part of the state would be a <u>desert</u> if it weren't for irrigation.

We didn't ask Mike to go with us on our weeklong fishing trip because we knew he would never <u>desert</u> his business responsibilities for that period of time.

dessert   the last course of a meal, often pastries or ice cream:

Gingerbread with lots of whipped cream is my son's favorite <u>dessert</u>.

Circle the correct answer:

1. We decided not to have any desert / (dessert) because we were too full from the delicious dinner.

2. Various kinds of flowers bloom in late winter and early spring in the (desert)/ dessert areas of the Southwest.

Write original sentences using these words:

1. **desert (meaning #1):** _____

2. **desert (meaning #2):** _____

3. **dessert:** _____

Learning United States History and Political Science Terms from Context Clues: Set 1

The United States is a republic, which means that the citizens exercise the powers of government through representatives. To meet this responsibility, citizens need to understand the country's heritage and political system; this is the overriding reason students are required to study history and government. In this regard, knowledge of the terms in this and the following two lessons is useful for the study of history and political science.

1. **amendment** (ə MEND mənt)—noun

   A change or addition to the Constitution, the basic document establishing the framework of the federal government. There are currently twenty-six amendments to the Constitution.

   The Thirteenth *Amendment* to the United States Constitution forbids slavery.

2. **Bill of Rights**—noun + preposition + noun

   Adopted in 1791 soon after the Constitution went into effect, the first ten amendments to the Constitution are known as the Bill of Rights. It is concerned with such important freedoms as religion and speech.

   Trial by jury is one of the important provisions in the *Bill of Rights*.

3. **boycott** (BOI kot)—noun or verb

   An economic means of influencing another nation or business by refusing to purchase its products.

   After the British government enacted the Stamp Act, colonial merchants decided to *boycott* English goods, especially tea.

4. **branches of government**—noun + preposition + noun

   The United States federal government comprises three branches:

   legislative (LEJ is lā tiv)—adjective, noun — Congress, made up of the House of Representatives and the Senate, which makes the laws

   executive (ig ZEK yə tiv)—adjective, noun — the president, who enforces the laws

   judiciary (joo DISH ē ər ē)—adjective, noun — the Supreme Court, which interprets the laws

5. **checks and balances** (CHEKS ănd BAL əns əs)—noun + conjunction + noun

Rights and procedures in the Constitution that reserve certain privileges to each of the three branches of government and that enable each branch to check, or limit, the powers of the other two.

Among the *checks and balances* existing in our government are the following: Congress (legislative) has the power to remove from office the president and Supreme Court justices; the president (executive) can refuse to sign bills passed by Congress and has the power to appoint Supreme Court justices when vacancies occur; the Supreme Court (judiciary) can declare bills approved by Congress and signed into law by the president unconstitutional.

6. **eminent domain** (EM ə nənt dō MĀN)—adjective + noun

The power of the government to acquire private property for public purposes.

The state government's power of *eminent domain* forced the O'Connors to sell a section of their farm so the highway could be altered.

7. **laissez-faire** (les ā FĀR)—adjective

Characterized by an economic policy that opposes government interference in business affairs.

Both presidential candidates stated they favor the *laissez-faire* doctrine, or government noninterference, when it came to such economic concerns as wages and prices.

8. **lobbyist** (LOB bē ist)—noun

A person who represents a special interest group that seeks to influence either the passage or defeat of certain bills.

The *lobbyist* for the oil company appeared before the committee to argue for the bill that would allow new offshore oil drilling.

9. **ratification** (rat ə fə KĀ shən)—noun

A power held by a legislative body to approve proposed agreements and amendments.

The Senate's *ratification* is necessary before the treaty becomes official.

10. **veto** (VĒ tō)—noun or verb

The president's refusal or act of refusing to sign a bill into law.

The president said he would *veto* the education bill passed by Congress.

Matching Academic Terms and Definitions: Set 1

Match each definition with the term it defines.

__d__	**1.** branches of government	**a.**	legislative power to approve certain government actions
__g__	**2.** amendment	**b.**	first ten amendments to the Constitution
__b__	**3.** Bill of Rights	**c.**	non-interference
__h__	**4.** checks and balances	**d.**	legislative, executive, judicial
__e__	**5.** veto	**e.**	president's refusal to sign a bill
__a__	**6.** ratification	**f.**	representative for a special concern
__i__	**7.** boycott	**g.**	change in the Constitution
__c__	**8.** laissez-faire	**h.**	ways government branches can limit one another
__j__	**9.** eminent domain	**i.**	refusal to buy
__f__	**10.** lobbyist	**j.**	government's right to secure private property

Fill-Ins with Academic Terms: Set 1

In each space, write the appropriate term from those listed below.

amendment	branches of government	laissez-faire	veto
Bill of Rights	checks and balances	lobbyist	
boycott	eminent domain	ratification	

1. The _____Bill of Rights_____ guarantees numerous personal freedoms.

2. Believing in as few restrictions on business as possible, the president is encouraging Congress to follow his _____laissez-faire_____ philosophy.

3. The striking workers are urging people to _____boycott_____ the company's products.

4. Some historians believe a(n) _____amendment_____ to the Constitution should be adopted to simplify presidential elections.

5. The president remains confident that the Senate's _____ratification_____ of the treaty will occur in two or three days.

6. The governor has suggested that the legislature exercise its right of _____eminent domain_____ to enlarge the state park near the coast.

7. The three _____branches of government_____ are the legislative, the executive, and the judicial.

8. The president warned that he would _____veto_____ any bills requiring an increase in taxes.

9. Mr. Tapley is a(n) _____lobbyist_____ for an environmental organization.

10. The _____checks and balances_____ contained in the Constitution are designed to prohibit any branch of government from exceeding its powers.

Related Meanings: Set 1

If the words opposite each other are similar in meaning, write Yes *in the space; if they are unrelated, write* No.

1. branches of government   <u>No</u>   legislative, executive, treasury
2. amendment   <u>Yes</u>   addition to or change in the Constitution
3. Bill of Rights   <u>No</u>   first twelve amendments
4. checks and balances   <u>No</u>   economic safeguards
5. veto   <u>Yes</u>   president's disapproval of a bill
6. ratification   <u>No</u>   presidential appointment
7. boycott   <u>Yes</u>   refusal to buy
8. laissez-faire   <u>No</u>   economic controls
9. eminent domain   <u>No</u>   power to declare war
10. lobbyist   <u>Yes</u>   representative for a special group

Writing Your Own Definitions: Set 1

Write either an original sentence or a definition for each term that clearly demonstrates your mastery of its meaning as used in United States history and political science.
Answers will vary.

1. **amendment** _____

_____

2. **Bill of Rights** _____

_____

3. **boycott** _____

_____

4. **branches of government** _____

_____

5. **checks and balances** _____

_____

6. **eminent domain** _____

_____

7. **laissez-faire** _____

_____

8. **lobbyist** _____

_____

9. ratification _____

_____

10. veto _____

_____

Learning United States History and Political Science Terms from Context Clues: Set 2

1. **filibuster** (FIL ə bus tər)—noun

   A technique by which a minority of senators attempts to block the passage of a bill through continuous talk, thus delaying the vote.

   The *filibuster* in the Senate has lasted six hours so far, so the controversial bill has never come to a vote.

2. **impeachment** (im PĒCH mənt)—noun

   The constitutional procedure for removing the president and other high federal officials from office for illegal activities.

   Andrew Johnson, who served as president from 1865 to 1869 after the assassination of Abraham Lincoln, and William Clinton, who served as president from 1993 to 2000, are the only presidents to have faced *impeachment;* both were acquitted by the Senate.

3. **lame duck** (LĀM DUK)—adjective + noun

   An elected official whose influence is weakened because he or she is soon to leave office, as a result of either an election defeat or a law that prohibits another term.

   The senator, a *lame duck* as a result of losing the fall election, announced he would be joining a Washington, D.C., law firm after his senate term expires.

4. **red herring** (RED HER ing)—adjective + noun

   An irrelevant topic that diverts attention from the main issue.

   The candidate running against the senator angrily claims that the senator's remarks about her divorce years ago is a *red herring* to draw attention away from his poor record regarding such important matters as education, universal medical coverage, and the national debt.

5. appropriation (ə PRŌ prē Ā shən)—noun

A grant of money to finance a government program.

Congress has approved an *appropriation* to improve the interstate highway system.

6. entitlement (en TĪ təl mənt)—noun

A law requiring the government to pay money to people who meet specific eligibility requirements.

Workers who have social security payments deducted from their salaries are eligible for an *entitlement* when they retire.

7. patronage (PĀ trə nij)—noun

The power given to political leaders to make appointments to government positions and to award contracts and favors to friends and supporters.

Patronage can lead to abuses, but it can also lead to benefits if political leaders appoint only well-qualified people to government positions.

8. referendum (REF ə REN dəm)—noun

An electoral device by which voters can either approve or disapprove of an action taken by their state legislature.

The *referendum* indicated overwhelming approval of the proposed dam project.

9. gerrymandering (JER ē MAN dər ing)—noun or verb

Establishment of a voting district in such a way as to give an advantage to one political party.

The Democrats accused the Republicans of *gerrymandering* the boundaries of the metropolitan area to obtain a voting advantage during elections.

10. sedition (sə DISH ən)—noun

Actions causing public disorder or rebellion against the government.

An illegal attempt to overthrow the government is called *sedition.*

Matching Academic Terms and Definitions: Set 2

Match each definition with the term it defines.

_e_	**1.** referendum	**a.** officerholder whose term is almost over
_g_	**2.** red herring	**b.** power to make appointments and
_i_	**3.** appropriation	grant favors to supporters
_f_	**4.** filibuster	**c.** redrawing voting boundaries to gain
_b_	**5.** patronage	an election advantage
_a_	**6.** lame duck	**d.** public disorder against the government

_h_	**7.** impeachment
_c_	**8.** gerrymandering
_j_	**9.** entitlement
_d_	**10.** sedition

e. enables citizens of a state to vote on action taken by its legislature

f. continuous talk designed to stop a bill from coming to a vote

g. something that distracts from the chief issue

h. method of removing high government officials from office

i. money budgeted for a government program

j. requires the government to pay money to qualified people

Fill-Ins with Academic Terms: Set 2

In each space, write the appropriate term from those listed below.

filibuster	appropriation	referendum	impeachment	entitlement
gerrymandering	lame duck	patronage	sedition	red herring

1. When Grover Cleveland became president, he exercised his power of _____patronage_____ by appointing thousands of Democrats to postal positions.

2. A(n) _____entitlement_____ is a financial obligation the government has to people meeting specific criteria.

3. Congress's _____appropriation_____ for space research has been increased for next year.

4. Attempts to overthrow the government through sabotage are considered _____sedition_____ .

5. A state _____referendum_____ to be held this fall will enable the voters of this state to express their feelings regarding the controversial environmental law.

6. _____Gerrymandering_____ is a term dating back to 1812 when Elbridge Gerry, the governor of Massachusetts, had the boundaries of voting districts redrawn to gain an election advantage.

7. The newspaper editorial maintains that the crime issue is a(n) _____red herring_____ that blurs the city's major problem, which, in the editor's opinion, is skyrocketing property taxes.

8. The mayor, now a(n) _____lame duck_____ , said she will resume her teaching career after her present term expires.

9. Many historians believe President Nixon would have faced certain _____impeachment_____ if he hadn't resigned after the Watergate scandal.

10. The senator's _____filibuster_____ lasted nine hours in an effort to delay the vote on the bill.

Related Meanings: Set 2

If the words opposite each other are similar in meaning, write Yes *in the space; if they are unrelated, write* No.

1. red herring ___Yes___ smokescreen that keeps attention away from the main issue
2. impeachment ___No___ presidential inauguration
3. lame duck ___No___ officerholder found guilty of a crime
4. filibuster ___Yes___ stalling talk
5. patronage ___No___ rebellion against the government
6. referendum ___Yes___ voters approve or reject an action of the state legislature
7. sedition ___No___ a bill that has been enacted into law
8. entitlement ___No___ officerholder's authority to appoint supporters to political jobs
9. gerrymandering ___No___ political bribery
10. appropriation ___No___ the seizing of illegal goods crossing state lines

Writing Your Own Definitions: Set 2

Write either an original sentence or a definition for each term that clearly demonstrates your master of its meaning as used in United States history and political science. Answers will vary.

1. **filibuster** _____

_____

2. **impeachment** _____

_____

3. **lame duck** _____

_____

4. **red herring** _____

_____

5. **appropriation** _____

_____

6. **entitlement** _____

_____

7. **patronage** _____

_____

8. referendum _____

_____

9. gerrymandering _____

_____

10. sedition _____

_____

Completing a Passage: United States History and Political Science

After reading the selection, fill in each space with one of the terms listed below.

laissez-faire	impeachment	judicial	appropriation	red herring
executive	lobbyist	sedition	legislative	boycott

WILLIAM H. SEWARD

The candidate heavily favored to win the Republican nomination for president in 1860 was William H. Seward, a senator from the state of New York. Seward, born in 1801, had also been a successful lawyer and a popular New York governor. He was well acquainted with all areas of governmental responsibilities, including those of the _____legislative_____ , _____executive_____ , and _____judicial_____ branches. In addition, he was aware that the slavery issue was no _____red herring_____ intended to distract voters from the important issues of the coming national election; he knew slavery was the main issue that had to be dealt with once and for all. Seward had been an abolitionist (person in favor of abolishing slavery) for many years. However, to the utter shock of many at the convention, including Seward, Abraham Lincoln of Illinois won the Republican nomination and later the national election that followed in the fall.

After the election, Lincoln selected Seward to serve in his Cabinet as secretary of state. Like many other members of the Cabinet, Seward initially underestimated Lincoln's political skills and intelligence as well as his determination to stamp out all acts of _____sedition_____ against the federal government. Soon, however, Seward and most of the others came to realize that Lincoln was a remarkable man who was uniquely gifted to lead the nation during the worst crisis it had ever faced. Along with Secretary of War Stanton, Seward became one of Lincoln's closest allies, admirers, and friends throughout his presidency.

During the Civil War, Seward was successful in persuading the European nations to adopt a policy of noninterference, or ___laissez-faire___, regarding the conflict, and many of these nations also agreed to ___boycott___ cotton and other products from the South.

On April 14, 1865, only days after Lee surrendered to Grant, President Lincoln was shot at Ford's Theater by John Wilkes Booth (he died on April 15). While this tragedy was taking place, one of Booth's co-conspirators, Lewis Powell, entered Seward's bedroom and repeatedly attacked him with a knife, slashing deep gashes in his face and neck. Only the fact that Seward was wearing a heavy neck brace because of a recent accident prevented Powell from landing a fatal blow.

Remarkably, Seward eventually recovered from both his carriage injuries and his knife wounds; tragically, however, Frances, his wife, and Fanny, one of his daughters, never recovered from the shock and anxiety caused by Lincoln's assassination and Powell's vicious attack on the family. Mrs. Seward died just three months later, and Fanny passed away the following year.

Seward, despite his injuries and deep personal sorrow, continued to perform his secretary of state duties, serving throughout President Andrew Johnson's extremely difficult term in office. In 1867, Seward secured an ___appropriation___ from Congress to purchase Alaska from Russia for $7,200,000. Critics of that day labeled the purchase "Seward's Folly" and "Seward's Icebox," but time has shown it to be the best territorial purchase ever made by the United States. Around this time, Congress, unhappy with President Johnson's policies, conducted ___impeachment___ proceedings against the president. Though President Johnson was eventually cleared by the slimmest of margins, his presidency was never free from bitter conflicts between him and Congress.

After Ulysses S. Grant was elected president in 1868, Seward finally retired from public life, but unlike so many retired politicians before and after him, he did not become a ___lobbyist___ for those seeking to do business with the federal government. Instead, Seward traveled around the world for fourteen months before returning to his beloved home in Auburn, New York, where he died in 1872.

William H. Seward was a hardworking, effective, and faithful servant to his nation during a critical time in its history, and as a result, he is fairly ranked among the best of those who have served our country as secretary of state.

FEATURED WORD: laissez-faire

Laissez-faire—a government's policy of non-interference in the nation's businesses and in the affairs of other countries:

- During the 19th century, the federal government followed a laissez-faire approach in the development of the nation's industries and businesses.

Origin: <French—*laissez* (let) and *faire* (to do)

Family words: laissez-faireism (n)

Image to remember: people who are tolerant of opinions other than their own

Write an original sentence using *laissez-faire*:

____

____

____

capital (1) a town or city that serves as the official seat of government; (2) wealth in the form of money or property:

>Washington, D.C., is the <u>capital</u> city of the United States.

>The couple raised enough <u>capital</u> to start a restaurant of their own.

capitol refers to the building where legislators meet:

>Congress meets in the <u>Capitol</u> Building in Washington, D.C.

Circle the correct answer:

1. Much of my aunt's (capital)/ capitol is invested in U.S. Savings Bonds.

2. The dome on the capital /(capitol) building looks like it is made of gold.

3. Is Trenton the (capital)/ capitol of New Jersey?

Write original sentences using these words:

1. **capital (meaning #1):** _____

2. **capital (meaning #2):** _____

3. **capitol:** _____

Learning Legal Terms from Context Clues: Set 1

The legal terms included in this chapter are among those that must be understood to gain insight into the fundamental concepts presented in introductory paralegal, law enforcement, criminal justice, and other such courses.

1. **acquittal** (ə KWIT əl)—noun

   The finding of the court or jury that the defendant is not guilty.

   After the defendant's *acquittal* was announced, her family rushed to embrace her.

2. **adjudicate** (a JOO də kāt)—verb

   To settle by legal decision as a judge or jury does; to judge.

   A judge will *adjudicate* the divorce settlement, including custody of the children.

3. **bail** (BĀL)—noun

   Security, usually in the form of money, used to release an accused person prior to a trial or hearing.

   The defendant would forfeit a *bail* of $10,000 if he failed to appear at his hearing.

4. **booking** (BOOK ing)—noun

   The process of entering the suspect's name, the offense with which the suspect is charged, and other pertinent information in the official arrest record.

   An officer at the police station used a computer to complete the *booking;* he typed information about the suspect and the crime with which he was charged.

5. **commute** (kə MYOOT)—verb

   To reduce a guilty person's sentence or punishment.

   The judge *commuted* the prisoner's sentence from eight to five years.

6. **culpability** (kul pə BIL ə tē)—noun

   Blameworthiness; guiltiness.

   The stockbroker admitted his *culpability* for the illegal business practices members of his firm had been following.

282

7. indict (in DĪT)—verb

To formally charge a person with a criminal offense.

The grand jury is deliberating whether to *indict* the driver for vehicular manslaughter.

8. perjury (PUR jə rē)—noun

Lying under oath.

Because it was later established that the defense witness had lied, she was indicted for *perjury*.

9. recidivism (ri SID ə viz əm)—noun

Relapsing into a previous behavior pattern, especially criminal behavior.

Because of the state's high rate of repeat offenders during the past decade, a special governor's commission has recommended new prison reform and rehabilitation programs in an effort to reduce such *recidivism*.

10. tort (TORT) **law**—noun + noun

Law that is concerned with wrongful acts resulting in injury or damage for which people can seek legal satisfaction.

Tort law is a branch of civil law (as opposed to criminal or contract law) concerned with compensating individuals for personal injury, property damage, or other losses.

Matching Academic Terms and Definitions: Set 1

Match each definition with the term it defines.

_f_	**1.** culpability	**a.** to reduce the severity of the punishment
_j_	**2.** tort law	**b.** process of entering suspect's name and other information in the official arrest record
_g_	**3.** recidivism	
_b_	**4.** booking	**c.** lying under oath
_i_	**5.** indict	**d.** to judge
_d_	**6.** adjudicate	**e.** a "not guilty" verdict
_a_	**7.** commute	**f.** the deserving of fault or blame
_e_	**8.** acquittal	**g.** backsliding to previous behavior
_h_	**9.** bail	**h.** security posted to gain the release of the accused before the trial
_c_	**10.** perjury	**i.** to formally charge a person with a crime
		j. branch of law specializing in personal injury and property damage cases

Fill-Ins with Academic Terms: Set 1

In each space, write the appropriate term from those listed below.

acquittal	bail	commuted	indict	recidivism
adjudicate	booking	culpability	perjury	tort law

1. The driver acknowledged his _____culpability_____ for the accident as he confessed to running a red light.

2. Libel suits are among the concerns of _____tort law_____.

3. The grand jury decided not to _____indict_____ the suspect because of a lack of compelling evidence.

4. Researchers are constantly attempting to identify the causes of _____recidivism_____ so steps can be taken to help former criminals lead productive lives and stay out of prison.

5. Though she knew her testimony would prove damaging to her friend's defense, she resolved to tell the truth about the incident rather than commit _____perjury_____.

6. The _____booking_____ of the suspect took considerable time because he was most uncooperative, even refusing to give his name, address, and date of birth.

7. The suspect's family rushed to embrace him after his _____acquittal_____.

8. Because his client has been a model prisoner, the lawyer is confident his client's sentence will be _____commuted_____ from twenty to ten years.

9. The business partners couldn't reach an agreement, so they consulted an expert in contract law to _____adjudicate_____ the matter.

10. The accused remained in jail after failing to raise the necessary money for his _____bail_____.

Related Meanings: Set 1

If the words opposite each other are similar in meaning, write Yes *in the space; if they are unrelated, write* No.

1. indict — _Yes_ charge with a crime
2. acquittal — _Yes_ free from the accusation
3. perjury — _No_ hung jury
4. adjudicate — _Yes_ judge
5. tort law — _No_ having to do with the legality of contracts
6. recidivism — _Yes_ backsliding into crime
7. commute — _No_ plead a case
8. bail — _No_ flee before a trial
9. booking — _No_ reduction of a sentence
10. culpability — _No_ lying under oath

Writing Your Own Definitions: Set 1

Write an original sentence or a definition for each term that clearly demonstrates your mastery of its meaning as used in law. Answers will vary.

1. **acquittal** _____
   _____

2. **adjudicate** _____
   _____

3. **bail** _____
   _____

4. **booking** _____
   _____

5. **commute** _____
   _____

6. **culpability** _____
   _____

7. **indict** _____
   _____

8. **perjury** _____
   _____

9. **recidivism** _____
   _____

10. **tort law** _____
    _____

Learning Legal Terms from Context Clues: Set 2

1. **appeal** (ə PĒL)—noun

   The request for a new hearing of a case already tried.
   After the guilty verdict was announced, the defendant's lawyer immediately announced she would seek an *appeal*.

2. **change of venue** (CHĀNJ uv VEN yoo)—noun + preposition + noun

A change in the place of the defendant's trial, generally from the county where the crime was committed to another judicial district.

The judge agreed to the defense lawyer's request for a *change of venue* because of the widespread publicity about the crime.

3. <u>concurrent</u> **sentencing,** <u>consecutive</u> **sentencing** (kən KUR ənt, kən SEK yə tiv)—nouns

<u>Concurrent</u> sentencing is when two or more sentences are handed out on the same occasion to be served during a common time period.

<u>Consecutive</u> sentencing is when two or more sentences are handed out on the same occasion and the time to be served is to be equal to the sum of the sentences.

The defendants, found guilty on all charges, hoped to receive *concurrent sentencing;* however, they received *consecutive sentencing,* so they must serve five years in prison for each crime they committed.

4. <u>ex</u>**tradite** (EK str ə dī t)—verb

To transfer an accused person to the authorities with the legal jurisdiction to try the case.

Texas officials agreed to *extradite* the suspect to Florida, where she had escaped from prison.

5. **felony** (FEL ə nē)—noun

A major crime punishable by death or a long prison sentence.

Kidnapping is a *felony* punishable by death in many states.

6. <u>mis</u>**demeanor** (mis də MĒ nər)—noun

A crime punishable by a fine and/or imprisonment, usually for less than a year; a misdemeanor is a less serious crime than a felony.

The protestors were warned they would be charged with a *misdemeanor* unless they stopped blocking the entrance to the building.

7. <u>sub</u>**poena** (sə PĒ nə)—noun

A legal order requiring a person to appear in court to give testimony.

The *subpoena* requires the supervisor to testify in court regarding the safety procedures being followed on the day the accident occurred.

8. **habeas corpus** (HĀ bē əs KOR pəs)—noun. Latin term meaning "you have the body."

A legal order commanding a person being held in custody to be produced before a court to determine the lawfulness of the person's confinement.

A request for *habeas corpus* was granted by the judge to determine whether the lawyer's client should be released until his scheduled deportation hearing.

9. **injunction** (in JUNGK shən)—noun

A legal order directing a person to refrain from doing some activity. An injunction is a preventive measure to guard against future injuries; it does not provide a remedy for past injuries.

An *injunction* prohibits the former employee from coming within three blocks of the business establishment where he once worked.

10. **jurisprudence** (JUR is PROOD ns)—noun

The science of law. Jurisprudence is also used as a synonym (word having the same meaning) for law.

Law courses are challenging because the study of *jurisprudence* encompasses all matters relating to our legal system.

11. **litigation** (lit ə GĀ shən)—noun

A legal suit in a court of law.

Unfortunately, *litigation* was necessary to settle our boundary dispute with our once-friendly neighbors.

12. **plaintiff** (PLAYN tif)—noun
defendant (də FEN dənt)—noun
litigants (LIT ə gənts)—noun

The plaintiff is the one who legally complains and initiates court action against someone; the defendant is the one being sued or, in a criminal case, the one being accused. The plaintiff and defendant are known as the litigants, that is, the parties involved in a lawsuit.

The *litigants* in the lawsuit are Mr. Dawson and Mr. Burnell. Mr. Dawson, the *plaintiff*, says he was never paid in full for building Mr. Burnell's house. Mr. Burnell, the *defendant*, contends Mr. Dawson was not paid in full because he had failed to fulfill all the terms of their contract.

Matching Academic Terms and Definitions: Set 2

Match each definition with the term it defines.

A

_c_	**1.** felony	**a.** the science of law
_f_	**2.** habeas corpus	**b.** legal suit in a court of law
_d_	**3.** extradite	**c.** major crime punishable by death or a severe prison sentence
_h_	**4.** misdemeanor	
_g_	**5.** defendant	**d.** to send a prisoner to authorities in another state
_b_	**6.** litigation	**e.** describes jail time served during the same time period
_e_	**7.** concurrent	
_a_	**8.** jurisprudence	**f.** requires a person be brought before the court to determine whether he or she is being held legally
		g. person being sued or accused of a crime
		h. crime punishable by a fine and/or imprisonment

B

_d_	**1.** subpoena	**a.** alteration of the location of a defendant's trial
_g_	**2.** appeal	
_f_	**3.** litigants	**b.** legal order barring a person from doing some activity
_e_	**4.** consecutive	
_a_	**5.** change of venue	**c.** person bringing court action against someone
_c_	**6.** plaintiff	
_b_	**7.** injunction	**d.** legal order requiring a person to testify in court
		e. describes sentences served one after the other
		f. parties involved in a lawsuit
		g. request for a new trial

Fill-Ins with Academic Terms: Set 2

In each space, write the appropriate term from those listed below.

A

appeal	consecutive	extradite	felony
subpoena	plaintiff	defendant	litigants

1. Nevada officials requested California authorities to _____extradite_____ the suspect to Nevada.

2. The prisoner received _____consecutive_____ sentencing, so he will serve a total of twenty years as each sentence called for ten years in prison.

3. The ___litigants___ in the case are a fired chauffeur; the
___plaintiff___ , who is suing his ex-boss; and the ___defendant___ ,
who is being sued for breach of contract.

4. Robbing a bank is a(n) ___felony___ , so the judge will undoubtedly
sentence the guilty person to a long prison term.

5. Because she was a close friend of the accused, my neighbor wasn't surprised
when she was served with a(n) ___subpoena___ requiring her to give testimony at his trial.

6. The defendant and her lawyer were stunned by the jury's verdict, and they made it
clear they would file a(n) ___appeal___ as soon as possible.

B

change of venue   concurrent   misdemeanor   habeas corpus
injunction   jurisprudence litigation

1. The teenagers were charged with a(n) ___misdemeanor___ after they were
caught spray-painting the front of the community swimming pool.

2. She was given ___concurrent___ sentencing, so she will serve a total of ten
years in federal prison even though the two crimes she was found guilty of each
carry a ten-year sentence.

3. The judge issued a(n) ___injunction___ prohibiting the young man from
having any further contact with his ex-girlfriend.

4. The lawyer assured his clients that the judge would agree to issue an order of
___habeas corpus___ , so they would either be brought to court and charged
with a crime or they would be released.

5. The community's widespread hostility against the defendant resulted in a(n)
___change of venue___ for the trial.

6. The former employee was threatened with ___litigation___ unless he
returned the company car within two days.

7. To earn a degree in ___jurisprudence___ generally takes three years of
full-time study beyond the bachelor's degree.

Related Meanings: Set 2

If the words opposite each other are similar in meaning, write Yes *in the space; if they
are unrelated, write* No.

1. extradite   ___No___ inconclusive evidence
2. litigation   ___Yes___ the taking of legal action leading to a court trial
3. appeal   ___No___ request for a different location for the trial
4. misdemeanor   ___No___ illegal arrest
5. felony   ___Yes___ major criminal offense
6. consecutive   ___Yes___ sentences served one after the other

7. concurrent	_Yes_	sentences served at the same time
8. change of venue	_No_	request for a new trial
9. plaintiff	_Yes_	person suing
10. injunction	_No_	requires a court appearance to give testimony
11. habeas corpus	_No_	crime victim's body
12. defendant	_Yes_	person being sued or accused of a crime
13. subpoena	_No_	the formal study of law
14. litigants	_Yes_	parties involved in a lawsuit
15. jurisprudence	_No_	a case decided by a jury rather than a judge

Writing Your Own Definitions: Set 2

Write an original sentence or a definition for each term that clearly demonstrates your mastery of its meaning as used in law. Answers will vary.

1. **appeal** _____

_____

2. **change of venue** _____

_____

3. **concurrent sentencing** _____

_____

4. **consecutive sentencing** _____

_____

5. **extradite** _____

_____

6. **felony** _____

_____

7. **misdemeanor** _____

_____

8. **subpoena** _____

_____

9. **habeas corpus** _____

_____

10. **injunction** _____

_____

11. jurisprudence _____

_____

12. litigation _____

_____

13. plaintiff _____

_____

14. defendant _____

_____

15. litigants _____

_____

Completing a Passage: Law

After reading the selection, fill in each space with one of the terms listed below.

booking	bail	felony	tort	jurisprudence
plaintiff	subpoenaing	appeal	defendant	adjudicated
indicted	acquittal	habeas corpus	misdemeanor	change of venue

PUBLIC DEFENDER

A public defender is a licensed lawyer, but unlike a defense attorney in private practice who is paid by the clients he or she chooses to represent, a public defender is paid with public funds (or by some non-profit agency) and assigned by the court to represent clients without financial resources. The 1963 *Gideon v. Wainwright* trial is responsible for guaranteeing that every person, even ones unable to pay, is entitled to legal counsel. Gideon, the ____defendant____, was accused by Wainwright, the ____plaintiff____, of breaking into his bar and stealing money and beer. Gideon was __indicted__ and charged with a ____felony____, not a ____misdemeanor____, because breaking and entering to commit a robbery is considered a major criminal offense.

At his trial, Gideon, who could not afford to hire a lawyer, maintained that it was fundamentally unfair that he had to attempt to defend himself against a trained prosecuting attorney. The Supreme Court agreed that Gideon was entitled to qualified legal counsel, and although some courts had provided free attorneys prior to the *Gideon v. Wainwright* ruling, this decision soon led to the creation of public defender programs throughout the country.

Full-time public defenders typically handle only criminal cases, so it is a rare occasion when they are assigned cases involving _____tort_____ law as they are usually not allowed to take cases involving personal injuries or civil disputes.

A public defender has the same rights as any defense lawyer, including that of being present during his or her client's _____booking_____ at the police station. During the pretrial hearing, a public defender may ask the judge to execute an order of _____habeas corpus_____ so that his or her client appears in court, which often makes possible the arrangement of _____bail_____ so that the client can be released until his or her case is _____adjudicated_____, or settled by legal decision. Also during a pretrial hearing, a public defender may ask the judge for a _____change of venue_____ because he or she feels the accused cannot receive a fair trial at the scheduled location. Before and during the trial, the public defender can request the _____subpoenaing_____ of witnesses to provide testimony on behalf of his or her client. And if the trial results in a conviction rather than an _____acquittal_____ for his or her client, the public defender may file an _____appeal_____, that is, a request for a new trial.

The 1963 Supreme Court ruling that poor people accused of serious crimes are entitled to legal counsel is considered by legal historians as a major advancement in _____jurisprudence_____. Public defenders provide evidence every day that this legal advancement is being observed in all of our nation's courts.

FEATURED WORD: subpoena

Subpoena—a legal order requiring a person to appear in court to give testimony:

- The passenger that was in the car fleeing from the accident scene received a <u>subpoena</u> to testify in court.

Origin: From the Middle English (1100–1500) word *suppena* <Latin *sub* (under) and *poena* (penalty). Has also been used as a verb since 1640: The bank's loan officer was <u>subpoenaed</u> to provide testimony in a bankruptcy case.

Family words: subpoenaed (v), subpoenaing (v), subpoenas (n)

Image to remember: someone giving testimony in a trial

Write an original sentence using *subpoena*:

_____

_____

_____

MASTERING CONFUSING WORDS	its / it's

its a possessive pronoun:

The car spun off the track when one of <u>its</u> tires came off <u>its</u> rim.

it's a contraction for "it is" or "it has":

Do you think <u>it's</u> time for us to go? (Do you think <u>it is</u> time for us to go?) <u>It's</u> been raining for three consecutive days. (<u>It has</u> been raining for three consecutive days.)

[Suggestion: If you could use <u>it is</u> in your sentence, use <u>it's</u>, that is, <u>its</u> with an apostrophe, as in this example: "Mary doesn't think <u>it's</u> likely she'll be able to go with us" because "Mary doesn't think <u>it is</u> likely she'll be able to go with us" is also correct. However, in "The dog cut <u>its</u> paw on a piece of glass," the <u>its</u> doesn't have an apostrophe because "The dog hurt <u>it is</u> paw on a piece of glass" doesn't work.]

Circle the correct answer:

1. Lana realizes that <u>its</u> / <u>it's</u> not too early to think about what she wants to major in.

2. Although <u>its</u> / <u>it's</u> star player was injured, the team won the tournament.

3. <u>Its</u> / <u>It's</u> been interesting working at a grocery store for the past three years, but I'd like to find a restaurant job now.

4. Why? Do you think <u>its</u> / <u>it's</u> easy to be on your feet for eight straight hours waiting on customers?

Write original sentences using these words:

1. **its:** _____

2. **it's (it is):** _____

3. **it's (it has):** _____

REVIEW TEST, CHAPTERS 18–23

Matching Academic Terms and Definitions

Match each academic term with its definition.

_e_	**1.** figures of speech	**a.**	evidence directly experienced or observed
_h_	**2.** genre	**b.**	anything that hinders communication
_a_	**3.** empirical	**c.**	behaviors reflecting society's moral standards
_b_	**4.** noise	**d.**	strategies adopted to protect one's self-image
_i_	**5.** placebo	**e.**	imaginative expressions used in writing and speaking
_j_	**6.** psychoanalysis	**f.**	describes an illness triggered by emotional troubles
_d_	**7.** defense mechanisms		
_g_	**8.** demography	**g.**	study of population figures
_f_	**9.** psychosomatic	**h.**	category or type of literature
_c_	**10.** social norms	**i.**	inactive substance used in experiments
		j.	therapy that emphasizes the exploration of one's childhood and dreams

Related Meanings

If the words opposite each other are similar in meaning, write Yes *in the space; if they are unrelated, write* No.

1.	branches of government	Yes	legislative, executive, judicial
2.	amendment	Yes	amendment or change to the Constitution
3.	indict	No	flee before a trial
4.	acquittal	No	a guilty verdict
5.	flashback	No	plot of a story
6.	antagonist	Yes	villain
7.	fallacies	No	jokes
8.	induction	Yes	drawing a conclusion after gathering evidence
9.	therapeutic	No	personality disorder
10.	superego	Yes	honest and moral side of one's personality
11.	values	Yes	ideas about what is good, wise, and worthwhile
12.	peer group	No	those of the upper class

Completing a Passage

After reading the selection, fill in each space with one of the terms listed below.

kinesics	premise	transitions	subjective	rapport	catalyst
decoding	venue	objective	impromptu	encoding	

GIVING A SPUR-OF-THE-MOMENT TALK

A major _____premise_____ of our speech teacher, Dr. Stillings, is that the steps involved in giving a(n) _____impromptu_____ speech are practically identical to those for giving any type of speech, with the major difference obviously being that little time can be devoted to each step. Nevertheless, Dr. Stillings insisted, we can usually make quick but helpful assumptions about our audience and the _____venue_____, or location, in which we're speaking; then, we likely will be in a position to begin establishing _____rapport_____ with our audience, perhaps by deciding to tell a joke, as humor often serves as a(n) _____catalyst_____ .

Related to the preceding steps is deciding when (or if) we should be _____objective_____ (not expressing any biases) and when (or if) we should be _____subjective_____ (expressing our personal feelings). In addition, Dr. Stillings reminded us that gestures and other forms of _____kinesics_____ generally contribute to the effectiveness of a speech, and _____transitions_____, such as *for example* and *on the other hand,* are helpful for linking information.

Finally, Dr. Stillings stressed that our responsibility in the _____encoding_____ of our thoughts into messages is to express what we wish to convey in the simplest and clearest way possible so that members of our audience will not struggle when _____decoding_____ our remarks.

Writing Your Own Definitions

Write either an original sentence or a definition for each of these academic terms that clearly demonstrates your mastery of its meaning.   Answers will vary.

1. veto _____

_____

2. Bill of Rights _____

_____

3. perjury _____

_____

4. bibliography _____

_____

5. nonsexist language _____

_____

Matching Academic Terms and Definitions

Match each academic term with its definition.

j	**1.** checks and balances	**a.**	sentence structure in which the verb "acts" upon the subject: "The solo <u>was sung</u> by Megan."
d	**2.** ratification		
f	**3.** adjudicate		
h	**4.** agrarian	**b.**	sentence structure in which the subject "does" the verb: "<u>Megan</u> <u>sang</u> the solo."
c	**5.** prose		
k	**6.** plagiarism	**c.**	writing that is not poetry
e	**7.** appeal	**d.**	legislative power to approve or disapprove treaties and government appointments
a	**8.** passive		
l	**9.** hypothesis	**e.**	legal request for a new trial
i	**10.** intrinsic	**f.**	to judge or to determine by legal means
b	**11.** active	**g.**	organization with numerous officials and rigid rules
g	**12.** bureaucracy		

h. relating to rural life

i. motivation coming from within a person

j. constitutional methods by which the branches of government can limit one another's actions

k. stealing the words of others

l. a reasonable assumption; a theory

Related Meanings

If the words opposite each other are similar in meaning, write Yes _in the space; if they are unrelated, write_ No.

1.	variable	Yes	factor manipulated in an experiment
2.	introvert	No	person with a friendly, outgoing personality
3.	laissez-faire	Yes	non-interference
4.	boycott	No	representative for a special group
5.	patriarchal	Yes	family headed by father
6.	booking	No	lying under oath
7.	bail	Yes	security pledged to gain the release of the accused
8.	denotation	No	word's suggested meanings
9.	literal	Yes	refers to the exact meaning of a word
10.	enunciation	Yes	precise pronunciation of words

Fill-Ins with Academic Terms

In each space, write the appropriate term from those listed below.

canon	experimental	anthology	personification	speaking
synopsis	id	multimedia	ego	alliteration
cognitive	metaphor	control	protagonist	

1. "The stars were winking at us" is an example of _____personification_____ .

2. "Funny Fred fell forward for Fiona" is an example of _____alliteration_____ .

3. "Jack became a roaring lion every time his computer broke down" is a figure of speech known as a(n) _____metaphor_____ .

4. I've finally finished my _____synopsis_____ of the book I read for my lit class.

5. Can you remember the name of the heroine, or _____protagonist_____ , in Pearl Buck's novel *The Good Earth*?

6. This thick _____anthology_____ includes short stories, essays, plays, and poems.

7. The best-known books in Mark Twain's _____canon_____ are, of course, those featuring Tom Sawyer and Huckleberry Finn.

8. The _____speaking_____ voice is concerned with such matters as volume, tone, and tempo.

9. A(n) _____multimedia_____ presentation features graphics often displayed by using a computer.

10. If you are assigned to the _____experimental_____ group, your meals will be supplemented with a high-potency multivitamin; on the other hand, if you are assigned to the _____control_____ group, you will receive the same meals as the other group but not the multivitamin.

11. _____Cognitive_____ therapy is a psychological approach designed to help individuals change harmful thought patterns to more constructive ones.

12. According to Freud, the _____ego_____ is responsible for logical thinking while the _____id_____ is the instinctive part of a person's personality.

Related Meanings

If the words opposite each other are similar in meaning, write Yes *in the space; if they are unrelated, write* No.

1. behavior therapy — No — psychological treatment emphasizing medications
2. Oedipus complex — Yes — child's subconscious sexual attraction to the parent of the opposite sex
3. neurosis — No — emotional disorder characterized by a loss of reality
4. psychosis — No — cleansing of unhealthy emotions

5. urbanism	Yes	relating to cities
6. acculturation	Yes	adopting new patterns of life after being exposed to a new society
7. culture	No	scientific study of mariners, art, music, and education
8. ethnic group	Yes	group within a society sharing the same traits, such as customs, nationality, and religion
9. ethnocentrism	No	person's social standing in society
10. gerontology	No	scientific study of adolescence
11. sanction	Yes	reinforces or discourages certain actions
12. status	No	relating to state government

Writing Your Own Definitions

Write either an original sentence or a definition for each of these academic terms that clearly demonstrates your mastery of its meaning. Answers will vary.

1. filibuster _____

_____

2. gerrymandering _____

_____

3. red herring _____

_____

4. change of venue _____

_____

5. plaintiff _____

_____

Matching Academic Terms and Definitions

Match each academic term with its definition.

f	**1.** eminent domain	**a.** legal notice requiring a person to give testi-mony in court
e	**2.** habeas corpus	
i	**3.** extradite	**b.** removal of the president or other high government officials from office
j	**4.** patronage	
h	**5.** sedition	**c.** crime punishable by death or a long prison sentence
k	**6.** recidivism	
b	**7.** impeachment	**d.** officeholder whose term is almost completed
l	**8.** misdemeanor	
d	**9.** lame duck	**e.** legal order requiring a person held in custody to be brought before the court

_____a_____ **10.** subpoena

_____g_____ **11.** appropriation

_____c_____ **12.** felony

f. gives government the legal right to seize private property

g. grant of money to finance a government program

h. public rebellion against the government

i. sending a prisoner to authorities in another state

j. elected officials' use of power to appoint supporters to government positions

k. backsliding to a previous behavior, such as a person returning to a life of crime

l. crime punishable by a fine and/or imprisonment

Mastering Confusing Words

Circle the correct answer.

1. After angrily slamming the door, Vicki (threw / through) her books on the table.

2. Would you like a piece of pecan pie for (desert / dessert)?

3. Jim keeps his (loose / lose) change in an old broken coffee cup.

4. Sharon went (farther / further) each day until she could comfortably jog three miles.

5. Anita cautioned, "Be careful that you don't (loose / lose) your car keys again."

6. It's hard to believe that this fertile region was once a vast (desert / dessert).

7. The judge asked the accused, "Do you have anything (farther / further) to say?"

8. After walking (threw / through) the lobby, you'll find the gift shop on your left.

9. Fred would never (desert / dessert) his friends if they needed his help.

10. The (capital / capitol) building was swarming with legislators, lobbyists, and media people.

11. Carson City, not Las Vegas, is the (capital / capitol) of Nevada.

12. I don't think (it's / its) going to snow because (it's / its) not cold enough.

13. I like the jacket, but I think (it's / its) color is too bright.

Crossword Puzzle

Solve the crossword by using the following academic terms:

foreshadowing	extrovert	hyperbole	injunction
sibling	satire	culpability	matriarchal
extrinsic	lobbyist	simile	critique
connotations	deduction	utopia	

(crossword grid)

Across down the grid: ¹s, ²f, ³m; ⁴c o n n o t a t i o n s, ⁵u t o p i a; m; ⁶s a t i r e; ⁷c l; ⁸h y p e r b o l e; i; t; ⁹c; ¹⁰e x t r i n s i c; q; ¹¹i; ¹²d ¹³e d u c t i o n; x e; r ¹⁴s i b l i n g; o; v; e ¹⁵l o b b y i s t; r; t

ACROSS

4. suggested meanings of words
5. imaginary place where everything is perfect
6. sarcastic humor
8. exaggeration
10. motivation coming from outside the person
12. reasoning starting with an accepted principle
14. a brother or a sister
15. a representative for a special-interest group

DOWN

1. comparison using *like* or *as*
2. hint as to what is going to happen
3. describes family headed by mother
7. an in-depth review
9. state of being guilty, deserving of blame
11. legal order barring a person from doing something
13. friendly, sociable person

Learning Business and Economic Terms from Context Clues: Set 1

A degree in business is the goal of thousands of college students; in addition, thousands of others elect, or are advised to take, a business or economics course so they can gain insight into the nation's economic system. Learning the terms included in this chapter will help you grasp the concepts dealt with in business and economics.

1. **commodities** (kə MOD i tēs)—noun

   Products bought, sold, or traded.

   Food, clothes, metals, and cars are among the country's chief *commodities*.

2. **GNP** (gross national product)—noun

   The total value of goods and services produced by a nation's business during a specific period, usually a year.

   GNP is the official measure of a nation's economic output.

3. **balance of trade** (BAL əns uv TRĀD)—noun + preposition + noun

   The relationship between a nation's exports (what it sells to other countries) and its imports (what it buys from other countries).

   The *balance of trade* for the United States in the past four months indicates that more goods were bought from other countries than were sold abroad.

4. **reciprocity** (RES ə PROS i tē)—noun

   A mutual exchange policy in which each part grants the other corresponding privileges. (Informally, this policy is sometimes referred to as "If you'll scratch my back, I'll scratch yours.")

   The two nations have a policy of *reciprocity* as they have removed the tariff on certain goods coming from each other's country.

5. **assets** (AS ets)—noun

   All items of value owned by a person or persons.

   The building, equipment, land, and patents are among the company's *assets*.

6. **liabilities** (LĪ ə BIL ə tēs)—noun

Debts owed to other firms or persons.

The store owner declared bankruptcy after his *liabilities* continued to exceed his assets.

7. **solvency** (SOL vən sē)—noun

The ability to meet one's financial obligations.

The firm's *solvency* enabled the board of directors to pay off all debts and to modernize the plant's equipment.

8. **fiscal** (FIS kəl)—adjective

Pertaining to financial matters.

The company's *fiscal* year begins on July 1.

9. **inflationary** (in FLĀ shə NER ē)—adjective

Describes a substantial rise in prices caused by an excessive expansion of paper money or bank credit.

The union representative argued that the company's salary offer did not match the rise in the cost of living caused by an extensive *inflationary* period.

10. **recession** (ri SESH ən)—noun

A prolonged economic period in which business is poor and unemployment is high. (Depression is used to describe a severe recession.)

A number of leading economists had predicted a *recession* during the second half of the year, but business and the employment rate continued to be good.

11. **bear market, bull market** (BĀR MAR kit, BUL MAR kit)—nouns

The stock market is the business of buying, selling, and trading of stocks, bonds, and other financial investments. A bear market refers to a falling stock market, that is, when such investments are declining in value. A bull market refers to a rising market, that is, when such investments are increasing in value.

Though my investments have continued to decline during the current *bear market,* my financial advisor said I shouldn't be discouraged because he was confident a *bull market* would occur before the year ended.

Matching Academic Terms and Definitions: Set 1

Match each definition with the term it defines.

_i_	**1.** liabilities	**a.** stocks show positive growth
_k_	**2.** fiscal	**b.** showing a significant rise in prices
_h_	**3.** GNP	**c.** period of poor business and high
_j_	**4.** commodities	unemployment
_c_	**5.** recession	**d.** ability to meet financial obligations
_a_	**6.** bull market	**e.** cash, property, and all other things of
_b_	**7.** inflationary	value
_f_	**8.** reciprocity	**f.** mutual exchange policy
_l_	**9.** bear market	**g.** comparison between what a country
_e_	**10.** assets	sells and what it buys
_d_	**11.** solvency	**h.** total value of goods and services of a
_g_	**12.** balance of trade	nation
		i. debts
		j. products bought, sold, or traded
		k. refers to financial concerns
		l. stocks show a decrease in value

Fill-Ins with Academic Terms: Set 1

In each space, write the appropriate term from those listed below.

commodities	balance of trade	assets	solvency	inflationary	bear
GNP	reciprocity	liabilities	fiscal	recession	bull

1. A(n) _____inflationary_____ period is especially hard on people with fixed incomes because an increase in their cost of living is not accompanied by a rise in their incomes.

2. Our company is one of the few I know of that uses a(n) _____fiscal_____ year of forty-eight weeks in order to have twelve months of four weeks each.

3. "In the black financially" is one way _____solvency_____ could be defined.

4. _____Commodities_____ sold by this diversified organization include fruit juices, appliances, and plywood.

5. My investments increased dramatically in value during last year's _____bull market_____ , but, unfortunately, they have decreased in value just as dramatically during this year's prolonged _____bear market_____ .

6. As a whole, the country's economy has suffered this year, resulting in a decline in the nation's _____GNP_____ .

7. Because of the economic _____recession_____ , car sales, property transactions, and factory production figures have been well below average.

8. One indicator of a country's economic health is its ___balance of trade___ , that is, how its export sales and import purchases compare.

9. The corporation's financial picture is excellent as it possesses ___assets___ worth over twelve billion dollars whereas its ___liabilities___ , or debts, total less than one billion.

10. "If you'll scratch my back, I'll scratch yours" is an informal definition of ___reciprocity___ .

Related Meanings: Set 1

If the words opposite each other are similar in meaning, write Yes *in the space; if they are unrelated, write* No.

1. commodities	No	worthless products
2. GNP	Yes	gross national product
3. assets	Yes	valuable possessions
4. balance of trade	Yes	ratio of imports to exports
5. fiscal	No	healthy financial condition
6. inflationary	No	downward plunge in prices
7. liabilities	Yes	debts
8. recession	No	booming economic period
9. reciprocity	Yes	exchange of rights and privileges
10. solvency	Yes	sound financial condition
11. bull market	Yes	investors are happy
12. bear market	Yes	investors are unhappy

Writing Your Own Definitions: Set 1

Write either an original sentence or a definition for each term that clearly demonstrates your mastery of its meaning as used in business and economics.   Answers will vary.

1. commodities _____

_____

2. GNP _____

_____

3. balance of trade _____

_____

4. reciprocity _____

_____

5. assets _____

_____

6. liabilities _____

_____

7. solvency _____

_____

8. fiscal _____

_____

9. inflationary _____

_____

10. recession _____

_____

11. bear market _____

_____

12. bull market _____

_____

Learning Business and Economic Terms from Context Clues: Set 2

1. **portfolio** (port FŌ lē Ō)—noun

   The collection of securities (stocks and bonds) held by a single investor.

   By carefully managing her *portfolio* over the years, my aunt was able to retire at age fifty-five.

2. **entrepreneur** (AN trə prə NUR)—noun

   A French term for an individual who develops an enterprise through innovation and risk taking.

   The *entrepreneur* risked a fortune in establishing her unique business, which is now showing an impressive profit.

3. **CEO** (chief executive officer)—noun

   The person ultimately responsible for all decisions affecting the management of an organization; generally reports to a board of directors.

   A. S. Robinson, the *CEO,* has successfully guided the company for the past seven years.

4. franchise (FRAN chīz)—noun

A legal agreement granting an individual or group the right to sell a firm's products or services. Can also mean the businesses that operate under this agreement.

After agreeing to the conditions stipulated in the contract, Mr. Sanchez was granted a *franchise* to operate one of the company's fast-food restaurants.

5. capital (KAP it ul)—noun

Wealth in the form of money or property.

Mr. Sanchez is also raising the necessary *capital* to secure a second franchise in another part of the city.

6. conglomerate (kən GLOM ər it)—noun

A corporation comprising companies that conduct a variety of unrelated businesses.

The *conglomerate* includes branches concerned with computers, batteries, and plumbing fixtures.

7. appreciation, depreciation (ə PRĒ shē Ā shən, di PRĒ shē Ā shən)—nouns

Appreciation is the increase in value of an asset; depreciation is the decline in value of an asset.

The land I owned near the city limits has shown a remarkable growth in *appreciation* over the past five years.
Years of mismanagement resulted in a *depreciation* of the company's manufacturing facilities.

8. affirmative action (ə FUR mə tiv AK shən)—adjective + noun

Action designed to increase opportunities for females and minorities through recruitment, training, and promotion so that they are fairly represented in the work force.

The company has hired many more women and Hispanics this past decade as a result of its *affirmative action* program.

9. divestiture (dī VEST i chər)—noun

The loss or voluntary surrender of property, interest, right, or title.

Because the corporation had an unfair advantage over its competitors, the court ordered a *divestiture* of certain of its assets.

10. obsolescence (OB sə LES əns)—noun

Condition when certain products are no longer marketable because of scientific or technological advances.

Typewriters are on the verge of *obsolescence* because of computers.

11. **audit** (AH dit)—noun, verb

An examination of the financial records of a business (noun); to examine the financial records of a business (verb).

Company officials have hired an accounting firm to conduct an independent *audit* of the company's financial records and procedures.

12. **golden parachute** (GŌL dən PAR ə SHOŌT)—adjective + noun

An exceedingly generous promise of pay and other benefits given to a top executive in case his or her company is taken over by another firm or he or she retires.

The CEO's *golden parachute,* which includes generous severance pay and other costly benefits, is being sharply criticized by the company's stockholders.

13. **tariff** (TAR if)—noun

Taxes on imported goods.

To protect domestic car makers, the government has placed a *tariff* on cars imported to this country.

14. **cartel** (kər TEL)—noun

A group of businesses that have joined together to control some industry.

An international oil *cartel* is responsible for the dramatic rise in gasoline prices.

15. **embargo** (em BAR gō)—noun

Official prohibition of trade by one nation against another.

Many countries have an *embargo* against that nation because of its failure to stop the export of illegal drugs.

Matching Academic Terms and Definitions: Set 2

Match each definition with the term it defines.

A

_e_	**1.** divestiture	**a.**	an increase in value
_d_	**2.** franchise	**b.**	banning of trade by one nation against another
_h_	**3.** conglomerate	**c.**	designed to promote fair career opportunities for females and minorities
_a_	**4.** appreciation		
_g_	**5.** cartel	**d.**	legal right to sell a firm's products
_c_	**6.** affirmative action	**e.**	act of shedding property
_b_	**7.** embargo	**f.**	securities owned by an investor
_f_	**8.** portfolio	**g.**	organization formed to establish a business monopoly
		h.	many companies owned by a corporation

B

b	**1.** tariff	**a.** products no longer marketable
f	**2.** entrepreneur	**b.** taxes on imported goods
h	**3.** golden parachute	**c.** wealth in the form of money or property
e	**4.** CEO	**d.** a decline in value
g	**5.** audit	**e.** chief executive officer of a business
c	**6.** capital	**f.** a bold, daring business person
d	**7.** depreciation	**g.** inspection of financial records
a	**8.** obsolescence	**h.** lavish severance pay and other benefits

Fill-Ins with Academic Terms: Set 2

In each space, write the appropriate term from those listed below.

A

portfolio	conglomerate	golden parachute	capital	audit
franchise	obsolescence	CEO	divestiture	

1. The corporation sold two of its overseas businesses; this voluntary _____divestiture_____ took its competitors by surprise.

2. Her _____portfolio_____ is diversified, ranging from oil and gas stocks to state and municipal bonds.

3. My brother is in an executive training program for a(n) _____conglomerate_____ that has numerous businesses here and abroad.

4. Before he agreed to become _____CEO_____ of the company, Mr. Andretti insisted on a(n) _____golden parachute_____ in case he retired, was fired, or the company was sold.

5. Quartz watches led to the _____obsolescence_____ of watches run by windup springs.

6. An independent _____audit_____ of the company's financial records uncovered only a few minor irregularities.

7. My cousin is trying to raise enough _____capital_____ to buy a _____franchise_____ from a nationally known bagel company.

B

entrepreneur	depreciation	tariff	embargo
appreciation	affirmative action	cartel	

1. Protestors are urging the United States to impose a(n) _____embargo_____ on that nation because of its widespread use of child labor.

2. A(n) _____cartel_____ was formed by neighboring countries in an attempt to control the price for their iron ore.

3. Our sociology professor said that our country has benefited in many ways from _____affirmative action_____ , such as by the greater number of women now admitted to medical schools.

4. Major stockholders are concerned because the plant's equipment is fast becoming worn and outdated, resulting in a(n) _____depreciation_____ of the plant's worth.

5. The dynamic _____entrepreneur_____ has earned the respect of the business world because her bold initiatives have helped to save what once was a failing company.

6. Lobbyists for the fruit-producing states are urging Congress to levy a(n) _____tariff_____ on all fruit, except for bananas, coming into this country.

7. The astounding _____appreciation_____ of real estate in this small community is due to the completion of a new highway, making possible a much easier commute to the city.

Related Meanings: Set 2

If the words opposite each other are similar in meaning, write Yes *in the space; if they are unrelated, write* No.

1. embargo	Yes	government banning of trade with a specific country
2. tariff	Yes	tax on goods coming into a country
3. capital	Yes	money and other forms of wealth
4. affirmative action	No	steps recommended to increase profits
5. cartel	No	license to operate a private business overseas
6. depreciation	No	an increase in value
7. entrepreneur	No	cautious investor
8. franchise	No	tax on luxury goods
9. audit	Yes	financial inspection
10. conglomerate	No	government regulations businesses must observe
11. divestiture	Yes	surrender of property
12. golden parachute	No	an agreeable business merger
13. CEO	No	Congressional Economical Opportunities
14. obsolescence	Yes	passing out of use
15. portfolio	Yes	person's financial holdings
16. appreciation	No	decrease in value

Writing Your Own Definitions: Set 2

Write either an original sentence or a definition for each term that clearly demonstrates your mastery of its meaning as used in business and economics.   Answers will vary.

1. **portfolio** _____

_____

2. entrepreneur _____

_____

3. CEO _____

_____

4. franchise _____

_____

5. capital _____

_____

6. conglomerate _____

_____

7. appreciation _____

_____

8. depreciation _____

_____

9. affirmative action _____

_____

10. divestiture _____

_____

11. obsolescence _____

_____

12. audit _____

_____

13. golden parachute _____

_____

14. tariff _____

_____

15. cartel _____

_____

16. embargo _____

_____

Completing a Passage: Business and Economics

After reading the selection, fill in each space with one of the terms listed below.

commodities   liabilities   GNP   capital   recession   solvency   bull
audit   CEO   assets   franchises   entrepreneurs   bear

RAY KROC, FAST-FOOD PIONEER

Ray Kroc, the founder of the international McDonald's hamburger empire, was born in Chicago in 1902 and attended the public schools in a nearby suburb. However, after he and two friends raised sufficient ___capital___ to rent a store building, Ray dropped out of high school. The ___commodities___, or products, these young and daring ___entrepreneurs___ had to sell were sheet music and musical instruments. Unfortunately for them, in only a few months their business lacked financial ___solvency___ (as a[n] ___audit___ would have clearly shown) because their ___liabilities___ far surpassed their ___assets___. Having no other alternative, the unfortunate trio had to go out of business. Shortly afterward, Ray volunteered to be an ambulance driver for the Red Cross during World War I.

After the war, Ray, who had learned to play the piano from his mother, became a pianist for a couple of orchestras. After marrying, he went to work for the Lily-Tulip Cup Company for a short time before becoming the musical director at a Chicago radio station.

As a result of a strong ___bull___ market, the country's economy in the early and mid-1920s was booming, and Ray decided to seek his fortune by entering the growing real estate business in Florida. However, soon after he moved there with his wife and young daughter, the state's economy suffered a lengthy ___recession___, putting the real estate business into a tailspin and making it necessary for Ray and his family to move back to Chicago, where he returned to the Lily-Tulip Cup Company as a sales representative.

In 1937, Ray Kroc came across a new invention, a machine that could mix five milkshakes at once. Despite the fact that the country was still feeling the effects of the ___bear___ market that triggered a prolonged economic depression, Ray, in 1941, decided to establish his own company to serve as the sole distributor of the "multimixer." This time, he experienced business success.

In 1954, Ray went to a San Bernardino, California, drive-in restaurant because he was curious about why its owners, Richard and Maurice McDonald, had bought not one but eight of his multimixers. Ray discovered that the McDonald brothers were running an extremely popular restaurant selling only hamburgers, French fries, and milkshakes at a rapid pace and at very low prices. He was fascinated by the "assembly-line" format the McDonalds used to operate their restaurant. Ray soon became convinced that the "McDonald" approach could be successful with other drive-in restaurants.

After some negotiating, the McDonalds agreed to let Ray buy, as well as sell, McDonald ____franchises____ , thereby granting others the legal right (in return for an initial fee and a share of gross sales) to open a McDonald's restaurant.

Ray Kroc opened the first of the chain of McDonald's restaurants in Des Plaines, Illinois, in 1955. By 1961, over 130 outlets had been established, and Ray bought out the McDonald brothers for $2.7 million. Now the sole _____CEO_____ of the company, Ray quickly displayed a gift for franchising, marketing, and advertising, and McDonald's restaurants continued to spring up and to succeed throughout the country.

Ray Kroc died in 1984 at the age of eighty-two, but his legacy continues to this day, as McDonald's has grown to be a multi-billion-dollar enterprise with over 30,000 restaurants worldwide. In addition, the phenomenal success of McDonald's has resulted in so many imitators over the years that the fast-food industry has become a major contributor to this nation's _____GNP_____ (value of goods produced).

Reciprocity—a mutual or cooperative interchange of favors or privileges:

- The long-established <u>reciprocity</u> between Canada and the United States regarding trade has resulted in economic benefits to both countries.

Origin: <Latin—*reciprocus* (returning the same way). <u>Reciprocal</u> (done in exchange) dates from 1570, and <u>reciprocate</u> (to return, to pay in kind) from 1820.

Family words: reciprocal (adj), reciprocate (v), reciprocation (n)

Image to remember: people agreeing to trade favors ("If you'll take care of my dog while I'm gone, then I'll take care of yours when you go on vacation.")

Write an original sentence using *reciprocity*:

_____

_____

_____

MASTERING CONFUSING WORDS | **disinterested / uninterested**

disinterested without favoritism (impartial), neutral, unbiased:

Judges, umpires, and referees should perform their duties in a <u>disinterested</u> manner.

uninterested bored, lacking interest, uncaring:

Reggie went to the game with Sandra, but he was <u>uninterested</u> in the outcome.

Circle the correct answer:

1. Whitney was <u>disinterested</u> /<u>uninterested</u> in the art exhibit, so she only stayed for a few minutes.

2. We need <u>disinterested</u> / <u>uninterested</u> people to serve on the panel so that the floats will be judged on their merits, not on who made them.

Write original sentences using these words:

1. **disinterested:** _____

2. **uninterested:** _____

Learning Mathematics Terms from Context Clues: Set 1

In addition to those students intending to major in math, computer science, business, accounting, nursing, or any of the sciences, most students, regardless of their major, are required to take at least one or two math courses. Mastery of the fundamental math skills—adding, subtracting, multiplying, dividing—is necessary to succeed in higher-level math courses such as algebra, geometry, and calculus. If it's been some time since you took a math course, you should benefit from reviewing the basic math terms presented in this chapter.

1. angles (ang gəls)—noun

Figures formed by two lines radiating from the same endpoint, called the **vertex** (VUR teks).

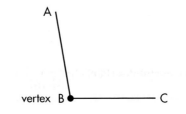

The three types of angles are the following:

A **right angle** is a 90° angle.

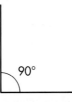

Right angle

An **acute** (ə KYOOT) **angle** measures <u>less</u> than 90°.

Acute angle

An **obtuse** (ob TOOS) **angle** measures <u>more</u> than 90°.

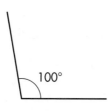

100°

Obtuse angle

2. **addition terms: addends** (AD ends), **sum** (sum)—nouns

Addends are the numbers being added; the answer is called the *sum* (sum).

$$\begin{array}{r} 29 \ addend \\ + \ 61 \ addend \\ \hline 90 \ sum \end{array}$$

3. **average** (AV rij)—noun

The sum of the addends in a row or column divided by the number of addends in the row or column.

$$46 + 52 + 39 + 43 = 180$$
$$180 \div 4 = 45 \ (\text{the } average)$$

4. **axioms** (AK sē əms), **postulates** (POS chə lāts)—nouns

Statements that are assumed to be true without proof.

Examples: "The whole is greater than its parts."
"Any straight line can be extended in either direction as far as is desired."

5. **circumference** (sər KUM fər əns)—noun

The distance around a circle (a circle's boundary).

6. **diameter** (dī AM ə tər)—noun

A straight line segment passing through the center of a figure, such as a circle.

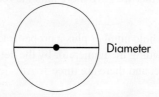

Diameter

7. **division terms: dividend** (DIV ə dend), **divisor** (də VĪ zər), **quotient** (KWŌ shənt)—nouns

The <u>dividend</u> is the number that the <u>divisor</u> divides to get the <u>quotient</u>, or the answer.

$$39 \div 13 = 3$$

dividend   divisor   quotient

8. **exponent** (ek SPŌ nənt)—noun

The raised number above a number or symbol that indicates how many times the number or symbol is to be used as a factor.

$$\text{exponent} \rightarrow 4^2 = 4 \times 4$$

$$\text{exponent} \rightarrow 2^4 = 2 \times 2 \times 2 \times 2$$

$$\text{exponents} \rightarrow 2^2 a^3 = 2 \times 2 \times a \times a \times a$$

An exponent is expressed in terms of <u>power</u>; for example, 4^2 is expressed as 4 to the *second power* (4×4), and 5^3 is expressed as 5 to the *third power* ($5 \times 5 \times 5$), etc.

9. **fractions** (FRAK shəns), **mixed numbers** (MIKST NUM bərs)—nouns

Fractions can be proper or improper; both contain a top number (the *numerator*) and a bottom number (the *denominator*).

A <u>proper fraction</u> represents part of a whole.

$$\frac{3}{4} \text{ numerator} \atop \text{denominator}$$

The <u>denominator</u> indicates that the whole has been divided into four parts; the <u>numerator</u> indicates how many parts are being considered. For example, a cake (the whole) is divided into four parts (indicated by the denominator), and three pieces (indicated by the numerator) have been eaten.

In an <u>improper fraction</u>, the numerator is larger than the denominator.

$$\frac{7}{4}$$

The denominator, 4, indicates that the whole is made up of four parts, but the numerator, 7, indicates that we have more than the four parts, so we have more than the whole.

A <u>mixed number</u> is a whole number plus a proper fraction; $\frac{7}{4}$ could be changed to a mixed number by dividing the numerator by the denominator, resulting in $1\frac{3}{4}$ ($\frac{4}{4}$ make a whole, or one, and there are three-fourths left over, making $1\frac{3}{4}$).

10. subtraction terms

Minuend is the number from which another number is subtracted.

Subtrahend is the number subtracted from the minuend.

Difference is the answer when you have completed the subtraction.

$$\begin{array}{r} 8 \text{ } minuend \\ -\ 5 \text{ } subtrahend \\ \hline 3 \text{ } difference \end{array}$$

Matching Academic Terms and Definitions: Set 1

Match each definition with the term it defines.

A

_h_	**1.** exponent	**a.** whole number plus a fraction
_g_	**2.** addends	**b.** angle of more than 90 degrees
_e_	**3.** circumference	**c.** answer for a division problem
_f_	**4.** axioms	**d.** number that divides another number
_d_	**5.** divisor	**e.** distance around a circle
_b_	**6.** obtuse	**f.** statements assumed to be true without proof
_i_	**7.** dividend	**g.** numbers being added
_a_	**8.** mixed number	**h.** raised number above a number or symbol
_c_	**9.** quotient	**i.** number being divided

B

_f_	**1.** numerator	**a.** bottom number of a fraction
_h_	**2.** right angle	**b.** angle of less than 90 degrees
_e_	**3.** diameter	**c.** when the top number of a fraction is smaller
_j_	**4.** vertex	than the bottom number
_a_	**5.** denominator	**d.** the sum of addends divided by the number
_c_	**6.** proper fraction	of addends
_d_	**7.** average	**e.** distance across a figure measuring from one
_b_	**8.** acute angle	side through the exact center to the other side
_g_	**9.** improper fraction	**f.** top number of a fraction
_i_	**10.** sum	**g.** when the top number of a fraction is larger
		than the bottom number
		h. angle of 90 degrees
		i. answer to an addition problem
		j. the common endpoint of two rays that form
		an angle

Related Meanings: Set 1

If the words opposite each other are similar in meaning, write Yes *in the space; if they are unrelated, write* No.

1. sum   <u>No</u>   answer obtained after dividing
2. axioms   <u>Yes</u>   postulates
3. mixed number   <u>No</u>   number with a value over 100
4. acute angle   <u>Yes</u>   angle less than 90°
5. addends   <u>Yes</u>   numbers that are added
6. numerator   <u>Yes</u>   top number of a fraction
7. exponent   <u>No</u>   answer obtained after adding
8. right angle   <u>Yes</u>   a 90° angle
9. proper fraction   <u>Yes</u>   when the numerator is smaller than the denominator
10. dividend   <u>No</u>   number obtained when you add up a row of addends and then divide by the number of addends
11. vertex   <u>No</u>   four-sided rectangle
12. obtuse angle   <u>Yes</u>   angle greater than 90°
13. diameter   <u>Yes</u>   a straight line passing through the center of a circle and meeting at opposite ends of the circumference
14. sum   <u>No</u>   raised number above another number or symbol
15. improper fraction   <u>Yes</u>   when the numerator is larger than the denominator
16. quotient   <u>No</u>   number being divided
17. average   <u>No</u>   statement generally known to be true
18. circumference   <u>Yes</u>   outer boundary of a circle
19. divisor   <u>Yes</u>   4 is the divisor in this problem: $12 \div 4 = 3$

Writing Your Own Definitions: Set 1

Write either an original sentence or a definition for each term that clearly demonstrates your mastery of its meaning as used in mathematics.   Answers will vary.

1. **proper fraction** _____

   _____

2. **average** _____

   _____

3. **dividend** _____

   _____

4. divisor _____

_____

5. quotient _____

_____

6. improper fraction _____

_____

7. addends _____

_____

8. sum _____

_____

9. obtuse angle _____

_____

10. exponent _____

_____

11. mixed number _____

_____

12. right angle _____

_____

13. diameter _____

_____

14. axioms _____

_____

15. circumference _____

_____

16. acute angle _____

_____

17. vertex _____

_____

Learning Mathematics Terms from Context Clues: Set 2

1. mean (MĒN)—noun

Mean is synonymous with <u>average</u>, that is, the sum of addends divided by the number of addends.

$$24 + 31 + 19 + 32 + 26 + 18 = 150; 150 \div 6 = 25 \text{ (the } mean\text{)}$$

2. median (MĒ dē ən)—noun

The number that separates the data into equal parts when the numbers are arranged from highest to lowest or lowest to highest. Here are the test scores for nine students arranged both ways:

99	73
97	76
94	78
88	82
85	85
82	88
78	94
76	97
73	99

The <u>median</u> is 85, as there are four numbers above 85 and four below 85; the median will be the same whether you arrange the numbers from highest to lowest or lowest to highest.

3. mode (MŌD)—noun

The number that occurs most frequently in a set of numbers.

17   19   22   17   15   19   21   17   22   17   25   17   14

Here the <u>mode</u> is 17 because it is the number occurring most frequently. This becomes clearer when you arrange the numbers again, either from highest to lowest or from lowest to highest:

25	I	14	I
22	II	15	I
21	I	17	ͰͰͰ
19	II	19	II
17	ͰͰͰ	21	I
15	I	22	II
14	I	25	I

To obtain the *mean* or *average* for this set of numbers, you would add all the numbers (including two 22s, two 19s, and five 17s), for a total of 242; then, dividing 242 by 13 (the total number of addends), you would get a <u>mean</u> or an average of 18.6, or 19 if you round off to the nearest whole number. To determine the <u>median</u> for these numbers, you would arrange them either from highest to lowest or from lowest to highest (it doesn't matter which):

25	17
22	17
22	17
21	17
19	15
19	14
17	

The <u>median</u> for these numbers is 17 because there are six numbers above 17 and six below 17.

Making computations like the preceding for a set of figures is often helpful in making decisions, gaining insights, and coming to conclusions. For example, if you were the president of a campus organization and the preceding numbers were the attendance figures for the past thirteen meetings, by computing the *mean, mode,* and *median* as was done, you likely could gain valuable insights regarding such matters as the type of programs the members seem to prefer, what time of day or day of the week seems to be best for the meetings, and how the organization's attendance figures compared to those of other years.

4. **multiplication terms: multiplicand** (MUL tə plə KAND), **multiplier** (MUL tə plī ər), **product** (PROD əkt)—nouns

The *multiplicand* is the number to be multiplied by another; the *multiplier* is the number that multiplies the multiplicand; and the *product* is the answer to a multiplication problem.

$$
\begin{array}{r}
46 = \textit{multiplicand} \\
\times\ \underline{32} = \textit{multiplier} \\
92 \\
\underline{138} \\
1{,}472 = \textit{product}
\end{array}
$$

Multiplicands and multipliers are also called *factors* (FAK tərs).

5. **perimeter** (pə RIM ə tər)—noun

The distance around a figure. (A circle's <u>perimeter</u> is the same as its <u>circumference</u>.)

6. radius (RĀ dē əs)—noun

A line segment from the exact center to a point on the circumference (or boundary) of the circle.

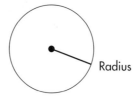

Radius

7. square root (SKWĀR ROOT)—adjective + noun

One of two identical factors of a number.

The <u>square root</u> of 25 is 5 (5 × 5 = 25).
The <u>square root</u> of 36 is 6 (6 × 6 = 36).
The <u>square root</u> of 49 is 7 (7 × 7 = 49).

<u>Squaring</u> a number is taking it to its *second power:* $8^2 = 64$ (8 × 8), and <u>cubing</u> a number is taking it to its *third power:* $9^3 = 729$ (9 × 9 × 9). Squaring or cubing a number is indicated by the exponent above it: 5^2, 6^3, etc.

8. variable (VAR ē ə bəl)—noun

The letter of the alphabet used to stand for an unknown number or one that can change or vary. For example:

If you were going to charge $8.00 for each ticket but you weren't sure how many tickets you would sell, you could represent this mathematically by using the <u>variable</u> *n*: 8 × *n*, or simply 8*n*.

9. math symbols

+   plus or add (7 + 5)
−   minus or subtract (7 − 5)
÷   divide (9 ÷ 3)
×   multiply (9 × 3)
•   also means to multiply (9 • 3)
=   equal ($5 = \frac{5}{1}$)
≠   not equal (4 ≠ 5)
<   less than (4 < 5)
>   greater than (5 > 4)
√   square root of a number ($\sqrt{4} = 2$)
%   percent (78%) (Percent refers to parts of 100, and a percent is often rewritten as a decimal: $^{78}/_{100} = 78\% = .78$.)

Matching Academic Terms and Definitions: Set 2

Match each definition with the term it defines.

__j__ **1.** mode
__h__ **2.** product
__k__ **3.** perimeter
__g__ **4.** multiplicand
__f__ **5.** variable
__b__ **6.** square root
__d__ **7.** cubing a number
__c__ **8.** radius
__e__ **9.** mean
__l__ **10.** median
__i__ **11.** multiplier
__a__ **12.** squaring a number

a. taking a number to its second power, such as 9^2, or $9 \times 9 = 81$

b. one of two identical factors of a number, such as 8 is for 64

c. line segment running from the exact center of a circle to a point on the circumference (or boundary) of the circle

d. taking a number to its third power, such as 4^3, or $4 \times 4 \times 4 = 64$

e. has the same meaning as *average*

f. a letter used for an unknown number, such as the *n* in $10 \times n$

g. number being multiplied

h. answer for a multiplication problem, such as 36 in $9 \times 4 = 36$

i. number that does the multiplying, such as 7 in 9×7

j. number occurring most often in a set of numbers

k. distance around a figure, such as a rectangle or square

l. number separating a column of numbers into two equal groups

Match each symbol with its meaning.

__f__ **1.** $\neq$
__g__ **2.** $>$
__b__ **3.** $+$
__h__ **4.** $\%$
__c__ **5.** $\times$
__j__ **6.** $<$
__e__ **7.** $=$
__c__ **8.** $\cdot$
__a__ **9.** $\sqrt{}$
__i__ **10.** $\div$
__d__ **11.** $-$

a. square root
b. plus or add
c. multiply
d. minus or subtract
e. equal
f. not equal
g. greater than
h. percent
i. divide
j. less than

Related Meanings: Set 2

If the words opposite each other are similar in meaning, write Yes *in the space; if they are unrelated, write* No.

1. product   <u>Yes</u>   <u>48</u> in $8 \times 6 = 48$
2. =   <u>Yes</u>   equal
3. median   <u>Yes</u>   number separating numbers into two equal groups
4. $\sqrt{}$ <u>Yes</u>   square root
5. perimeter   <u>No</u>   angle less than $90°$
6. %   <u>Yes</u>   percent
7. variable   <u>No</u>   number occurring most often in a set of numbers
8. cubing   <u>Yes</u> 6^3 or $6 \times 6 \times 6 = 216$
9. >   <u>No</u>   less than
10. multiplier   <u>Yes</u>   <u>6</u> in $12 \times 6 = 72$
11. <   <u>No</u>   greater than
12. squaring   <u>Yes</u> 8^2 or $8 \times 8 = 64$
13. ≠   <u>Yes</u>   not equal
14. +   <u>Yes</u>   add or plus
15. ×   <u>Yes</u>   multiply
16. multiplicand   <u>Yes</u>   <u>9</u> in $9 \times 7 = 63$
17. •   <u>Yes</u>   multiply
18. mean   <u>No</u>   largest number in a group of numbers
19. mode   <u>No</u>   letter of the alphabet standing for an unknown number

Writing Your Own Definitions: Set 2

Write either an original sentence or a definition for each term or symbol that clearly demonstrates your mastery of its meaning as used in mathematics.   Answers will vary.

1. **mean** _____

    _____

2. **multiplicand** _____

    _____

3. **+** _____

    _____

4. **squaring a number** _____

    _____

5. **=** _____

    _____

6. • _____

_____

7. % _____

_____

8. mode _____

_____

9. product _____

_____

10. multiplier _____

_____

11. > _____

_____

12. perimeter _____

_____

13. × _____

_____

14. cubing a number _____

_____

15. variable _____

_____

16. median _____

_____

17. $\sqrt{}$ _____

_____

18. ≠ _____

_____

19. < _____

_____

20. ÷ _____

_____

Completing a Passage: Mathematics

After reading the selection, fill in each space with one of the terms or symbols listed below.

numerator	quotient	%	+ dividend < × ± divisor −
exponents	denominator	variables	> = √ ÷ •

MATH SYMBOLS

There are many languages in the world—Spanish, French, Italian, English, Arabic, Chinese, Bengali, German, Portuguese, Japanese, and many, many others—and no one knows them all. But math concepts are the same for people the world over; 2 plus 2 equals 4 is true in all countries. In addition, Arabic numerals (1, 2, 3, etc.) are universally used, so if a person can solve a math problem in the United States, he or she can solve the same problem anywhere in the world.

Math symbols (+, −, ×, etc.) are also used universally, but unlike math concepts that were discovered, math symbols were invented. For example, _____+_____ , the sign to add, was adapted from the Latin word for "and" (*et*) by a French mathematician in the 1300s. A math book published in Belgium in 1514 used _____−_____ , the minus symbol, as well as the plus symbol. Both of these symbols came into general use in much of Europe by the late 1500s. _____×_____ , the symbol for multiplication, first appeared in *Clavis Mathematicae* (*Keys to Mathematics*), published in London in 1631. The other symbol for multiplication, _____•_____ , was first used by a German mathematician in the 1600s because he thought the existing multiplication symbol was too easily confused with the letter x. The obelus, or _____÷_____ , was first used as a division symbol in an algebra textbook published in 1659. However, by the 1800s, math textbooks in the United States were showing the _____dividend_____ (number being divided), the _____divisor_____ (number doing the dividing), and the _____quotient_____ (answer) in the manner students are most familiar with, as in this example:

$$13\overline{)52}^{\,4}$$

The equal sign, _____=_____ , first appeared in 1557 in a book by Robert Recorde, and the sign of inequality, _____≠_____ , is attributed to an 18th-century mathematician by the name of Euler. The symbols for "greater than," _____>_____ , and "less than," _____<_____ , came into use after Thomas Harriet published his textbook in 1631. The use of _____exponents_____, or raised numbers, such as the 3 in 12^3, was adopted by other mathematicians after René Descartes (1596–1650) began using them.

_____%_____, or the percent symbol, is believed to have evolved from a symbol used in an anonymous Italian manuscript published in the late 1400s. The use of _____variables_____, that is, letters that stand for numbers, can be traced back thousands of years to the ancient Greek civilization.

Fractions were commonly used centuries ago by both Hindus and Arabs, and the horizontal bar separating the _____numerator_____ and _____denominator_____ is attributed to al-Hassan, who lived in the 1200s. _____$\sqrt{}$_____, the square root symbol, first appeared in 1525, and it is credited to Rudolf Coss, a German mathematician.

Because the same math principles, numerals, and symbols are used throughout the world, it can be said that math is a universal "language" we all share.

Postulate—statement assumed to be true without proof; used as a basis for argument and reasoning:

- Euclid, a Greek who lived in the third century B.C., is credited with developing the principles of geometry based on five <u>postulates</u>, or <u>axioms</u>. One of Euclid's <u>postulates</u> is this: All right angles are congruent (correspond or coincide).

Origin: <Latin—*postulare* (to assume)

Family words: postulated (v), postulating (v), postulation (n), postulator (n)

Image to remember: students solving challenging math problems

Write an original sentence using *postulate*:

_____

_____

_____

who's a contraction of *who is*:

Who's going to volunteer to go to the post office to mail this package?

(If you can say, "Who is going to volunteer to go to the post office to mail this package?" then you can use Who's; if you can't substitute who is for who's, then use whose.)

whose a possessive (showing ownership) pronoun:

Whose car is parked in the driveway?

(It is nonsensical to say, "Who is car is parked in the driveway?" If you are in doubt as to whether to write who's or whose, substitute who is for who's; if the sentence sounds okay, then who's can be used, but if the sentence sounds awkward, use whose.)

Circle the correct answer:

1. Does anyone know who's / (whose) books these are?

2. Jake's a nice guy (who's) / whose going to do well in the business world.

3. Marjorie, (who's) / whose thinking of transferring to a smaller college, is in the second semester of her sophomore year.

4. Gary, who's / (whose) personality has really blossomed this year, was recently elected to the student senate.

Write original sentences using these words:

1. who's: _____

2. whose: _____

Learning Biological Science Terms from Context Clues: Set 1

The biological sciences, which are devoted to the study of the functions and structures of living organisms, include biology, zoology, botany, entomology, microbiology, physiology, genetics, and a number of other sciences as well. A major in one or more of the biological sciences is a popular choice for students interested in careers in medicine, wildlife, forestry, the environment, teaching, and careers having to do with various types of animal or plant life.

Knowledge of the terms in this chapter will be a major asset to you when you take a biological science course.

1. **biology** (bī OL ə jē)—noun

   The study of living organisms, including their structure, function, development, and distribution.

   Natalie has enjoyed all of her high school science courses, but particularly those having to do with animals and plants, so she is seriously considering *biology* as her college major.

2. **zoology** (zō OL ə jē)—noun

   The branch of biology specializing in the study of animals.

   Matthew is majoring in *zoology* as he hopes to be a veterinarian some day.

3. **botany** (BOT ə nē)—noun

   The branch of biology specializing in the study of plants.

   My cousin's landscaping business resulted from his initial interest in *botany.*

4. **entomology** (en tə MOL ə jē)—noun

   The branch of biology specializing in the study of insects.

   Mr. Bryson, who has a master's degree in *entomology,* was consulted by the Peach Growers Association when some type of insect began infesting the peach orchards in the state.

5. **microbiology** (MĪ krō bī OL ə jē)—noun

   The branch of biology specializing in the study of microorganisms and their effects on other living organisms.

   Since *microbiology* involves the study of living organisms too small to be seen by the unaided eye, powerful microscopes must be used.

Entomologists study insects such as butterflies. *(Royalty Free/Jupiter Images)*

6. physiology (FIZ e OL ə je)—noun

The biological study of the functions of living organisms and their parts.

The nursing degree program includes a challenging course in *physiology* because nurses must understand the functions of the human body.

7. genetics (jə NET iks)—noun

The branch of biology devoted to the study of genes, which are responsible for the hereditary characteristics of people and other living organisms.

In *genetics* class, our professor discussed the possibility of altering an organism's genes to prevent the development of abnormalities and disease.

8. chromosomes (KRO mə soms)—noun

Microscopic, threadlike bodies in the nucleus of a cell that determine the particular characteristics of an organism; each cell in a human body has forty-six chromosomes. The majority of animal and plant species have between ten and fifty *chromosomes.*

9. genes (JENZ)—noun

Elements in chromosomes that control the development of hereditary characteristics.

The color of a person's eyes is determined by *genes*.

10. mutation (mu TĀ shən)—noun

A change in the genes of an organism that is transmitted to the offspring, resulting in offspring differing in some significant way from the parents.

Professor Bailey said that while the effects of a *mutation* on offspring can sometimes be beneficial, generally a *mutation* results in harmful abnormalities.

11. symbiosis (sim bē Ō sis)—noun

The general meaning of this term is "living together." In biology, it refers to two different types of organisms living together for their mutual benefit.

The *symbiosis* between an Egyptian plover bird and a crocodile results in mutual benefit for them both, as the bird eats parasites that are harmful to the crocodile, while the crocodile protects the bird from those who would otherwise prey on it.

12. fauna, flora (FON ə, FLOR ə)—nouns

Fauna are the animals and flora are the plants of a particular region or period.

Some citizens are protesting the planned draining of the bog because they fear the draining will destroy the *fauna* and *flora,* that is, the animals and plants native to the bog region.

13. habitat (HAB ə tat)—noun

The natural physical area where an animal or a plant lives and thrives.

The *habitat* for seals is the seashore and the ocean.

Matching Academic Terms and Definitions: Set 1

Match each definition with the term it defines.

___i___	**1.** microbiology	**a.** study of the parts and functions of living organisms
___e___	**2.** mutation	**b.** threadlike bodies in cells responsible for hereditary characteristics
___m___	**3.** genetics	
___b___	**4.** chromosomes	**c.** animals of a particular region or period
___j___	**5.** flora	**d.** branch of biology devoted to the study of animals
___d___	**6.** zoology	**e.** abnormality caused by a change in a parent's genes
___l___	**7.** habitat	**f.** mutual relationship that benefits both species
___k___	**8.** biology	**g.** study of insects
___c___	**9.** fauna	**h.** elements in chromosomes responsible for eye color and other characteristics
___n___	**10.** botany	
___a___	**11.** physiology	**i.** study of microorganisms

_f_	**12.** symbiosis	**j.** plant life of a particular region or period
_h_	**13.** genes	**k.** study of living organisms (plants and animals), including their structure, function, development, and distribution
_g_	**14.** entomology	**l.** natural physical area where an animal or a plant lives
		m. concentrated study of genes
		n. branch of biology specializing in the study of plants

Fill-Ins with Academic Terms: Set 1

In each space, write the appropriate term from those listed below.

mutation	habitat	physiology	genes	flora
fauna	chromosomes	genetics	microbiology	symbiosis
biology	zoology	entomology	botany	

1. The hereditary factors lying within chromosomes are called _____genes_____ .

2. Meat ants and leaf hoppers live in _____symbiosis_____ , as the ants receive a rich food source from the hoppers, and the hoppers in return are protected from their enemies by the ants.

3. Surprisingly, glacial ice is the natural _____habitat_____ of numerous plants, which are considered among the world's hardiest _____flora_____ .

4. A sudden change, called a(n) _____mutation_____ , in an organism's makeup usually results in detrimental effects.

5. _____Chromosomes_____ contain genes, or hereditary units.

6. The _____fauna_____ of Montana include(s) a variety of many large and small animals.

7. Because you've been intrigued with insects since you were a youngster, you should consider majoring in _____entomology_____ .

8. I like my _____botany_____ class, but learning the Latin names of the many plants we study takes me hours.

9. During the next three years, Nancy, a pre-med major, said she would be taking courses in _____physiology_____ to learn about the functions and structures of the human body, another in _____microbiology_____ to learn about microorganisms and their effects on humans, and a course her senior year in _____genetics_____ , to learn how genes determine certain human characteristics.

10. My introductory course in _____biology_____ is a challenge because it includes an extensive study of both animal and plant life as well as a three-hour laboratory session every week.

11. Zachary took a course in _____zoology_____ during the fall semester, and this opportunity to study animals in depth has sparked an interest in veterinarian medicine.

Related Meanings: Set 1

If the words opposite each other are similar in meaning, write Yes *in the space; if they are unrelated, write* No.

1. chromosomes   <u>No</u> essential vitamins
2. genes   <u>Yes</u> hereditary units
3. habitat   <u>Yes</u> home
4. mutation   <u>No</u> maturity
5. botany   <u>No</u> study of insects
6. biology   <u>Yes</u> study of plant and animal life
7. flora   <u>Yes</u> plant life of a particular region or period
8. microbiology   <u>No</u> study of the effects of electricity on humans
9. entomology   <u>No</u> study of flowers and other plant life
10. zoology   <u>Yes</u> study of animal life
11. fauna   <u>Yes</u> animal life of a particular area or period
12. genetics   <u>Yes</u> study of genes
13. physiology   <u>Yes</u> study of the functions and parts of living organisms
14. symbiosis   <u>No</u> destruction of harmful fauna and flora

Writing Your Own Definitions: Set 1

Write either an original sentence or a definition for each term that clearly demonstrates your mastery of its meaning as used in the biological sciences.   Answers will vary.

1. **mutation** _____

_____

2. **physiology** _____

_____

3. **biology** _____

_____

4. **flora** _____

_____

5. **genes** _____

_____

6. **botany** _____

_____

7. **habitat** _____

_____

8. symbiosis _____

_____

9. zoology _____

_____

10. fauna _____

_____

11. microbiology _____

_____

12. genetics _____

_____

13. entomology _____

_____

14. chromosomes _____

_____

Learning Biological Science Terms from Context Clues: Set 2

1. <u>**congenital**</u> (kən JEN ə təl)—adjective

   Inborn or existing since birth.

   Jeremy says that he has never been able to distinguish between certain colors, including shades of blue and brown, very well. Color blindness like Jeremy's is a *congenital* condition.

2. **homeo<u>sta</u>sis** (hōm ē ō STĀ sis)—noun

   A body's tendency to maintain its internal systems in a normal stable condition. *Homeostatsis* occurs when a person, in an effort to maintain a normal oxygen level, automatically breathes deeply after running.

3. **dormant** (DOR mənt)—adjective

   Describes an organism at rest and not developing.

   Seeds will remain *dormant* until the temperature and other environmental conditions are suitable for sprouting.

4. prolific (prō LIF ik)—adjective

Producing offspring in abundance.

As a result of their frequent litters, rabbits are well known as *prolific* breeders.

5. taxonomy (tak SON ə mē)—noun

The systematic classification of animals and plants into categories.

Taxonomy places organisms with similar structures in the same category.

6. vertebrates, invertebrates (VUR tə brātes, in VUR tə brātes)—nouns

Animals with backbones are vertebrates; animals without backbones are invertebrates.

Dogs are included in the taxonomy classifying *vertebrates* because they have backbones; worms, on the other hand, are listed in the taxonomy classifying *invertebrates,* because they have no backbones.

7. carnivorous (kar NIV ə rəs),
herbivorous (hur BIV ə rəs),
omnivorous (om NIV ə rəs)—adjectives

A taxonomy relating to animals makes these distinctions for these terms: carnivorous animals eat primarily meat; herbivorous animals eat primarily plants; omnivorous animals eat both meat and plants.

Wolves are *carnivorous*; cows are *herbivorous;* humans, because we eat both plants and animals, are *omnivorous.*

8. hominids (HOM ə nids)—noun

The human family and their ancestors, including extinct humanlike types.

Prehistoric humans are considered *hominids.*

9. plankton (PLANK tən)—noun

The microscopic plants and animals floating near the surface in almost all bodies of water.

Important food sources for most fish are the tiny animals and plants, known as *plankton,* drifting in the water.

10. hybrid (HĪ brid)—noun

The crossbreed of offspring of two animals or plants from different species.

A mule is a *hybrid* resulting from the mating of a horse and a donkey.

11. **protoplasm** (PRŌ tə plaz əm)—noun

A chemically complex, colorless semifluid considered the physical basis of life.
Scientists believe that *protoplasm* is the building block of all animal life.

12. **metabolism** (mə TAB ə liz əm)—noun

An inclusive term used to refer to all the chemical reactions by which the cells
of an organism transform energy, maintain their identity, and reproduce.

All life forms, from single-celled plants to multicelled humans, depend on
hundreds of precisely regulated processes known collectively as *metabolism*.

13. **ossification** (os ə fə KĀ shən)—noun

Formation and hardening of the bones.
As people mature, their bones harden, a process called *ossification*.

Matching Academic Terms and Definitions: Set 2

Match each definition with the term it defines.

A

_h_	**1.** vertebrates	**a.**	hardening of the bones
_g_	**2.** prolific	**b.**	eating plants
_f_	**3.** hominids	**c.**	the systematic classification of plants and animals
_e_	**4.** plankton	**d.**	the tendency for a body to balance itself internally
_b_	**5.** herbivorous	**e.**	extremely small animals and plants living near
_d_	**6.** homeostasis		the surface of water
_a_	**7.** ossification	**f.**	humans and their ancestors
_c_	**8.** taxonomy	**g.**	producing a large number of offspring
		h.	animals with backbones

B

_d_	**1.** invertebrates	**a.**	in a state of inactivity
_f_	**2.** omnivorous	**b.**	result when two plants or animals of different
_e_	**3.** congenital		species are bred
_a_	**4.** dormant	**c.**	semifluid substance considered the basis of all
_h_	**5.** carnivorous		life
_c_	**6.** protoplasm	**d.**	animals lacking spines
_b_	**7.** hybrid	**e.**	inborn, existing since birth
_g_	**8.** metabolism	**f.**	eating both plants and animals
		g.	term referring to all of a body's chemical and
			physical processes
		h.	eating meat

Fill-Ins with Academic Terms: Set 2

A

In each space, write the appropriate term from those listed below.

metabolism	herbivorous	protoplasm	dormant
hominids	ossification	omnivorous	vertebrates

1. Flower bulbs are _____dormant_____ in the winter, but they develop shoots in the spring.

2. The primitive Java man is classified with _____hominids_____ because he is considered a human ancestor.

3. Birds are _____vertebrates_____ because they have spines.

4. Because of _____ossification_____ , bones are more brittle as a person ages.

5. _____Protoplasm_____ is a semifluid substance considered the building block of all animal life.

6. _____Metabolism_____ is the term used for the normal chemical and physical activities, such as those involved in digestion and circulation, taking place within living organisms.

7. Horses and zebras are _____herbivorous_____ animals as they eat only grass and other plant life, whereas crows and raccoons are _____omnivorous_____ as they eat both plant life and meat.

B

prolific	homeostasis	invertebrates	carnivorous
plankton	taxonomy	congenital	hybrid

1. The veterinarian said my puppy was born with a defective heart valve, a _____congenital_____ condition that wasn't correctible.

2. Cheetahs and snow leopards eat mainly meat, so they are _____carnivorous_____ animals.

3. That particular brand of corn is a _____hybrid_____ developed by cross-pollinating two different varieties.

4. _____Taxonomy_____ is concerned with the systematic classification of plants and animals based on similar features; for example, crocodiles, lizards, and snakes are classified as reptiles because they all have horny skins and their offspring are hatched from eggs.

5. _____Plankton_____ are tiny animals and plants that drift in most bodies of water.

6. _____Homeostasis_____ is the term used to describe an organism's natural tendency to keep its system in normal condition, such as by maintaining the same internal temperature despite external conditions.

7. Snails and spiders don't have backbones, so they are classified as _____invertebrates_____ .

8. Fish are _____prolific_____ as they produce thousands of eggs.

Related Meanings: Set 2

If the words opposite each other are similar in meaning, write Yes *in the space; if they are unrelated, write* No.

1. plankton	Yes	tiny water plants and animals
2. taxonomy	No	dissection of animals
3. vertebrates	Yes	animals with spines
4. invertebrates	Yes	animals with no backbones
5. hominids	No	organisms that live only in water
6. herbivorous	Yes	primarily plant eating
7. carnivorous	No	eating both plants and animals
8. omnivorous	No	primarily meat eating
9. homeostasis	No	organisms native to a specific region or period
10. congenital	Yes	inborn
11. protoplasm	No	hardening of the bones
12. metabolism	Yes	sum of body's internal chemical and physical activities
13. ossification	No	semifluid considered to be the building block for all animals
14. hybrid	Yes	offspring of two different species
15. dormant	No	active state
16. prolific	No	intelligent

Writing Your Own Definitions: Set 2

Write either an original sentence or a definition for each term that clearly demonstrates your mastery of its meaning as used in the biological sciences. Answers will vary.

1. **taxonomy** _____

   _____

2. **dormant** _____

   _____

3. **congenital** _____

   _____

4. **vertebrates** _____

   _____

5. invertebrates _____

_____

6. prolific _____

_____

7. homeostasis _____

_____

8. carnivorous _____

_____

9. herbivorous _____

_____

10. omnivorous _____

_____

11. ossification _____

_____

12. plankton _____

_____

13. protoplasm _____

_____

14. hominids _____

_____

15. metabolism _____

_____

16. hybrid _____

_____

Completing a Passage: Biological Sciences

After reading the selection, fill in each space with one of the terms listed below.

prolific	congenital	botany	symbiosis	flora
dormant	habitat	hybrids	mutations	genetics

GREGOR JOHANN MENDEL

Gregor Johann Mendel (1822–1884) is considered to be the "father of modern ____genetics____" because he is recognized as the first scientist to study heredity in a comprehensive, systematic manner.

Mendel was born in what was then a part of the Austrian Empire but is today a part of the Czech Republic. When he was twenty-one, he entered St. Thomas Monastery in Moravia to study for the priesthood. In addition to being a monastery, St. Thomas was also an outstanding center for all types of study, including those focused on the sciences. The monastery grounds included a botanical garden that featured the ____flora____ of the area as well as cultivated plants that could also thrive in that particular ____habitat____ .

Mendel did become a priest, but it soon became obvious he was better suited to be a teacher. As a result, he was sent to study science and mathematics at the University of Vienna, returning to St. Thomas Monastery after two years. Inspired by his university teachers, Mendel became intensely interested in ____botany____ , particularly in the many variations of plants. He had learned scientific research skills while at the University of Vienna. Shortly after his return to St. Thomas, Mendel began his experiments relating to heredity by using thirty-four different kinds of peas. One of his interests was developing ____hybrids____ through crossbreeding. His research required the use of thousands of plants, and because peas are reasonably ____prolific____ in reproducing, they were well suited for his purposes.

During an eight-year period, Mendel cultivated and tested over 28,000 pea plants, carefully analyzing pairs of seeds and plants for their hereditary characteristics, which included unexpected ____mutations____ that were sometimes advantageous but most often were not. He also discovered that plants and other organisms, such as certain types of worms, often lived in ____symbiosis____ , an arrangement that helped each to benefit in a significant way.

Mendel believed it was essential to observe his experimental plants in all their stages, including when they were ____dormant____ , or inactive. As a result of long and careful studies, Mendel eventually discovered that he could predict with great accuracy the pattern of hereditary features that would appear in the various species of the plants in each generation.

Mendel published his important findings on heredity in 1866. His research abilities enabled him to express his results mathematically and statistically, and his findings were eventually recognized as being among the most important ones in the history of science.

In fact, Gregor Johann Mendel's pioneer work relating to heredity heralded the development of genetics into a specialized science. This field of science has advanced to the point that many of today's geneticists confidently say that we will be able to prevent ____congenital____ diseases and abnormalities that currently afflict thousands of newborns every year.

FEATURED WORD: homeostasis

Homeostasis—an organism's innate tendency to maintain its physiological processes in equilibrium:

- Jack said he was dizzy after his first ride on a roller coaster, but thanks to good old homeostasis, he laughingly added, his balance returned to normal after a few minutes.

Origin: <Greek—*homoios* (like) and *stasis* (stoppage, standing)
Family words: homeostatic (adj)
Image to remember: someone regaining his or her breath after running

Write an original sentence using *homeostasis*:

_____

_____

_____

imply   to throw out a suggestion without directly stating it:

Joanna's smiles seem to <u>imply</u> she had been accepted at the college she most wanted to attend.

infer   to draw a conclusion:

I could <u>infer</u> from my dad's scowl that he wasn't happy I hadn't shoveled the snow from the driveway.

Cricle the correct answer:

1. From our professor's coy remarks, she seemed to (imply)/ infer that we would have a pop quiz at our next class meeting; what did you imply /(infer) from what she said?

2. I didn't mean to (imply)/ infer from my snickering that Jackson isn't a good player, so you'd be wrong to imply /(infer) that he isn't; to tell you the truth, I snickered in sympathy with you because you're going to have your hands full trying to keep him from scoring points.

Write original sentences using these words:

1. **imply:** _____

2. **infer:** _____

Learning Physical Science Terms from Context Clues: Set 1

Physical sciences can refer to general science courses or courses focused primarily on geology, astronomy, chemistry, physics, or other specialties. Physical science courses contribute to our understanding of the hows and whys of our world and universe. Developments in the various subdivisions of physical science have led to advances in agriculture, industry, engineering, medicine, and many other fields. This chapter presents an opportunity to become familiar with some of the basic terms used in physical science courses.

1. **geology** (jē OL ə jē)—noun

   The scientific study of the origin, history, and structure of the earth.
   Earthquakes, landslides, volcanoes, and mineral resources are among the many subjects that are studied in *geology*.

2. **topography** (tə POG rə fē)—noun

   The detailed mapping or description of the surface features of a region.
   The state of New York's varied *topography* includes lakes, rivers, mountains, valleys, forests, and plains.

3. **sedimentary rocks** (sed ə MEN tə rē ROKS)—adjective + noun

   Rocks formed from the deposits of sediment (sand or other small fragments of solids).
   Sedimentary rocks are soft rocks, and they are often found in layers (strata).

4. **metamorphic rocks** (met ə MOR fik ROKS)—adjective + noun

   Rocks formed from sedimentary rocks that have been subjected to great pressure and heat beneath the earth's surface; they are the most common rocks in the earth's crust.
   Metamorphic rocks are hard; marble, for example, is a *metamorphic rock.*

5. **igneous rocks** (IG nē əs ROKS)— adjective + noun

   Rocks formed from cooled magma (hot liquid rock formed within the earth).
   Granite and basalt are *igneous rocks.*

6. **stalactites** (stə LAK tīts)—noun

   Icicle-shaped rocky deposits hanging from the <u>roofs of caves</u>.
   Stalactites are formed on the <u>roofs of caves</u> from the drippings of water containing certain minerals.

This photo of Chinese Theater in Carlsbad Caverns shows both *stalactites* and *stalagmites.*
(© David Muench/CORBIS)

7. **stalagmites** (stə LAG mīts)—noun

Rocky deposits that build up on the <u>floors of caves</u>.

Stalagmites are formed by the drippings of water containing certain minerals; they resemble upside-down stalactites. (To distinguish between stalactites and stalagmites, remember that stala<u>gmites</u> MIGHT reach the ceiling of the roof someday.)

8. **meteorology** (mē tē ə ROL ə jē)—noun

The science concerned with the earth's atmosphere, particularly its weather and climate.

In *meteorology,* <u>weather</u> refers to atmospheric conditions at a particular time; <u>climate</u>, on the other hand, refers to the average weather conditions over a period of years.

9. astronomy (ə STRON ə mē)—noun

The science concerned with the study of the universe beyond the earth's atmosphere.

Astronomy includes the study of the moon, sun, stars, planets, and asteroids (asteroids are sometimes referred to as minor planets).

10. solar, lunar (SŌ lər, LOO nər)—adjectives

<u>Solar</u> refers to the sun, and <u>lunar</u> refers to the moon.

Some houses are built or modified to take advantage of *solar* energy.
The period between full moons is called a *lunar* month.

11. celestial (sə LES chəl)—adjective

Relating to the sky or the heavens.
The Big Dipper is among the best-known *celestial* figures formed by stars.

12. zenith, nadir (ZĒ nith, NĀ dər)—nouns

<u>Zenith</u> is the <u>highest</u> point in the sky, or the point directly above the observer; <u>nadir</u> is the <u>lowest</u> point, or the point directly beneath a given position.

This month, the Big Dipper is at its *zenith,* or highest point, but in a few months, it will be at its *nadir,* or lowest point.

Matching Academic Terms and Definitions: Set 1

Match each definition with the term it defines.

<u>i</u>	**1.** igneous	**a.** rocky deposits that have formed on cave floors
<u>c</u>	**2.** astronomy	
<u>j</u>	**3.** nadir	**b.** rocks most common in the earth's crust
<u>l</u>	**4.** meteorology	**c.** study of the solar system and other matter beyond the earth's atmosphere
<u>a</u>	**5.** stalagmites	
<u>h</u>	**6.** zenith	**d.** study of a region's surface features
<u>m</u>	**7.** geology	**e.** relating to the sky or the heavens
<u>k</u>	**8.** solar	**f.** rocks formed from deposits of sediment
<u>b</u>	**9.** metamorphic	**g.** rocky deposits hanging from cave roofs
<u>n</u>	**10.** lunar	**h.** highest point
<u>g</u>	**11.** stalactites	**i.** rocks formed from cooled magma
<u>f</u>	**12.** sedimentary	**j.** lowest point
<u>e</u>	**13.** celestial	**k.** pertains to the sun
<u>d</u>	**14.** topography	**l.** science of weather and climate
		m. study of the earth's origin, history, and structure
		n. pertains to the moon

Fill-Ins with Academic Terms: Set 1

In each space, write the appropriate term from those listed below.

geology	topography	stalagmites	metamorphic	solar
astronomy	stalactites	nadir	sedimentary	
igneous	zenith	meteorology	lunar	

1. Granite, used to create buildings, stairs, and other structures, is a(n)
   _____ igneous _____ rock.

2. Oddly shaped _____ stalactites _____ could be seen hanging from the cave's roof
   while large _____ stalagmites _____ had built up on the cave's floor.

3. _____ Topography _____ includes the study of cartography (mapmaking) because
   maps contribute to a comprehensive understanding of an area's surface features.

4. _____ Sedimentary _____ rocks are soft rocks often found in layers, or strata.

5. The Raymonds have _____ solar _____ panels on their house roof, and they
   say the sun's rays provide them with an economical source of heat.

6. During July, that particular constellation, viewed from our country, is at its
   _____ zenith _____ , or highest location.

7. Sierra is majoring in _____ geology _____ as she's interested in the study of
   earthquakes, volcanoes, and other matters relating to the earth's structure.

8. By the third week in December, the sun is at its _____ nadir _____ , or
   lowest point in this part of the world.

9. _____ Metamorphic _____ rocks, which are the most common rocks in the earth's
   crust, are formed from another class of rocks after being subjected to tremendous
   pressure and heat beneath the earth's surface.

10. _____ Meteorology _____ is the scientific study of weather and climate.

11. Is a(n) _____ lunar _____ month the same as a calendar month? And is the
    moon really responsible for the tides of oceans?

Related Meanings: Set 1

*If the words opposite each other are similar in meaning, write Yes in the space; if they
are unrelated, write No.*

1. stalactites   _Yes_ rocky deposits on cave roofs
2. astronomy   _Yes_ study of matter in the universe beyond the earth
3. lunar   _No_   pertains to stars
4. zenith   _No_   circular orbit of the earth
5. meteorology   _No_   study of matter in space smaller than planets
6. nadir   _Yes_ lowest point
7. metamorphic   _Yes_ hard rocks like granite

8. stalagmites	Yes	rocky deposits on cave floors
9. celestial	No	relates to bodies of water
10. igneous	Yes	rocks formed from hot liquid rock (magma)
11. geology	Yes	study of the origin, structure, and history of the earth
12. topography	No	science devoted to the study of weather and climate
13. sedimentary	Yes	soft rocks formed from sediment
14. solar	No	pertains to the boiling lava found deep inside the earth

Writing Your Own Definitions: Set 1

Write either an original sentence or a definition for each term that clearly demonstrates your mastery of its meaning as used in the physical sciences.   Answers will vary.

1. **astronomy** _____

_____

2. **nadir** _____

_____

3. **meteorology** _____

_____

4. **zenith** _____

_____

5. **celestial** _____

_____

6. **stalactites** _____

_____

7. **solar** _____

_____

8. **lunar** _____

_____

9. **stalagmites** _____

_____

10. **geology** _____

_____

11. **igneous rocks** _____

_____

12. **metamorphic rocks** _____

_____

13. **sedimentary rocks** _____

_____

14. **topography** _____

_____

Learning Physical Science Terms from Context Clues: Set 2

1. **chemistry** (KEM ə strē)—noun

   The composition, structure, properties, and reactions of substances.

   The study of *chemistry* includes the investigation of substances' atomic and molecular systems.

2. **organic, inorganic chemistry** (or GAN ik, in or GAN ik KEM ə strē)— adjectives + noun

   Organic chemistry is concerned with basic substances and matter containing carbon, which include all organisms.

   The compounds (see **8**) of plants and animals, which contain carbon, are among the topics studied in *organic chemistry*.

   In contrast, inorganic chemistry is concerned with basic non-carbon substances and matter.

   Acids and minerals containing no carbon are studied in *inorganic chemistry*.

3. **element** (EL ə mənt)—noun

   A fundamental substance that cannot be separated into other substances by chemical means; there are more than a hundred elements.

   Hydrogen is classified as an *element* because it cannot be broken down into other substances.

4. **atom** (AT əm)—noun

   The smallest unit of an element that still retains all the chemical properties of the element.

   One oxygen *atom* combines with two hydrogen *atoms* to form water.

This diagram shows the locations of *protons, electrons,* and *neutrons* within an *atom*.

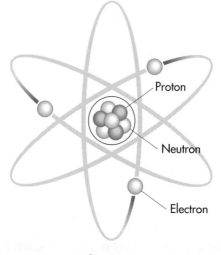

The Atom

5. **proton, electron, neutron** (PRŌ ton, ə LEK tron, NOO tron)—nouns

   A <u>proton</u> is a very small particle in all atoms; it has a <u>positive</u> electric charge.

   An <u>electron</u> is a very small particle in all atoms; it has a <u>negative</u> electric charge.

   A <u>neutron</u> is a very small particle in all atoms except hydrogen, and it has <u>no</u> electric charge.

   Atoms contain minute particles containing *protons, electrons,* and *neutrons.*

6. **nucleus** (NOO cle əs)—noun

   The central part of an atom containing protons and neutrons.

   The *nucleus* of an atom has a positive charge because of its protons. Electrons, which have a negative charge, are not a core part of the nucleus.

7. **molecule** (MOL ə kūl)—noun

   Smallest particle of any material capable of existing independently; it contains all the chemical properties of the material.

   A *molecule* is formed from atoms with balancing attractive forces.

8. <u>**compound**</u> (KOM pound)—noun

   A pure substance composed of two or more elements chemically united in a specific proportion; therefore, it can be broken down into two or more other pure substances by a chemical change.

   Water is a *compound* whose molecules contain two atoms of hydrogen and one atom of oxygen (H_2O).

9. <u>synthesis</u> (SIN thə sis)—noun

The process of combining elements to form a compound.
The *synthesis* of various chemical processes led to the development of nylon.

10. **catalyst** (KAT ə list)—noun

A substance that initiates or accelerates a chemical reaction without itself undergoing any permanent change.
Chlorophyll is the *catalyst* responsible for the increased rate at which food is made in plants.

11. **solute** (SOL ūt)—noun

Any gas or solid that will dissolve or disappear when water or other liquid is added.
Salt is a *solute;* when added to water, the salt dissolves.

12. **physics** (FIZ iks)—noun

The study of matter and energy and the interactions between the two.
Acoustics (relating to sound), optics (relating to vision), and mechanics are among the subjects studied in *physics.*

13. **kinetic, potential energy** (kə NET ik, pə TEN shəl EN ər jē)—adjectives + nouns

<u>Kinetic</u> energy is energy in motion; <u>potential</u> energy is stored energy.
A swinging hammer displays *kinetic energy;* a hammer at rest has *potential energy.*

14. **centrifugal, centripetal forces** (sen TRIF ə gəl, sen TRIP ə təl FŌRS əs)— adjectives + noun

<u>Centrifugal</u> refers to the force that propels an object outward from the center of rotation; <u>centripetal</u> refers to the force that tends to draw an object inward toward the center of rotation.
When a rock is swung at the end of a string, the rock exerts an outward force on the string as it seeks to fly off in space; this is *centrifugal* force at work. On the other hand, the string pulls inwardly on the moving rock to keep it in its circular path; this is *centripetal* force at work.

15. **oscillate** (OS ə lāt)—verb

To swing to and fro, vibrate, or fluctuate; to make a wavelike motion.
The pendulum will *oscillate* when it is released.

16. malleable (MAL ē ə bəl)—adjective

Describes objects that can be hammered or shaped without breaking.

Metals are *malleable*; that is, they can be processed into desired shapes.

Matching Academic Terms and Definitions: Set 2

Match each definition with the term it defines.

A

_a_	**1.** inorganic	**a.** branch of chemistry concerned with the study of non-carbon materials
_c_	**2.** proton	
_i_	**3.** chemistry	**b.** combining process
_b_	**4.** synthesis	**c.** has a positive charge
_f_	**5.** atom	**d.** substance that cannot be broken down into other substances
_g_	**6.** electron	
_d_	**7.** element	**e.** branch of chemistry concerned with the study of materials containing carbon
_j_	**8.** neutron	
_e_	**9.** organic	**f.** the smallest unit of an element
_h_	**10.** nucleus	**g.** has a negative charge
		h. atom's central part
		i. study of the composition, structure, properties, and reactions of substances
		j. has no electric charge

B

_g_	**1.** solute	**a.** describes objects that can be hammered and molded
_h_	**2.** kinetic	**b.** stored energy
_d_	**3.** compound	**c.** outward force
_f_	**4.** physics	**d.** a pure substance containing two or more elements
_i_	**5.** centripetal	**e.** increases chemical reaction rate
_b_	**6.** potential	**f.** study of energy and matter and their interactions
_a_	**7.** malleable	**g.** gas or solid that dissolves in liquid
_j_	**8.** molecule	**h.** energy in motion
_k_	**9.** oscillate	**i.** inward force
_c_	**10.** centrifugal	**j.** smallest particle of any material capable of existing independently
_e_	**11.** catalyst	
		k. to vibrate

Fill-Ins with Academic Terms: Set 2

In each space, write the appropriate term from those listed below.

A

chemistry	synthesis	inorganic	neutrons	potential	solutes	atoms
nucleus	electrons	organic	kinetic	catalyst	protons	

1. Over the years, combining substances and procedures, a process known as
   _____synthesis_____ , has led to the improvement of innumerable products as
   well as the development of countless new ones.

2. _____Atoms_____ , the smallest particles of elements, contain
   _____protons_____ (positive electric charges), _____electrons_____
   (negative electric charges), and _____neutrons_____ (no electric charges).

3. An atom's _____nucleus_____ is a very dense region with a positive charge.

4. The project the scientists are working on in the laboratory is to develop a
   _____catalyst_____ that will speed up the chemical reaction rate necessary to
   produce the special dyes used in medical diagnoses and research.

5. Water cascading over a dam is _____kinetic_____ energy, while water held
   in reserve behind a dam is _____potential_____ energy.

6. My high school _____chemistry_____ course was about the structure, properties, and reactions of a wide variety of substances, but my current college course
   in _____organic_____ chemistry concentrates solely on substances containing
   carbon, like animals and plants. Then next fall, I'll be taking a course in
   _____inorganic_____ chemistry, a course focusing exclusively on non-carbon
   substances, like acids and minerals.

7. Carbon dioxide and oxygen are gases that dissolve in water, so they are
   considered _____solutes_____ .

B

malleable	molecule	compound	centripetal
centrifugal	physics	elements	

1. _____Elements_____ are fundamental substances consisting of atoms of only
   one kind, so they cannot be broken down into other substances and, either singly
   or in combination, they compose everything that exists.

2. Chemists use symbols to represent the 100+ elements. For example, the
   element sodium is represented by Na and the element chlorine by Cl. When
   these elements are combined, salt (NaCl) is formed. Salt, then, is a
   _____compound_____ because it is made by joining elements.

3. Formed by atoms, the smallest particle of a material that can exist independently
   is a _____molecule_____ .

4. Metals, such as aluminum, steel, and titanium, are _____malleable_____ , so they are used to make thousands of objects, ranging from airplanes to golf clubs.

5. _____Physics_____ is the study of matter and energy and the interactions between the two, including the effects of _____centrifugal_____ (outward) and _____centripetal_____ (inward) forces that characterize objects in circular motion.

Related Meanings: Set 2

If the words opposite each other are similar in meaning, write Yes *in the space; if they are unrelated, write* No.

1. malleable	Yes	describes something that can be molded or shaped, such as steel
2. potential energy	No	magnetic power
3. centrifugal force	Yes	outward force
4. oscillate	Yes	swing to and fro
5. kinetic energy	Yes	energy in motion
6. centripetal force	No	causes objects to stay upright
7. catalyst	Yes	something that speeds chemical reaction rate
8. molecule	No	atom's center
9. physics	Yes	study of matter and energy and their interactions
10. element	Yes	a basic substance that cannot be divided into other substances
11. organic chemistry	Yes	study of basic substances containing carbon
12. solute	No	liquid oxygen
13. nucleus	No	study of hydraulics containing hot fluids
14. inorganic chemistry	No	study of basic substances containing no acids
15. proton	Yes	positive electric charge
16. synthesis	No	separating process used in chemistry
17. neutron	No	negative electric charge
18. compound	Yes	contains two or more elements
19. chemistry	No	study focusing exclusively on hereditary factors
20. electron	No	no electric charge
21. atom	No	salt, sugar, and similar compounds

Writing Your Own Definitions: Set 2

Write either an original sentence or a definition for each term that clearly demonstrates your mastery of its meaning as used in the physical sciences.   Answers will vary.

1. proton _____

_____

2. centrifugal force _____

_____

3. **atom** _____

_____

4. **chemistry** _____

_____

5. **organic chemistry** _____

_____

6. **electron** _____

_____

7. **nucleus** _____

_____

8. **neutron** _____

_____

9. **inorganic chemistry** _____

_____

10. **centripetal force** _____

_____

11. **kinetic energy** _____

_____

12. **synthesis** _____

_____

13. **malleable** _____

_____

14. **element** _____

_____

15. **potential energy** _____

_____

16. **catalyst** _____

_____

17. **solute** _____

_____

18. molecule _____

_____

19. physics _____

_____

20. oscillate _____

_____

21. compound _____

_____

Completing a Passage: Physical Sciences

After reading the selection, fill in each space with one of the terms listed below.

catalysts	molecules	neutrons	solutes	elements	synthesis
organic	chemistry	electrons	compounds	chemistry	protons

MARY PETERS FIESER, CHEMIST

Mary Peters Fieser was born in 1909 in Atchison, Kansas, but her family moved to Harrisburg, Pennsylvania, when she was still a child. She attended Bryn Mawr College, located near Philadelphia, with the intention of becoming a doctor. However, she changed her major to ____*chemistry*____ after becoming interested in the composition, properties, and reactions of substances. Her decision to major in this subject was also influenced by her chemistry professor, Dr. Louis Fieser.

After graduating from Bryn Mawr in 1930, she moved to Massachusetts to work on a master's degree in chemistry. Although she took most of her courses at Harvard University, Mary had to enroll at nearby Radcliffe College because Harvard did not admit women students at that time. Louis Fieser had accepted a faculty position at Harvard, and Mary was able to work in his research group, which centered on *organic chemistry*, the branch concerned with substances containing carbon. While Professor Fieser was open to allowing women to work in his lab to study ____*elements*____, such as hydrogen, and ____*compounds*____, such as salt (formed by combining sodium and chorine), other Harvard faculty certainly were not. One of Mary's chemistry professors would not even allow her to do the lab assignments in *his* laboratory, so she had to do them unsupervised in the basement of a nearby building. Despite such obstacles, Mary received her master's degree in 1932, and she and Louis Fieser were married shortly afterward.

Mary Peters Fieser
(Courtesy Bryn Mawr Library)

    Mary and Louis Fieser collaborated in their research, much of which was devoted to _____synthesis_____ , including the combining of _____molecules_____ , the smallest particles of materials capable of existing independently. During World War II in the 1940s, they synthesized sources of quinine, a compound used to treat malaria, a serious illness soldiers fighting in the tropics often contracted. Such projects required the Fiesers to search for _____catalysts_____ to speed up chemical reactions and to experiment with _____solutes_____ to discover which ones dissolved faster in various liquids. The Fiesers also synthesized cortisone and other steroid hormones.

While their research brought the Fiesers a great deal of international attention, their real fame came after they wrote their immensely popular textbook *Organic Chemistry*. First published in 1944, it went through many new editions over the years and was translated into many foreign languages. Mary is credited with writing the widely admired and influential chapters having to do with real-world applications of organic chemistry. This textbook also contained biographical information about 454 different chemists, including those whose work centered on the particles in atoms: ____protons____ (positive charges), ____electrons____ (negative charges), and ____neutrons____ (no charges). Louis and Mary's writing is known for its originality, charm, clarity, and elegance—a notable accomplishment given the complexity of much of their subject matter.

In 1971, Mary was awarded the American Chemical Society's Garvan Medal. After Louis died in 1977, she continued her research and writing at Harvard. Throughout her nearly sixty-year association with Harvard, Mary never received a salary, even after she held the title of research associate.

In 1996, Harvard dedicated the Louis and Mary Fieser Laboratory for Undergraduate Organic Chemistry. The following year, Mary Peters Fieser, universally recognized as one of the outstanding chemists of the 20th century, died at the age of eighty-seven.

Chemistry—the science of the composition, structure, properties, and reactions of matter, especially of atomic and molecular systems:

- One of the first things I learned in my <u>chemistry</u> course was that the molecules in liquids are in constant motion and tend to escape from the surface and become gaseous molecules, with some liquids doing so even at temperatures far below the boiling point. (Water's boiling point is 212 degrees Fahrenheit or 100 degrees Celsius.)

Origin: Originally, chemistry was called "alchemy," which referred to the "natural physical process." Alchemy became a so-called art or practice during the Middle Ages (350–1450), first in Egypt, then in other parts of the Middle East, and eventually in Europe. The major goal of alchemy was to discover a way to convert common metals to gold and silver. Though this goal was never realized, it did lead to the discovery of new substances. The term *alchemy* can be traced to the Greek word *khymeia* (that which is poured out). *Chemistry*, as a term and as a scientific study, dates to the late 1700s.

Family words: chemical (adj), chemist (n)

Image to remember: experiments being conducted by people in white lab coats

Write an original sentence using *chemistry*:

_____

_____

_____

can   able to do something:

Vanessa is confident she <u>can</u> be at the airport in half an hour.

may   permission to do something:

<u>May</u> I borrow your car this evening?

Circle the correct answer:

1. You <u>can</u> / (may) borrow my car this evening if you (can) / may fill it up with gas.

2. If I can / (may) talk with you for a few minutes, I'm sure I (can) / may help you understand Troy's point of view.

Write original sentences using these words:

1. **may:** _____

2. **can:** _____

Learning Computer Science Terms from Context Clues: Set 1

Computer science is changing so rapidly that keeping up with its technological innovations and ever-expanding vocabulary is a major challenge. However, the terms that are featured in this chapter remain at the heart of computer language.

1. **terminal** (TUR mə nəl)—noun

   Consists of a keyboard that enters information into the computer and a screen that displays the computer's responses.

   A computer *terminal* combines the features of a typewriter and a television screen.

2. **monitor** (MON ə tər)—noun

   The screen displaying computer information. A monitor is also known as a CRT (cathode ray tube).

   This *monitor* displays tables and graphs in vivid colors.

3. **peripheral** (pə RIF ər əl)—noun

   An extra device, such as a printer or a data storage component, that is added to the computer.

   A *peripheral* you should consider adding to your computer is a letter-quality printer.

4. **port** (PORT)—noun

   A connector on the back of a computer where a peripheral is attached.

   The printer cable must be attached to the correct *port*.

5. **cursor, mouse** (KUR sor, MOWSE)—nouns

   A cursor is a movable pointer on a computer screen that indicates where an insertion, deletion, or other operation can take place.

   The *cursor* moves automatically to the next space after you type. You can also move the *cursor* up, down, backward, or forward.

   A mouse is a hand-held device for moving a cursor and entering simple commands and information.

   After selecting the symbol you want, press the button on the *mouse*.

6. **icons** (Ī kons)—noun

Small pictures representing the various options available to the user of that particular computer program. Icons are displayed on the monitor, or computer screen.

You can get rid of your old e-mail by clicking your mouse on the wastepaper basket *icon.*

7. **fonts** (FONTS)—noun

The various type sizes, styles, and symbols a computer is capable of producing, such as italics, script, and boldface.

A special set of *fonts* will give you the ability to change the type size and style.

8. **modem** (MŌ dem)—noun

A device used to link a computer to a telephone network, permitting information to be transmitted from one computer system to another. A fax/modem allows data to be transmitted to a fax (facsimile) machine, which prints the data out on paper.

The college has a local computer bulletin board accessible by a *modem.*

9. **memory** (MEM ə rē), **RAM** (Random Access Memory), **ROM** (Read Only Memory)—nouns

Memory refers to the computer's capacity for storing information. Today, most memory is stored on a hard disk (as opposed to a floppy disk or diskette) permanently installed inside the computer. RAM is the part of the computer's memory that can be added to or deleted from; because RAM can be changed, it is also called read/write memory. ROM is the computer's preprogrammed memory; it cannot be added to or deleted from.

RAM is the computer's electronic *memory;* it contains instructions and data a specific computer program can execute.

ROM is the preprogrammed *memory* that loads the computer's operating system.

10. **binary, bit, byte** (BĪ nə rē, BIT, BĪT)—nouns

Binary refers to two digits: 0 and 1.
Computer operations are based on a *binary* number system.
A bit is a single binary digit.
A *bit* is the smallest piece of information stored in a computer.
Byte is the unit of data or memory now universally taken to mean eight bits.
The size of a computer's memory is described in terms of *bytes.*

Matching Academic Terms and Definitions: Set 1

Match each definition with the term it defines.

A

_c_	**1.** peripheral	**a.** computer screen
_d_	**2.** binary	**b.** memory that can be added to or deleted from
_e_	**3.** ROM	**c.** accessory added to a computer
_a_	**4.** monitor	**d.** based on 0 and 1
_g_	**5.** icons	**e.** computer's preprogrammed memory
_b_	**6.** RAM	**f.** hand-held device used for entering commands
_f_	**7.** mouse	**g.** small pictures representing various computer options

B

_d_	**1.** bit	**a.** consists of eight bits
_e_	**2.** terminal	**b.** various typefaces, such as italics
_b_	**3.** fonts	**c.** connector on the back of a computer
_f_	**4.** cursor	**d.** a single binary digit
_g_	**5.** modem	**e.** computer keyboard and screen
_a_	**6.** byte	**f.** movable screen pointer
_c_	**7.** port	**g.** permits computers to communicate over telephone wires

Fill-Ins with Academic Terms: Set 1

In each space, write the appropriate term from those listed below.

terminal	port	icon	RAM	bits
monitor	cursor	fonts	ROM	byte
peripheral	mouse	modem	binary	

1. A(n) _____modem_____ is a device used to link a computer to a telephone network.

2. A computer uses a(n) _____binary_____ number system, that is, of two digits, 0 and 1.

3. A(n) _____mouse_____ , controlled by one hand, is used to enter commands into the computer.

4. This set of _____fonts_____ contains a number of decorative typefaces.

5. A(n) _____byte_____ is a unit of data or memory consisting of eight _____bits_____ .

6. Reggie moved the _____cursor_____ on the screen and clicked on "Edit."

7. You'll have to connect the printer cable to a(n) _____port_____ on the back of the computer.

8. My roommate bought a new _____monitor_____ , or computer screen, that is one of the largest I've seen, but it is less than two inches thick.

9. _____ROM_____ is the computer's preprogrammed memory, so it can't be changed; on the other hand, _____RAM_____ is memory that can be added to or deleted from.

10. Because a keyboard is a necessity, it is not considered a(n) _____peripheral_____.

11. The _____icon_____ I clicked on the most is the one showing a tiny picture of an envelope, which gets me to my e-mail.

12. The keyboard and screen of a laptop or notebook computer are significantly smaller than the _____terminal_____ of a desktop computer.

Related Meanings: Set 1

If the words opposite each other are similar in meaning, write Yes *in the space; if they are unrelated, write* No.

1.	fonts	Yes	keyboard's assortment of typefaces
2.	ROM	Yes	Read Only Memory
3.	bit	No	a computer timing device
4.	port	No	popular Internet website
5.	peripheral	Yes	computer accessory, such as a printer
6.	mouse	No	computer screen saver
7.	cursor	No	a computer error
8.	RAM	No	one of the most popular computer models
9.	monitor	Yes	computer screen
10.	terminal	No	an outdated computer program
11.	binary	No	movable pointer
12.	byte	Yes	a unit of information consisting of eight bits
13.	icons	Yes	small pictorial representations representing options
14.	modem	No	memory-saving part of the computer

Writing Your Own Definitions: Set 1

Write either an original sentence or a definition for each term that clearly demonstrates your mastery of its meaning as used in computer science.   Answers will vary.

1. **terminal** _____

_____

2. **monitor** _____

_____

3. **peripheral** _____

_____

4. **port** _____

_____

5. cursor _____

_____

6. mouse _____

_____

7. icons _____

_____

8. fonts _____

_____

9. modem _____

_____

10. memory _____

_____

11. RAM _____

_____

12. ROM _____

_____

13. binary _____

_____

14. bit _____

_____

15. byte _____

_____

Learning Computer Science Terms from Context Clues: Set 2

1. **hardware, software** (HARD WĀR, SOFT WĀR)—nouns

   <u>Hardware</u> refers to the physical parts of the computer system, such as the terminal and monitor. <u>Software</u> refers to computer programs written to perform specific tasks.

   The insurance company is spending thousands of dollars to update its computer *hardware* and *software*.

2. **file** (FĪL)—noun

A collection of related information stored on a disk. A file can contain a professionally prepared program or a user-created document.

A *file* must be given a specific title, such as "Team Statistics," and steps must be taken to save it on the computer's hard disk or the *file* will be lost when the computer is shut off.

3. **database** (DĀ tə bāys)—noun

A computer program used to manage large collections of information related to a particular subject or purpose.

Mailing lists, phone numbers, e-mail addresses, and payroll information are examples of information often contained in *databases.*

4. **spreadsheet** (SPREED shēt)—noun

A computer program that organizes numerical data into rows and columns.

The accountant entered the numbers on the *spreadsheet* program, which then presented the data in rows and columns on the screen.

5. **hacker** (HAK ər)—noun

A person who "hacks" or breaks into other people's computer files to look at, copy, change, or destroy their data. A hacker is able to do this by figuring out the password being used to protect such data; this is called "cracking" the password.

Hackers are electronic outlaws because they illegally tamper with other people's computer files.

6. **virus** (VĪ rəs)—noun

A program that attaches itself to other programs and then reproduces itself, damaging the data in the other programs.

Most computer *viruses* are deliberately written by *hackers* who either want to destroy data or want to frustrate other computer users.

7. **crash** (KRASH)—noun

A slang word for when a computer stops working properly. A crash can occur when the operating system or software application malfunctions. Viruses also can cause a crash, as can a severe storm that disrupts electrical service. Because *crashes* are not uncommon, you should always "save" your work in a file, even when the file is incomplete. You do this by clicking on "File" on the top left of your screen, then clicking on "Save."

8. **menu bar** (MEN yoo BAR)—adjective + noun

The horizontal bar across the top of the computer screen that allows a user to point-and-click the mouse on functions he or she wants the computer to do, such as retrieve, save, or print a file. A "menu" drops down from the horizontal bar displaying the various options available for that specific function.

Tova went to the *menu bar* at the top of the screen and clicked on "Format" as she wanted to change the font size she was using for her report.

9. **download** (DOWN lohd)—verb

To copy a file onto one's computer.

Shane is *downloading* an antivirus program onto his computer.

10. **Internet** (IN tər net)—noun

A computer network is a group of computers connected together so they can communicate with one another; the Internet connects thousands of such computer networks. The Internet, then, is actually a network of networks.

Computer networks of governments, libraries, businesses, universities, and other organizations throughout the nation and the world make up the *Internet.*

11. **e-mail** (Ē MĀL)—noun

The Internet has made possible e-mail, or electronic mail. E-mail provides instantaneous personal and business communication.

"Spam" is unsolicited *e-mail* on the Internet; it is considered junk mail by most computer users, much like unsolicited phone marketing generally is.

12. **domain name** (dō MĀN NĀM)—adjective + noun

The name located to the right of the @ sign in an e-mail address. The most common domain names are .com (commercial site); .gov (government site); .edu (educational institution site); .net (network site); and .org (nonprofit organization site).

You can get the homepage of the University of McKay by using this e-mail address, which includes the *domain name* edu: umckay@umk.edu.

13. **World Wide Web** (WURLD WĪD WEB)—noun

The World Wide Web (WWW), or Web, is the powerful Internet facility that permits access to information from hundreds of sources and from all parts of the world. Web "pages" feature hypertext, a system that highlights key words; when you "click" your mouse on a key word, the screen provides more in-depth information relating to your topic. Hypermedia is similar, but it displays pictures and other types of illustrations as well.

The *World Wide Web* provided me with numerous sources about Monticello, Thomas Jefferson's home near Charlottesville, Virginia. Then by clicking my mouse on a number of hypertext and hypermedia words, I was able to secure the information and illustrations I needed to complete my research project.

14. **search engine** (surch EN jin)—adjective + noun

A website used to locate other websites that will lead you to the specific information you desire.

After an appropriate word or phrase is typed at the top of the web page, a *search engine,* such as Google or Yahoo!, will list the most promising sites for the information being sought.

15. blog (BLOG)—noun

Short for <u>weblog</u>, which is essentially a computer journal that is frequently updated by its author and available to anyone who has access to the Internet.

A *blog* generally reflects the author's opinions, which can range from humorous to outrageous, about a particular topic, such as politics or celebrities.

Matching Academic Terms and Definitions: Set 2

Match each definition with the term it defines.

A

_c_	**1.** database	**a.** facility that locates information available on the Internet
_f_	**2.** spreadsheet	
_a_	**3.** World Wide Web	**b.** network of networks
_h_	**4.** hacker	**c.** program used to manage large data collections
_g_	**5.** hardware	
_b_	**6.** Internet	**d.** related information stored on a disk
_e_	**7.** download	**e.** to copy a file or program onto a computer
_d_	**8.** file	**f.** organizes data into rows and columns
		g. a computer's physical equipment
		h. breaks into other computer users' programs

B

_e_	**1.** software	**a.** a horizontal band at the top of the computer screen that allows a computer user to point-and-click on specific functions
_c_	**2.** virus	
_h_	**3.** search engine	
_f_	**4.** e-mail	**b.** computer stops working properly
_a_	**5.** menu bar	**c.** damages other programs by reproducing itself
_g_	**6.** blog	**d.** unsolicited and usually unwanted e-mail
_i_	**7.** domain name	**e.** programs written to perform specific tasks
_b_	**8.** crash	**f.** electronic mail
_d_	**9.** spam	**g.** a site in which a person writes his or her opinions about a topic or topics
		h. a website used to locate information available on the Internet
		i. registered name to the right of the @ in an e-mail address

Fill-Ins with Academic Terms: Set 2

In each space, write the appropriate term from those listed below.

A

e-mail	spreadsheets	crash	hackers	files	spam
domain name	software	viruses	download	Internet	

Most computer _____viruses_____ are caused by _____hackers_____ who wish to break into another user's program, either to obtain private information or to simply cause mischief. Fortunately, there are _____software_____ programs that can provide a high degree of protection against this type of invasion. Business enterprises find such protection crucial to their success because many of their _____files_____ are _____spreadsheets_____ containing rows and columns of sensitive financial information.

Of course, there are other reasons why a computer may _____crash_____ , such as an extensive power outage, a major operating system malfunction, or a foolish attempt to _____download_____ a protected program from the _____Internet_____ .

In addition, sometimes unsolicited _____e-mail_____ , known as _____spam_____ , can trigger a virus, so even though you may recognize the _____domain name_____ (such as .edu) of the sender, if the rest of his or her address is unfamiliar or suspicious looking, you would be wise to delete the message rather than open it.

B

menu bar   blog   hardware   database   search engine   World Wide Web

1. This _____database_____ contains the names, addresses, phone numbers, and e-mail addresses of the college's alumni.

2. The horizontal _____menu bar_____ enables you to click on numerous functions, including "File," "Edit," "Format," "Tools," and others.

3. I went to the popular _____search engine_____ known as Google to find information about the community college I was interested in attending.

4. The _____blog_____ I check out periodically is one having to do with surfing.

5. Over the years, computer _____hardware_____ , especially monitors, has become lighter and slimmer.

6. The _____World Wide Web_____ "pages" feature hypertext, a system highlighting key words, and hypermedia, a system displaying illustrations.

Related Meanings: Set 2

If the words opposite each other are similar in meaning, write Yes *in the space; if they are unrelated, write* No.

1. virus   <u>No</u>   upgrades computer programs
2. Internet   <u>Yes</u>   the network of computer networks
3. WWW   <u>Yes</u>   World Wide Web
4. file   <u>No</u>   instrument used to speed up computer feedback
5. database   <u>Yes</u>   a computer program used to manage large collections of information
6. search engine   <u>No</u>   a computer's recycle bin
7. hardware   <u>Yes</u>   a computer's physical equipment
8. software   <u>No</u>   term used for outdated equipment
9. spreadsheet   <u>No</u>   an anti-virus program
10. hacker   <u>No</u>   computer beginner
11. download   <u>Yes</u>   to duplicate a file or program onto another computer
12. e-mail   <u>Yes</u>   electronic mail
13. domain name   <u>No</u>   name to the left of the @ in e-mail addresses
14. crash   <u>Yes</u>   malfunction that stops the computer from working
15. spam   <u>No</u>   computer journal an author makes available on the Internet
16. menu bar   <u>Yes</u>   allows user to point-and-click on specific functions
17. blog   <u>No</u>   junk e-mail

Writing Your Own Definitions: Set 2

Write either an original sentence or a definition for each term that clearly demonstrates your mastery of its meaning as used in computer science.   Answers will vary.

1. **search engine** _____

   _____

2. **spam** _____

   _____

3. **Internet** _____

   _____

4. **World Wide Web** _____

   _____

5. **hardware** _____

   _____

6. file _____

_____

7. menu bar _____

_____

8. database _____

_____

9. crash _____

_____

10. spreadsheet _____

_____

11. domain name _____

_____

12. hacker _____

_____

13. blog _____

_____

14. download _____

_____

15. e-mail _____

_____

16. software _____

_____

17. virus _____

_____

Completing a Passage: Computer Science

After reading the selection, fill in each space with one of the terms listed below.

terminal	peripherals	World Wide Web	mouse	binary
ROM	spreadsheets	e-mail	RAM	cursor
Internet	search engine	software	bytes	
databases	icons	bits	monitor	

A BRIEF HISTORY OF PERSONAL COMPUTERS

The history of computers can, in a sense, be traced back hundreds of years to the abacus. An abacus consists of a wooden frame, inside of which beads are moved to make arithmetic calculations. In fact, this simple but clever device is still being used in some parts of the world. But the origin of computers as we know them dates back to the 1940s. However, these early computers such as ENIAC (Electronic Numerical Integrator And Computer), were enormous and as expensive to build as large airplanes, and they were limited for the most part to mathematical calculations.

By the early 1970s integrated electronic circuits and microprocessors had been developed, paving the way for a new generation of computers, as it now became possible to combine the basic elements of a computer onto tiny silicon computer chips. A computer's capacity for storing information increased dramatically, making possible all types of computer operations based on the ____binary____ number system, which uses the two digits 0 and 1, with ____bytes____ (each consisting of eight ____bits____) determining the size of a computer's memory. Eventually, ____RAM____ (Random Access Memory) and ____ROM____ (Read Only Memory) became familiar acronyms to computer users.

In 1977, Steven Jobs and Stephen Wozniak created Apple II, the first PC (personal computer) to have color graphics and a keyboard, or ____terminal____ . In 1984, the Apple Macintosh was introduced, a computer that featured a graphical user interface (GUI) that combined ____icons____ (small pictures that represent files or programs) with windows (boxes containing an open file or program). The Macintosh also introduced the hand-held device, dubbed a(n) ____mouse____ , that could move a pointing device (called a[n] ____cursor____) on the ____monitor____ , or screen.

In 1981, IBM (International Business Machines Corporation) introduced a PC purposely designed so that other computer companies could create similar machines (clones) that could also use IBM's ____software____ , or computer programs. Computer ____peripherals____ , such as printers, also became available to the public. In 1984,

Michael Dell, a college student at the time, began a computer company with just $1,000; by 2007, the Dell Computer Corporation showed gross sales of over $14 billion.

The first independent version of Microsoft Windows 1.0, developed by Bill Gates and others, appeared on the scene in 1985. Windows became extremely popular with people of all ages, including those who play computer games and those who create ___databases___ (large collections of information) and ___spreadsheets___ (numerical data).

With the development of the ___Internet___ , that superhighway of computer networks, and the ___World Wide Web___ (WWW) in the 1990s, computer users could now, by using a(n) ___search engine___ like Yahoo!, access thousands—if not millions—of sources of information. In addition, the development of ___e-mail___ enabled companies to conduct business quickly and people to stay in touch easily.

In a relatively short period, PCs have revolutionized all segments of our society. In fact, it is undoubtedly hard for most of us to imagine when our country and the rest of the world was "computer-less." One thing is for sure: PCs will continue to develop in ways unimaginable to us at the present time, resulting in even more changes in how we lead our lives.

FEATURED WORD: peripheral

Peripheral—(1) relating to an outer boundary; (2) superficial, of minor importance; (3) a computer accessory, such as a printer:

- Fans were lining the <u>peripheral</u> fence of the track to watch the mile race.
- Gaylord has only <u>peripheral</u> interest in sports, but he loves music.
- A <u>peripheral</u> you should consider getting is a scanner, which is like having a camera for your computer.

Origin: <Greek—*peripheria* (circumference, outer surface). "Peripheral" as an accessory to a computer dates back to the 1950s.

Family words: peripherally (adv), periphery (n)

Image to remember: someone on the outer edge of a group, not one of the "ins"; a piece of hardware attached to a computer

Write original sentences demonstrating the three common definitions of *peripheral*:

1. _____

2. _____

3. _____

council   an assembly of people called together to discuss or to deliberate a topic or topics:

The city council is meeting Monday evening to discuss whether a new sports auditorium is needed in our community.

counsel   to offer advice:

The lawyer counseled those living in the neighborhood when they learned that someone was planning to build a large condo complex at the far end of the street.

Circle the correct answer:

1. Mrs. Pelletier agreed to council / counsel the drama club this semester.

2. Mr. Stewart is a member of the council / counsel advising the governor on environmental matters.

Write original sentences using these words:

1. **council:** _____

2. **counsel:** _____

Learning Medical Terms from Context Clues: Set 1—Word Parts

Although knowledge of the word parts and frequently used medical terms presented in this chapter is beneficial to all students, those planning to enter a medical-related profession will find this knowledge particularly valuable.

1. **algia**—pain

   Neuralgia is pain extending along a nerve or group of nerves.

2. **arteri**—blood vessel

   Arteries are blood vessels carrying blood away from the heart.

3. **arthr**—joint

   Arthritis is inflammation of the joints.

4. **cardi**—heart

   Bradycardia is a heart rate of less than 60 beats per minute in an adult; *tachycardia* is a heart rate exceeding 100 beats per minute in an adult.

5. **derm**—skin

   Dermatology is the branch of medicine concerned with the skin and its diseases.

6. **gastr**—stomach

   Gastrology is the branch of medicine concerned with the stomach and its diseases.

7. **hem**—blood

   Hematology is the study of blood and the blood-producing organs.

8. **itis**—inflammation

   Bronchitis is inflammation of the membrane lining the bronchial tubes.

9. **my**—muscle

   Myalgia is muscular pain.

10. neur—nerve

Neuritis is inflammation of a nerve (see also <u>neuralgia</u> above).

11. osteo—bone

Osteoporosis is a disease in which the bones become weak and brittle, often leading to curvature of the spine.

12. phleb—vein

Phlebitis is inflammation of a vein.

13. psych—mind

Psychiatry is the branch of medicine concerned with mental disorders.

14. pulmo—lung

Pulmonary pneumonia occurs in the lungs.

15. tomy—act of cutting

Splenectomy is removal of the spleen.

Matching Academic Terms and Definitions: Set 1

Use your knowledge of the underlined word parts to match the definitions and terms.

A

d	**1.** osteo<u>genesis</u>	**a.** chronic pain in the muscles
f	**2.** gastro<u>scope</u>	**b.** relating to the lungs
b	**3.** pulmonic	**c.** inflammation of a saclike body cavity containing a lubricating fluid
a	**4.** fibro<u>myalgia</u>	**d.** the formation and development of bony tissue
h	**5.** psychosomatic	**e.** examination of arteries using x-rays
g	**6.** cardiograph	**f.** instrument used to examine the interior of the stomach
c	**7.** bur<u>itis</u>	**g.** instrument that records heart movements
e	**8.** arteriography	**h.** concerned with the influence of the mind on the body

B

f	**1.** phlebology	**a.** abnormal weakness of the muscles
c	**2.** hemoglobin	**b.** skin disease
e	**3.** neural	**c.** iron pigment in the red blood cells
g	**4.** lobo<u>tomy</u>	**d.** examination or treatment of a joint using an instrument inserted through a small opening
a	**5.** myasthenia	

e. relating to a nerve or the nervous system

f. study of veins and their diseases

g. surgical incision in the front part of the brain

Learning Medical Terms from Context Clues: Set 2

List One

1. **acute** (ə KYOOT)—adjective

   Describes an illness or pain with a rapid onset and a short, severe course.

2. **<u>asymptomatic</u>** (ā simp tə MAT ik)—adjective

   Not showing any symptoms of disease.

3. **atrophy** (AT rə fē)—noun

   Wasting away of muscles or a decrease in the size of a body part due to disease or lack of use.

4. **benign** (bə NĪN)—adjective

   Harmless, not deadly.

5. **cauterize** (KƏ tə rīz)—verb

   To burn or sear away abnormal tissue by using an instrument, such as a laser or an electrical current.

6. **<u>chronic</u>** (KRON ik)—adjective

   Describes a pain or illness of long duration.

7. **<u>coagulate</u>** (kō AG yə lāt)—verb

   To thicken or clot (as of blood).

8. **cyanosis** (sī ə NŌ sis)—noun

   Blue or gray discoloration of the skin because of reduced oxygen levels in the blood.

9. **<u>dementia</u>** (dē MEN shə)—noun

   A progressive decline in cognitive (mental) abilities; also referred to as Alzheimer's disease.

10. edema (ə DĒ mə)—noun

The swelling of body tissues with fluids; bloating.

11. etiology (ē tē OL ə jē)—noun

The causes or origins of a disease; the study of these causes.

12. febrile (FĒ brəl)—adjective

Having a fever.

13. triage (TRĒ əzh)—noun

A process followed for sorting injured people into groups based on their need for medical attention. Triage is from a French word meaning "sorting," and it reflects the Greek word *tria* ("three"). In its strictest sense, then, triage means sorting patients into three categories based on the seriousness of their medical condition.

List Two

1. gerontology (jer ən TOL ə jē)—noun

Study of the processes and problems of the elderly.

2. hospice (HOS pis)—noun

Type of care of the terminally ill founded on the concept of allowing individuals to die with dignity surrounded by those who love them.

3. malaise (mə LĀZ)—noun

A general feeling of sickness; a general sense of depression or unease.

4. malignant (mə LIG nənt)—adjective

Deadly, terminal, threatening to life.

5. natal (NĀ təl)—adjective

Pertaining to birth.

6. oncology (on KOL ə jē)—noun

The branch of medicine having to do with cancer.

7. palliative (PAL ē ə tiv)—adjective

Describes medical care that relieves symptoms but does not cure.

8. **pathology** (pə THOL ə jē)—noun

   The scientific study of diseases and their causes, including the examination of corpses to determine the cause of death.

9. **prognosis** (prəg NŌ sis)—noun

   The forecast of the probable course and outcome of a disease.

10. **protocol** (PRŌ tə kəl)—noun

    Series of standing medical orders or procedures that should be followed under specific conditions.

11. **remission** (rə MISH ən)—noun

    The lessening of a disease's symptoms.

12. **trauma** (TRə mə)—noun

    A life-threatening injury resulting from an accident or violence; a serious emotional shock.

13. **vertigo** (VUR tə gō)—noun

    Dizziness; sensation of the head spinning.

Matching Academic Terms and Definitions: Set 2

Match each definition with the term it defines.

A

| coagulate | edema | palliative | malignant | asymptomatic |
| vertigo | cauterize | febrile | pathology | |

cauterize	**1.** to burn away abnormal tissue
palliative	**2.** medical care that relieves symptoms but does not cure
coagulate	**3.** to clot
febrile	**4.** feverish
malignant	**5.** deadly
edema	**6.** swelling of body tissue with fluids; bloating
asymptomatic	**7.** not showing any indications of disease
pathology	**8.** study of diseases and their causes; studying what caused a death
vertigo	**9.** dizziness

B

trauma	natal	cyanosis	benign
atrophy	prognosis	hospice	oncology

prognosis   **1.** forecast of the probable course and outcome of a disease

cyanosis   **2.** blue or gray complexion due to the lack of oxygen

oncology   **3.** medical specialty concerned with cancer

trauma   **4.** life-threatening injury due to an accident or violence

hospice   **5.** compassionate approach designed to allow patients to die with dignity

natal   **6.** refers to birth

atrophy   **7.** wasting away of muscles

benign   **8.** mild, harmless

C

gerontology	etiology	triage	malaise	chronic
protocol	remission	dementia	acute	

dementia   **1.** Alzheimer's disease

chronic   **2.** describes a long-lasting pain or illness

gerontology   **3.** scientific study of aging

remission   **4.** decline in a disease's symptoms

acute   **5.** describes a sudden illness or pain having a short but severe course

protocol   **6.** standard medical procedures to follow under certain circumstances

etiology   **7.** the origins or causes of diseases

malaise   **8.** a vague feeling of illness or unease

triage   **9.** the sorting of injured patients into groups based on their medical need

Completing a Passage: Medicine

After reading the selection, fill in each space with one of the terms listed below.

cyanosis	triage	chronic	asymptomatic	cauterizing
palliative	acute	febrile	protocols	coagulate
prognosis	malaise	trauma	natal	oncology

EMERGENCY MEDICINE

Emergency medicine, though a medical specialty, encompasses a great deal of general medicine, such as treating nauseated and _____*febrile*_____ children suffering from the flu and _____*cauterizing*_____ a patient's wound with an electrical instrument so the blood from the wound will _____*coagulate*_____ and the healing process can begin. But emergency physicians are especially trained to treat those suffering from physical _____*trauma*_____, that is, from life-threatening injuries or illnesses. For example, they are the ones who are counted on to save patients brought into the emergency room with disturbing grayish or bluish complexions indicating _____*cyanosis*_____. Emergency physicians must quickly diagnose and stabilize such patients, then transfer them to the appropriate hospital unit, such as cardiology, or, if they are a cancer patient, _____oncology_____ . In addition, an emergency physician must be capable of diagnosing and then stabilizing recently born babies brought to the emergency room in distress before transferring them to the _____natal_____ unit. On the other hand, patients with _____chronic_____ conditions such as arthritis or those exhibiting _____malaise_____ indicated by _asymptomatic_ findings are often referred to their private doctors.

In addition to physicians, EMTs (emergency medical technicians), also known as paramedics, are trained to provide life-saving care in any location and to transport patients to the hospital by ambulance or, in some cases, by helicopter. Hospital emergency rooms are also staffed with nurses who are specially trained to help treat seriously injured or critically ill patients, including those with _____acute_____ ailments, that is, those whose severe illnesses came on suddenly and whose ____prognosis____ for relief from pain and possibly recovery would have been impossible had they not been brought to the emergency room.

_____Protocols_____ exist in emergency rooms to ensure that vital medical procedures are followed in certain situations. For example, to cope with large-scale accidents (as well as extremely crowded waiting rooms), emergency personnel are trained in the _____triage_____ system so that priority is given to those patients suffering from the most serious trauma. For example, patients suffering from strokes, poisonings, drug overdoses, heart attacks, car injuries, and acute asthma attacks are given priority over those with minor cuts and sore throats. Though immediate ____palliative____ care to relieve extreme pain is often standard practice, relief of symptoms is sometimes delayed to make sure that an accurate diagnosis leading to a cure is not obscured.

Those seeking a career in emergency medicine must undergo lengthy, specialized training, culminating in the passing of certification tests. Emergency physicians, for example, must obtain a four-year medical degree, complete a three-year residency, and pass a national certification exam. The stress for those in emergency medicine is often great, but, fortunately, so is the satisfaction that results from helping those people in the greatest need of medical aid.

Etiology—the causes of diseases:

- It took many years of medical research to unravel the <u>etiology</u> of poliomyelitis, but once the cause was traced to a specific virus, preventive vaccines could be developed.

Origin: 1555 <Greek—*aitiologia* (statement of cause); *aitia* (cause) and *logia* (speaking)

Family words: etiological (adj), etiologically (adv), etiologist (n)

Image to remember: public health officials scouring farms, stores, and restaurants seeking to find the source of a major outbreak of a disease

Write an original sentence using *etiology*:

_____

_____

_____

fewer   used with individual things that can actually be counted:

Because of the threatening weather, there were <u>fewer</u> people at the game than there were yesterday.

less   used when referring to a smaller quantity of something that can't be counted:

Fortunately, we've had <u>less</u> rain this week, so we were able to plant our garden.

Circle the correct answer:

1. We sold ⟨fewer⟩ / less cakes today than we did at last year's bake sale.

2. I'm disappointed that my new car gets ⟨fewer⟩ / less miles per gallon than my old one did, and its tank also holds fewer / ⟨less⟩ gas.

3. This summer, the Department of Transportation has fewer / ⟨less⟩ money, so there will be ⟨fewer⟩ / less roads built and repaired, and ⟨fewer⟩ / less part-time workers hired.

4. According to the labels, this cereal has ⟨fewer⟩ / less calories than that one does, and this widely advertised brand of bottled water actually has fewer / ⟨less⟩ liquid in it than that generic brand does.

Write original sentences using these words:

1. **fewer:** _____

2. **less:** _____

REVIEW TEST, CHAPTERS 24–29

Matching Academic Terms and Definitions

Match each academic term with its definition.

_d_	**1.** commodities	**a.** cash, property, and other things of value
_i_	**2.** vertex	**b.** accessory added to a computer
_f_	**3.** biology	**c.** concerned with a region's surface features
_l_	**4.** geology	**d.** products bought, sold, or traded
_b_	**5.** peripheral	**e.** angle of more than 90°
_k_	**6.** asymptomatic	**f.** study of living organisms
_a_	**7.** assets	**g.** small pictures representing various
_j_	**8.** zoology	computer options
_e_	**9.** obtuse	**h.** wasting away of muscles
_c_	**10.** topography	**i.** the point where two lines meet to form
_g_	**11.** icons	an angle
_h_	**12.** atrophy	**j.** study of animals
		k. no symptoms of disease
		l. study of the earth's origin, history, and structure

Related Meanings

If the words opposite each other are similar in meaning, write Yes *in the space; if they are unrelated, write* No.

1. GNP	_No_	general national policy
2. botany	_Yes_	study of plants
3. stalactites	_Yes_	deposits hanging from cave roofs
4. cursor	_No_	computer keyboard
5. benign	_No_	hardening of the bones
6. malignant	_Yes_	deadly
7. fonts	_Yes_	various computer typefaces, such as italics
8. homeostasis	_No_	virus causing paralysis
9. zenith	_Yes_	highest point
10. CEO	_Yes_	chief executive officer
11. right angle	_Yes_	90° angle
12. meteorology	_No_	study of microscopic life

Completing a Passage

After reading the selection, fill in each space with one of the terms listed below.

genes	symbiotic	prolific	mutations	habitat
invertebrates	entomology	taxonomy	dormant	flora

SOME TIDBITS ABOUT INSECTS

_____Entomology_____, the scientific study of insects, is a branch of zoology. Students taking a course in this subject learn some mind-boggling information about insects. For example, 95 percent of all animal species are insects, and, according to research reports, there are 10 quintillion (10,000,000,000,000,000,000) living insects! When it comes to reproducing, insects are unbelievably _____prolific_____, laying thousands of eggs throughout their life span, which can vary from a few hours (certain microorganisms) to seventeen years (certain locusts).

The _____habitat_____ of insects has no boundaries, as they live and thrive in all parts of the world, including the Arctic and Antarctic regions. Many types of _____flora_____, including a variety of water plants, and certain species of insects have a _____symbiotic_____ relationship, enabling each to survive. In addition, many species of insects are _____dormant_____ during certain parts of the year, while others remain constantly active.

Insects are _____invertebrates_____, as they lack backbones. The extensive _____taxonomy_____ for insects classifies thirty-two different orders; beetles make up the largest order, with over 500,000 different species. It is unlikely that the classification of insects will ever be completed, as _____mutations_____, which result from changes in the _____genes_____ of a parent, will no doubt add many more species as the years go by.

Writing Your Own Definitions

Write either an original sentence or a definition for each of these academic terms that clearly demonstrates your mastery of its meaning.   Answers will vary.

1. **liabilities** _____

   _____

2. **acute angle** _____

   _____

3. **fauna** _____

   _____

4. nadir _____

_____

5. hacker _____

_____

Matching Academic Terms and Definitions

Match each academic term with its definition.

l	**1.** quotient	**a.** deterioration of mental abilities; Alzheimer's disease
k	**2.** circumference	**b.** describes objects that can be shaped
f	**3.** fiscal	**c.** describes energy in motion, such as a swinging hammer
g	**4.** obsolescence	**d.** lessening of a disease's symptoms
c	**5.** kinetic	**e.** website used to locate other websites on the Internet
i	**6.** potential	**f.** pertaining to financial matters
b	**7.** malleable	**g.** describes products no longer in style or marketable
j	**8.** blog	**h.** the causes or origins of diseases
e	**9.** search engine	**i.** describes stored energy, such as a hammer on a shelf
h	**10.** etiology	**j.** individual's weblog used to express personal views
a	**11.** dementia	**k.** distance around a circle
d	**12.** remission	**l.** answer to a division problem

Related Meanings

If the words opposite each other are similar in meaning, write Yes *in the space; if they are unrelated, write* No.

1. bear market	Yes	falling stock market
2. bull market	Yes	rising stock market
3. average	Yes	mean
4. axioms	Yes	postulates
5. genetics	No	study of successful business practices
6. vertebrates	Yes	animals with backbones
7. lunar	No	relating to the sun
8. solar	No	relating to the moon
9. catalyst	Yes	speeds up chemical action
10. capital	Yes	money

Fill-Ins with Academic Terms

In each space, write the appropriate term from those listed below.

febrile   conglomerate   edema   solvency   celestial   numerator   audit
hospice   divestiture   denominator   protocol   diameter   balance of trade

1. Nurses receive training regarding the _____protocol_____ to follow when certain medical situations arise.

2. In the fraction 7/8, 7 is the _____numerator_____ and 8 is the _____denominator_____ .

3. _____Hospice_____ is compassionate care designed for the terminally ill so they are permitted to die with as much comfort and dignity as possible.

4. An indicator of a nation's economic health is its _balance of trade_ , that is, how its export sales and import purchases compare.

5. Though not complaining of any discomfort, the young man was found to be _____febrile_____ with a temperature of over 100 degrees and clear indications of _____edema_____ , or bloating, of his ankles.

6. The _____diameter_____ of the room, that is, the distance from one wall to the opposite with the tape measure running through the exact center, is 32 feet.

7. Throughout the centuries, people have given names to the _____celestial_____ figures formed by the stars.

8. Because the corporation had a virtual monopoly regarding the selling of many agricultural products in various countries, the court ordered a(n) _____divestiture_____ of its fertilizing company.

9. The business _conglomerate_ includes TV stations, publishing companies, and paper mills, and its _____solvency_____ is beyond question, according to an independent _____audit_____ of its financial records.

Related Meanings

If the words opposite each other are similar in meaning, write Yes *in the space; if they are unrelated, write* No.

1. sum _____Yes_____ total
2. proton _____Yes_____ positive electric charge
3. neutron _____No_____ negative charge
4. electron _____No_____ no electric charge
5. 14⅝ _____Yes_____ mixed number
6. 3/2 _____No_____ proper fraction
7. 4/11 _____No_____ improper fraction
8. > _____No_____ equal to
9. < _____Yes_____ less than
10. recession _____No_____ substantial increase in business and employment

11. depreciation   <u>Yes</u> decline in value
12. chronic   <u>No</u> of short duration
13. ≠   <u>No</u> greater than
14. malaise   <u>No</u> feeling of well-being
15. palliative   <u>Yes</u> eases symptoms but does not cure

Writing Your Own Definitions

Write either an original sentence or a definition for each of these academic terms that clearly demonstrates your mastery of its meaning.   Answers will vary.

1. **computer hardware** _____

   _____

2. **prognosis** _____

   _____

3. **franchise** _____

   _____

4. **golden parachute** _____

   _____

5. **tariff** _____

   _____

Matching Academic Terms and Definitions

Match each academic term with its definition.

<u>j</u>	**1.** triage	**a.**	describes rocks formed by sediment deposits
<u>k</u>	**2.** centripetal	**b.**	study of the universe beyond the earth's atmosphere
<u>l</u>	**3.** physics	**c.**	study of substances not containing carbon
<u>n</u>	**4.** physiology	**d.**	result when two organisms of different species are bred
<u>h</u>	**5.** igneous	**e.**	a substance dissolved in a solution
<u>a</u>	**6.** sedimentary	**f.**	combining process
<u>d</u>	**7.** hybrid	**g.**	composed of two or more elements
<u>b</u>	**8.** astronomy	**h.**	describes rocks formed by cooled magma
<u>e</u>	**9.** solute	**i.**	force propelling objects outward
<u>m</u>	**10.** organic chemistry	**j.**	the sorting of the injured into groups
<u>o</u>	**11.** inflationary		
<u>c</u>	**12.** inorganic chemistry		

_____i_____	**13.** centrifugal	**k.** force drawing objects inward
_____g_____	**14.** compound	**l.** study of matter and energy
_____f_____	**15.** synthesis	**m.** study of substances containing carbon
		n. study of the functions and parts of living organisms
		o. describes substantial rise in prices

Mastering Confusing Words

Circle the correct answer.

1. The city ((council) / counsel) is scheduled to meet this evening at 7:30.

2. Did your advisor (council / (counsel)) you regarding what courses you should take next semester?

3. We need at least three ((disinterested) / uninterested) people to serve as judges for the art show.

4. Jaye prefers swimming to jogging, so she was (disinterested / (uninterested)) in going running with us.

5. I have (fewer / (less)) money now than I did last month, but, fortunately, I also have ((fewer) / less) debts.

6. Do you know (who's / (whose)) wristwatch this is?

7. Lesley, you'll never believe ((who's) / whose) studying by himself in the library!

8. The clerk asked the customer, "(Can / (May)) I help you?"

9. You (can / (may)) borrow my car if you ((can) / may) get it back here within two hours.

10. Did you (imply / (infer)) from what I said that I don't like your cousin? I didn't mean to ((imply) / infer) that.

Crossword Puzzle

Solve the crossword by using the following academic terms.

acute — carnivorous — cartel — dividend — embargo — entrepreneur
median — metabolism — mode — natal — omnivorous — ossification
oscillate — plankton — reciprocity — variable

ACROSS

1. official banning of trade with a specific country
2. number separating numbers into two equal groups
4. mutual, beneficial exchange
6. securities owned by an investor
9. letter standing for an unknown number
11. semifluid considered to be the building block of life
13. hardening of bones
14. angle of less than 90°
15. business group that controls some industry
16. eating both plants and meat

DOWN

1. a bold, daring business person
2. number occurring most often in a set of numbers
3. body's total chemical and physical processes
5. meat eating
7. to vibrate
8. microscopic organisms floating in water
10. number being divided
12. pertaining to birth

Parts of Speech

1. Adjectives

An **adjective** describes or modifies a noun or pronoun.

Did you see that <u>gray</u> cat?

<u>Two</u> cars were parked in the driveway.

He is <u>tall</u>, <u>dark</u>, and <u>handsome</u>.

Specific suffixes are associated with adjectives, including -able, -ible, -al, -ful, -ous, -ive, and -y:

She is a cap<u>able</u> worker.

This is a revers<u>ible</u> coat.

We celebrated the nation<u>al</u> holiday in Alaska.

Martin is a care<u>ful</u> driver.

They own a spaci<u>ous</u> ranch in Wyoming.

The plaintiff is suing for punit<u>ive</u> damages as well.

Sharon is cleaning her mess<u>y</u> room.

Demonstrative adjectives: <u>these</u> people, <u>this</u> office

Descriptive adjectives: <u>lovely</u> day, <u>pale</u> color

Interrogative adjectives: <u>What</u> program? <u>Whose</u> coat?

Limiting adjectives: <u>three</u> children, <u>several</u> cars

Possessive adjectives: <u>our</u> apartment, <u>my</u> uncle

Proper adjectives: <u>American</u> flag, <u>Canadian</u> imports

2. Adverbs

An **adverb** describes or modifies a verb, an adjective, or another adverb.

modifying a verb: Brittany walked <u>quickly</u> to the door.

modifying an adjective: She was <u>extremely</u> happy to get the news.

modifying another adverb: Time went by <u>very</u> slowly.

Adverbs often indicate when, where, how, and to what extent.

> when: The Andersons will arrive <u>tomorrow</u>.

> where: Steve, place the chair <u>here</u>.

> how: The children sang <u>loudly</u>.

> to what extent: We were <u>completely</u> bewildered by the news.

Adverbs often end in the suffix -ly, as a number of preceding examples illustrate.

3. Conjunctions

A **conjunction** is a word used to join words or groups of words. There are coordinating, subordinating, adverbial, and correlative conjunctions.

Coordinating conjunctions: and, but, for, nor, or, yet, so

> Rain <u>and</u> fog made driving difficult.

> We had the day off, <u>but</u> Sheila had to work.

> My husband bought a ticket, <u>for</u> he loves that type of music.

> Meredith couldn't answer the question, <u>nor</u> could I.

> You can have ice cream <u>or</u> pudding for dessert.

> Shane had his car repaired, <u>yet</u> it is still giving him trouble.

> We were tired, <u>so</u> we didn't attend the ceremony.

Subordinating conjunctions: after, although, because, if, etc.

> <u>After</u> they left, the party broke up.

> <u>Although</u> it was cloudy, Sandy still got a sunburn.

> He refused dessert <u>because</u> he is on a diet.

> The game will be played next week <u>if</u> it has to be canceled today.

Adverbial conjunctions: consequently, however, therefore, etc.

> Bob never heard from him again; <u>consequently</u>, he rented the apartment to someone else.

> I knew that he had applied for that position; <u>however</u>, I was surprised that he got it.

> Our plane leaves at 6:30 A.M.; <u>therefore</u>, we will have to get up early.

Correlative conjunctions: either-or, neither-nor, not only–but also

I think that <u>either</u> the cat <u>or</u> the dog broke the lamp.

It is clear that <u>neither</u> the owners <u>nor</u> the workers want the strike to continue.

We were <u>not only</u> surprised <u>but also</u> embarrassed by the news.

4. Interjections

An **interjection** is a word or phrase that expresses strong emotion.

<u>Ouch</u>! I've been stung by a bee.

<u>Look out</u>! There's ice on the sidewalk.

5. Nouns

A **noun** is a person, place, or thing.

person: Emily

place: Prince Edward Island

thing: wrench

Common nouns refer to general classes: woman, city, building.

Proper nouns refer to particular people, places, or things: Anne, Detroit, Empire State Building.

Collective nouns name groups: family, team, class.

Concrete nouns name tangible things: rock, flower, table.

Abstract nouns name intangible things: idea, bravery, democracy.

6. Prepositions

A **preposition** is a word that combines with a noun or pronoun to form a phrase; prepositional phrases generally serve as adjectives or adverbs.

prepositional phrase
↓
Laura mowed the grass [after lunch.]
↗   ↖
preposition   noun

prepositional phrase

We have full confidence [in him.]

preposition   noun

These words often function as prepositions:

above	behind	during	from	of	to
before	by	for	in	over	with

7. Pronouns

A **pronoun** is a word used in place of a noun.

noun: <u>Paul</u> is coming home tomorrow.

pronoun: <u>He</u> is coming home tomorrow.

These words are among those that serve as pronouns:

I	he	it	they	themselves	which	these	anybody
you	she	we	myself	who	what	those	somebody

8. Verbs

A **verb** is a word or group of words expressing action or the state of being of a subject.

action verb: Yolanda <u>laughed</u>.

state of being verb: Our guests <u>are</u> here.

A **transitive verb** expresses action and has an object.

verb   object

Janet <u>set</u> the <u>package</u> on the table.

verb   object

Wayne <u>flipped</u> the <u>pages</u> of the telephone directory.

An **intransitive verb** does not have an object.

verb

The boy <u>shivered</u>.

verb

The ice and snow <u>melted</u>.

A **linking verb** connects the subject and a complement that renames or describes the subject.

>   Jamie <u>is</u> the captain.

>   The clothes <u>seemed</u> inexpensive.

An **auxiliary** or **helping verb** combines with other verbs to form phrases.

helping verb
↓

>   Katherine <u>can paint</u>.

helping verb
↓

>   The windows <u>were closed</u>.

These words function as auxiliary or helping verbs:

am	been	can	did	does	has	is	might	shall	was
are	being	could	do	had	have	may	must	should	were

Using the Dictionary

A dictionary is the best source for learning the precise meanings of words; moreover, it provides other valuable information about words, including their pronunciation, spelling, parts of speech, and origin.

Printed below is the entry for **exonerate** found in the fourth college edition of *The American Heritage Dictionary*, one of the most recommended dictionaries for college students. By becoming familiar with the key parts that have been identified and explained, you will be able to take better advantage of the information a college-level dictionary provides.

```
 A              B          C           D
 |              |          |          /\
ex • on • er • ate (ĭg-zŏn′ ə rāt′) tr. v.   -at • ed,   -at • ing, -ates.
To free from blame. [< Lat. exonerare, to free from a burden.]—ex on er a tion. —ex on er a tive adj.
 |              |                           |
 E              F                           G
```

A. The **entry word** is printed in boldface type and divided into syllables.

B. The **pronunciation** of the word is shown in parentheses, with the pronunciation indicated by specific letters, lines, and symbols. A guide to the pronunciation is generally found in the inside cover of the dictionary as well as at the bottom of every other page.

C. The **parts of speech** of a word are indicated by an abbreviation; parts of speech are commonly abbreviated in this manner:

adj.—adjective   prep.—preposition
adv.—adverb   pron.—pronoun
conj.—conjunction   v.—verb
interj.—interjection   intr. v. (or vi)—intransitive verb
n.—noun   tr. v. (or vt)—transitive verb

See Appendix A for a review of the parts of speech.

D. The **verb tenses** of *exonerate* are provided (exonerated, exonerating, exonerates).

E. The word's **definition.** (Keep in mind that a word may have more than one definition, so it is sometimes necessary to select the definition appropriate to the context in which the word is being used.)

F. The **etymology** of the word is enclosed in brackets; etymology is concerned with the origin and history of words. In our example, it is disclosed that *exonerate* comes from the Latin word *exonerare,* which means "to free from a burden." The following are typical of the abbreviations used to indicate the language from which a word originated.

OE—Old English, the language spoken in England from the years 700 to 1100
ME—Middle English, the language spoken in England from 1100 to 1500
OF—Old French, the language spoken in France from 800 to 1200
F—French, the language spoken in France today
Lat.—Latin, spoken by the Romans approximately 2,000 years ago
GK—Ancient Greek, spoken in Greece approximately 2,500 years ago

G. "Relatives" of the word are indicated; in our example, the noun *exoneration* and the adjective *exonerative* are related to the verb *exonerate.*

Guide words are printed in boldface type at the top of each dictionary page; they indicate the first and last words printed on that particular page. Because words in a dictionary are listed in alphabetical order, the guide words reveal whether the word you are looking for can be found on that particular page. For example, the guide words *exodus* and *expectancy* in *The American Heritage Dictionary* indicate that *exonerate* can be found on that page.

Most college-level dictionaries also include numerous introductory and supplementary pages devoted to a variety of topics like the following:

- Directions for using the dictionary
- Pronunciation guide and other explanatory notes
- Directories and tables of useful information
- Basic manual on grammar, punctuation, and style
- Brief history of the English language
- Biographical entries

Index for Word Parts

Index for Challenging Words

Index for Academic Terms

acculturation, 258
acquittal, 282
acute, 377
addition terms
    addends, 315
    sum, 315
adjudicate, 282
affirmative action, 306
agrarian, 258
alliteration, 226
amendment, 270
analogy, 226
angles
    acute, 314
    obtuse, 315
    right, 314
antagonist, 226
anthology, 227
appeal, 285
appreciation, 306
appropriation, 275
assets, 301
astronomy, 346
asymptomatic, 377
atom, 349
atrophy, 377
audit, 306
average, 315
axioms, 315

bail, 282
balance of trade, 301
bear market, 302
behavior therapy, 251
benign, 377
bibliography, 222
Bill of Rights, 270
binary, 362
biology, 330
bit, 362
blog, 367
booking, 382
botony, 330
boycott, 270

branches of
    government, 270
bull market, 302
bureaucracy, 262
byte, 362

canon, 226
capital, 306
carnivorous, 336
cartel, 307
catalyst, 233, 351
centrifugal, 351
centripetal, 351
CEO (chief executive
    officer), 305
change of venue, 286
checks and balances,
    271
chemistry, 349
chromosomes, 331
chronic, 377
circumference, 315
coagulate, 377
congenital, 335
cognitive, 246
cognitive therapy, 252
commodities, 301
commute, 382
compound, 350
concurrent sentencing,
    286
conglomerate, 306
connotation, 222
consecutive
    sentencing, 286
context, 233
control group, 245
crash, 366
critique, 239
culpability, 282
culture, 258
cursor, 361
cyanosis, 377

database, 366
decoding, 233
deduction, 239
defendant, 287
defense mechanisms,
    250
dementia, 377
demography, 258
denotation, 222
depreciation, 306
divestiture, 306
division terms
    dividend, 316
    divisor, 316
    quotient, 316
domain name, 367
dormant, 335
download, 367

edema, 378
ego, 249
electron, 350
element, 349
e-mail, 367
embargo, 307
eminent domain,
    271
empirical, 246
encoding, 233
entomology, 330
enunciation, 234
entitlement, 275
entrepreneur, 305
ethnic group, 262
ethnocentrism, 262
etiology, 378
executive, 270
experimental group,
    245
exponent, 316
extradite, 286
extrinsic motivation,
    246

fallacies, 238
fauna, 232
febrile, 278
felony, 286
figures of speech, 222
file, 366
filibuster, 247
fiscal, 302
flashback, 277
flora, 332
folkways, 227
fonts, 362
foreshadowing, 227
fractions
    improper, 316
    proper, 316
franchise, 306

genes, 332
genre, 222
geology, 344
geriatrics, 263
gerontology, 263, 378
gerrymandering, 275
GNP (gross national
    product), 301
golden parachute, 307

habeas corpus, 287
habitat, 332
hacker, 366
hardware, 365
herbivorous, 336
homeostasis, 335
hominids, 336
hospice, 378
hybrid, 336
hyperbole, 226
hypothesis, 246

icons, 362
id, 249
igneous rocks, 344

impeachment, 274
impromptu speaking, 234
indict, 283
induction, 239
inflationary, 302
injunction, 287
inorganic chemistry, 349
Internet, 367
intrinsic motivation, 246
introvert, 246
invertebrates, 336

judiciary, 270
jurisprudence, 287

kinesics, 237
kinetic energy, 351

laissez-faire, 271
lame duck, 274
legislative, 270
liabilities, 302
literal, 223
litigants, 287
litigation, 287
lobbyist, 271
lunar, 346

malaise, 378
malleable, 352
malignant, 378
Malthusian theory, 262
math symbols, 322
matriarchal family, 262
mean, 320
median, 320
memory, RAM, ROM, 362
menu bar, 366
metabolism, 337
metamorphic rocks, 344
metaphor, 223

meteorology, 345
microbiology, 330
misdemeanor, 286
mixed numbers, 316
mode, 320
modem, 362
molecule, 350
monitor, 361
mores, 258
mouse, 361
multimedia presentation, 239
multiplication terms
    multiplicand, 321
    multiplier, 321
    product, 321
mutation, 332

nadir, 346
natal, 378
neurosis, 251
neutron, 350
noise, 234
nonsexist language, 238
nucleus, 350

objective, 239
obsolescence, 306
Oedipus complex, 251
omnivorous, 336
oncology, 378
organic chemistry, 349
oscillate, 351
ossification, 336

palliative, 378
pathology, 379
patriarchal family, 263
patronage, 275
peer group, 258
peripheral, 361
perjury, 283
personification, 223
physics, 351
physiology, 331

placebo, 346
plagiarism, 226
plaintiff, 287
plankton, 336
port, 361
portfolio, 305
postulates, 315
potential energy, 351
premise, 238
prognosis, 379
prolific, 336
prose, 223
protagonist, 226
protocol, 379
proton, 350
protoplasm, 337
psychoanalysis, 250
psychosis, 251
psychosomatic, 251

radius, 322
rapport, 238
ratification, 271
recession, 302
recidivism, 283
reciprocity, 301
red herring, 274
referendum, 275
remission, 379

sanction, 263
satire, 226
search engine, 367
sedimentary rocks, 344
sedition, 275
sibling, 259
simile, 223
social norms, 259
software, 365
solute, 351
solvency, 302
spam, 367
spreadsheet, 366
square root, 322
stalactites, 344
stalagmites, 345

status, 263
stereotype, 259
subjective, 239
subpoena, 286
subtraction terms
    difference, 317
    minuend, 317
    subtrahend, 317
superego, 249
symbiosis, 332
synopsis, 227
synthesis, 351

tariff, 307
taxonomy, 336
terminal, 361
therapeutic, 251
topography, 344
tort law, 283
transitions, 237
trauma, 379
triage, 378

urbanism, 259
utopia, 263

values, 259
variable, 245, 322
venue, 233
vertebrates, 336
vertigo, 379
veto, 271
virus, 366
voice
    active, 234
    passive, 234
    speaking, 234

World Wide Web (WWW), 367

zenith, 346
zoology, 330

Index for Mastering Confusing Words